STREETWISE®
INCORPORATING YOUR BUSINESS

From Legal Issues to Tax Concerns, All You
Need to Establish and Protect Your Business

Michele Cagan, C.P.A.

BUSINESS

Avon, Massachusetts

A Streetwise® Publication. Streetwise® is a registered trademark of F+W Publications.

Published by Adams Media, an F+W Publications Company
57 Littlefield Street
Avon, MA 02322
www.adamsmedia.com

ISBN 10: 1-59869-094-9
ISBN 13: 978-1-59869-094-1

Printed in the United States of America.

J I H G F E D C B A

Library of Congress Cataloging-in-Publication Data

Cagan, Michele.
  Streetwise incorporating your business / Michele Cagan.
      p. cm. – (A streetwise series book)
  Includes index.
  ISBN-13: 978-1-59869-094-1 (pbk.)
  ISBN-10: 1-59869-094-9 (pbk.)
  1. Incorporation–United States–Popular works. I. Title.

  KF1420.Z9C3 2007
  346.73'06622–dc22   2007002038

This book is available at quantity discounts for bulk purchases.
For information, please call 1-800-289-0963.

CONTENTS

Dedication

To my mom, and to my best boy and best friend.

Introduction

For more than thirteen years I have worked with all sorts of small-business clients. Back in the beginning, everyone I dealt with was incorporating because that was really the only way to ensure limited liability protection. Then, with the advent of the LLC and the LLP, corporations began to lose favor. Now they've come back around to be the entity of choice for many small businesses looking for that same legal protection with a side order of flexible tax-planning capabilities.

Whether you already have a business that's structured in some other way or are just launching your first enterprise, one of the available corporate entities may be the best choice for your company. It doesn't matter what industry you are in or how long you've already been in business: Every company is vulnerable to lawsuits; every successful business owner has to pay taxes; and almost every company needs outside funding to help it grow. Corporations offer you the most options, the best ways to minimize tax bites, and the simplest way to bring in investors without losing control. Both you and your company could very well benefit in the long run through the simple process of incorporation. And, contrary to popular belief, it isn't that hard to do.

Incorporating your business really is a simple step-by-step process. When you have all the steps laid out for you, as they are in this guide, you can create a secure and profitable corporation, no sweat. *Streetwise® Incorporating Your Business* tells you which steps you can take on your own and which are better taken with professional guidance. From choosing the most advantageous corporate entity to filing the legal paperwork to paying out the first dividend, this book will show you how it's all done.

It takes guts to start a business, sweat to make it a success, and a lockbox to preserve those hard-earned profits. The marketplace is increasingly competitive, and the economic climate makes it harder than ever to hold on to your wealth. Starting and growing a profitable business is tough, but holding on to everything you've built can be even harder. Incorporating your business gives you an extra layer of protection for both your personal nest egg and your burgeoning business, leaving your money in your hands. This book gives you all the tools you need to create a rock-solid corporation, one that will help you to grow and protect your fortune.

Getting Started

PART 1

How Structure Impacts Your Business

Like the foundation upon which your house is built, a business structure provides support and framework for your business. This structure, or entity, is the legal form of your company, but it comes with a wide-ranging set of implications beyond the legal ones. Among other things, the entity you choose for your company directs the following:

- ➲ How many owners your business can have
- ➲ The type of owners your business can have
- ➲ Your (and your co-owners') personal liability for business debts
- ➲ Your company's liability for your (and your co-owners') personal debts
- ➲ What type of funding is available to the business
- ➲ How your business is perceived by others
- ➲ How much paperwork you will have to do
- ➲ Who pays the income taxes
- ➲ How much income tax will be paid

Many novice business owners overlook the importance of entity choice; in fact, many don't even actively make a choice before jumping into business, and they end up stuck with the most basic (and often least protective) structures. But even those entrepreneurs who have made painstaking decisions regarding their business entities may find themselves in the position of needing to make a change.

While every business entity can be changed after the fact, that often involves extra paperwork and sometimes invokes a tax consequence as well. Those pitfalls of switching can be managed with some careful planning, but choosing the best entity for your business—either at start-up or after your company has grown enough to merit a change in entity—in the first place can help you avoid potential difficulties.

A Natural Progression

When it comes to small business, there is a typical pattern of progression when it comes to structure. Many novice entrepreneurs, whether they have planned to start a business or just slid into it without really knowing what's what, start off as sole proprietors (when they are flying solo) or as general partnerships (when at least two people are involved). These business structures are the default settings: If you do nothing, these are the entities you will have created. As you might expect, these entities are the least beneficial in virtually all ways except the simplicity of formation.

Once business owners get into the swing of things—read this as "start making money, paying taxes, and owning something too good to lose"—they begin to think about better ways to manage their companies. They may search around online for advice or talk to their CPAs, attorneys, or other professional advisors. Whichever path they take, they will likely end up transforming their companies into other entities, usually limited liability companies (LLCs) or S corporations.

The final destination comes into play when the company has grown beyond expectations, pulling in revenues measured in (at least) millions of dollars each year. At that point, most businesses become C corporations, and they live that way forevermore.

Do You Have a Business?

Sometimes, a person can be in business and not fully realize it. Sound crazy? Think about this. A man employed at a plumbing supply company does a little bit of light plumbing work on the side. That's a business. Or a secretary types up term papers for her son's classmates for a small fee. That's a business.

Here's the basic rule. If you perform a service for money, or sell something for more than you originally paid, and you are not acting as an employee for someone else, you have engaged in a business transaction . . . for your own business.

Before the First Transaction

The instant you complete your first transaction, you have a business. It does not matter if any money has changed hands; the simple act of agreeing to provide a product or service for money, even if that money won't come into play for months, counts as a business transaction. Once you're in business, it can cost extra time and money to make an entity switch.

In the absence of LLC or incorporation papers, and depending on the number of owners involved, your business will automatically be a sole proprietorship or general partnership for accounting, tax, and legal purposes. If you do want to start a business, but you want to enjoy the benefits of a more sophisticated entity (such as protection from business debts), it's better to fill out all the paperwork and mail in the fees before you do anything else. The things you do to form the business count as entity set-up costs, not regular transactions, and will not make you an inadvertent sole proprietor or partner.

If you have already started, do not worry; you can switch to another structure. It just costs more and involves more legalities and paperwork (not to mention potential tax implications) than if you had formed the desired entity at the very start.

A Brief Look at the Choices

When you create a business, you have four basic entity choices and a few options inside those. The big four are sole proprietorship, partnership, corporation, and limited liability company (or LLC, the baby of the bunch). Sole proprietorships and LLCs come in one flavor only, but corporations and partnerships have several varieties from which to choose. Once you have a good understanding of your options, you will be better able to select the best business structure for your company right now. You should also know that as your company grows and changes, you can always switch to another.

Partnerships

Partnerships come in three basic varieties and one twist that's currently available only in some states. The three main types, and the one twist, are the following:

1. General
2. Limited
3. Limited liability (LLP)
4. Limited liability limited (the twist)

There are vast differences among these entities when it comes to liability protection for and involvement by partners, but the differences are very small when it comes to taxation.

In general partnerships, each partner is both jointly and severally liable for all debts of the partnership. That means every single partner is 100 percent personally liable for every dime owed to anyone by the partnership, but he can sue his partners for some of the money back if he's the only one forced to pony up at first. Wait, it gets worse! For example, you could end up responsible for a fellow partner's personal debts. Your partner could also run up ridiculous bills, charge them to the business, take a hike, and leave you holding the bag. Just in case the point here hasn't poked you in the eye already, a general partnership is the very worst business entity you could ever possibly form.

▶▶ **A limited partnership has two different types of partners: general (who fare just as described above) and limited.** Limited partners can never lose more than their investment, and they can never be held liable for the company's business debts—unless, that is, they participate in the business in any way other than to supply money in exchange for shares. The instant they participate in the business—in any capacity—they become general partners and lose all protection.

LLPs (limited liability partnerships) offer some level of personal liability protection for general partners; the amount of protection varies somewhat according to state law. Usually, though, it shields each partner from responsibility for business debts. Many professional partnerships (like accounting firms and law offices) are set up as LLPs when state law prohibits them from forming either LLCs or corporations.

Finally, the limited liability limited partnership (or LLLP) offers limited liability protection to the general partners of a limited partnership. This twist on the standard is not available in most states, at least not yet. The setup and maintenance are fairly tricky, and the entity hasn't been around long enough for proven reliability.

The LLC

Not quite a corporation, not really a partnership, the LLC offers your company the best features of these two entities with few (if any) of the drawbacks. As the name suggests, all owners—called members—are afforded limited liability protection. When it comes to taxation, you and your fellow members can actually choose whether you prefer to be taxed as a partnership or as a C corporation, adding an extra dimension of flexibility. On the operations front, you can run your company like a normal partnership; that's referred to as member-managed. Or you can run it more like a corporation, with the owners making all the major top-down decisions but none of the day-to-day operating ones; that is called (rather awkwardly) manager-managed.

With all of this seeming flexibility, why would anyone choose a corporation over an LLC? A couple of reasons can land you squarely in the corporate camp. First, LLCs are relatively new and not even remotely as vigorously tested as corporations, which have been around for centuries. To you, that means a corporate entity offers the most comprehensive and reliable personal liability protection available, which is no small thing. Second, it's easier to raise equity capital with a corporation (especially a standard C corporation) than with any other business structure.

Corporations

For centuries, corporations have afforded their owners with highly beneficial limited liability protection, their strongest selling point. Close behind, when it comes to selling points, are their virtually unlimited life and their relative ease in raising fresh capital. ▶▶ **All corporations are state-chartered entities, bound by the laws of both the state (or states) in which they are incorporated and those in which they conduct business.**

For federal tax purposes, there are two major types of corporations: the regular C variety and the subchapter S version. In addition to these two major categories, there are also some spin-offs, like the personal-service corporation and the qualified small-business corporation. While C and S corporate entities have several similarities, such as liability protection and capital structure, there are also some glaring differences (such as the way each is taxed and the legal restrictions on ownership). Every corporation starts out as a C; some stay that way, but some elect S status instead. However, not every corporation is eligible for S status, as you will learn in Chapter 2.

At the state level, in addition to the C or S variety, many small corporations opt for statutory close (pronounced "cloze," like you do with a door) status. This distinction allows for a reduction in the somewhat overwhelming paperwork requirements necessary to maintain a corporation, making it easier for smaller companies to remain in compliance at all times.

Consider These Factors

When you decide which entity makes the most sense for your business, you have to look at those determining factors that are most important to you. You will consider several business and personal issues, which together make your situation unique. At first glance, some of these factors may seem like they impact either your business or your personal situation. The truth is, though, that most of them will affect both sides of your life, so both sides should be taken into account.

When trying to figure out which entity is best for your company, the four biggest issues you will need to consider are ownership, liability, taxes, and transferability. You will add some other factors into the picture, such as costs and ongoing maintenance chores, but entity choice will impact those four issues most strongly. Making the best choice for your business now can save time and aggravation later, so carefully consider your options before committing to one. Remember, what worked best for someone else's business, or even for another business you own (or owned), may not work as well for this one.

At the same time, you must carefully consider your personal situation, particularly if you've already built up a substantial nest egg that needs protecting. Part of that protection comes from limiting liability through your business entity, and part comes from minimizing the overall tax bite (leaving more money in your hands and less sent in to fill the government's coffers).

The Number of Owners

The number of owners your company has will eliminate some of your choices. When there will be more than one owner, sole proprietorship is off the table. On the other hand, having a single owner knocks out all forms of partnership. And should you plan on having more than a hundred owners, the S corporation is not an option; for close corporations, the limit (depending on state law) is normally thirty-five or fifty.

When it comes to LLCs and C corporations, you can have any number of owners, from one to you name it. Some of the paperwork and tax issues may be different for single-owner LLCs or corporations, but the binding legal structure does not alter.

What Do You Have to Lose?

The second piece of the liability issue is money. That's typically the whole point of liability claims and lawsuits. Your business allegedly caused someone to suffer some kind of injury, and that person wants your business to pay for it. Insurance is often your company's first line of defense, but those payouts are almost always capped. When the insurance doesn't satisfy the people suing, they may try to attach the company's assets. If your business has minimal assets, though, there is really no point in suing it. In that case, the plaintiff could turn to you and your co-owners for satisfaction—unless you are protected by your business structure.

Is Liability Really an Issue?

Some businesses are more naturally prone to liability claims than others. This means it is likely that for certain types of businesses someone at some point will sue your company. Some business enterprises come with blatantly obvious lawsuits waiting to happen: you produce hazardous chemicals, you and your crew build bridges, or you run an amusement park (the kind with rides and roller coasters). Others may be less overtly risky but still liability-prone, such as businesses that serve food and alcohol or delivery services, for example. Some businesses fall very low on the liability scale (think bookkeeping, interior design) until you add one very volatile ingredient—employees.

If your business involves any of the following, you are facing potential liability problems:

- ➲ Employees
- ➲ Customers who come to your place of business
- ➲ Delivery vehicles
- ➲ Hazardous materials
- ➲ Dangerous activities

Very Different Tax Bills

Though it may seem illogical, the same exact income earned by two different business structures could be taxed completely differently, and the gap in the amount of taxes paid could be fairly large. The biggest tax difference concerns exactly which entity is taxed: the business itself or the owners.

Under current law, only C corporations pay taxes on their own income. As the owner, you would be personally taxed only on money that you took out of the business, regardless of the form, including salary and dividends. That salary is taxable to you, and tax deductible to the company, for a sort of tax wash. Dividends, on the other hand, are subject to the much-debated double taxation. That happens when the corporation pays tax on its income and then distributes some of that income as dividends to its owners, who then pay tax on that dividend income. There are some distinct tax advantages with C corporations, despite that very vexing double taxation issue. More employee-oriented expenses are fully deductible, even when the employee is the owner. Plus, you have more tax-shifting capabilities to let you take advantage of which tax rate is lower right now, personal or corporate.

All other entities (unless they have specifically designated that they wish to be taxed as C corporations) enjoy what is known as pass-through taxation. For these business structures, the income of the company passes through directly to the tax returns of the owners. The company still has to file an informational return, but it pays no taxes on its own behalf. Instead, the various pieces of income show up in various places on the owners' personal income tax returns. With pass-through corporate entities, owners still receive salaries and dividends, which can still impact the ultimate tax bill; for the other entities, though, no money you take out of the company has any impact on taxes.

Passing Down or Selling Your Company

Whether you are just starting out as an entrepreneur or have been your own boss for decades, at some point you will want to stop and hand over the reins to someone else. You may want to keep some fingers in the company pie, retaining at least some portion of ownership; or you may just want to get out completely and sever all ties. You may want to sell the company in one big chunk to outsiders; you may want to sell off your big assets and then simply dissolve the business; or you may want to pass the business down to someone in your family. No matter what you want to do, when the time comes to shift the ownership to someone else, your entity will dictate how that can be done.

Corporations are the easiest companies to transfer, in part or in whole, to other parties. C corporations offer the most flexibility here, as there are no legal limits on either the number or types of shareholders. However, as long as you stay within legal guidelines for an S or close corporation, the mechanics of transferring shares are still pretty simple. Also, in addition to legal regulations, you may also be subject to limitations as spelled out in your shareholders' agreement.

As for multimember LLCs and partnerships, their internal restrictions are typically pretty comprehensive, as spelled out in either a members' or partners' agreement. These agreements usually require that anyone a partner or member sells to must be approved by a majority of the remaining partners or members. Partnerships may have the added complication of dissolution. A partnership technically only exists while the originating general partners participate. When one leaves, that original partnership does not really exist anymore (though you may be allowed to carry on using the same name in some cases).

Sole proprietorships cannot be transferred; the entities themselves are commingled with the owner. The sole proprietorship itself will be dissolved, and the sale will count as a sale of individual assets. It works the same way when the business is passed down to the next generation.

Rather than the business as a whole being counted as a gift or inheritance, it is viewed as a collection of assets. When the business resumes as a sole proprietorship, it will be that of the new owner.

Why Incorporating Is Better

The most significant benefit of forming a regular corporation—and this is a benefit you cannot find anywhere else—comes thanks to the current corporate tax structure. C corporations are the only entities that pay their own taxes; all other business structures are pass-through entities, meaning business income shows up on personal tax returns. Though tax rates are subject to change (and they do change rather frequently), right now C corporations enjoy some of the lowest income-tax rates around. Plus, corporations offer the most opportunity for income shifting, allowing for significant tax planning and reduction capabilities.

▸▸ **When it comes to solid personal liability protection, corporations offer their owners the most secure form of the benefit.** Proven over and over in court, literally for centuries, this shield has stood the test of time and uncountable lawsuits. Even in very public cases of grievous corporate conduct, the shareholders—even those directly involved in the daily business of the corporation—were not held personally financially accountable to plaintiffs. With small companies, the threat of lawsuits that reach your personal holdings looms even larger, and the corporate umbrella can deflect that threat handily.

In addition to those very big benefits, you also get continuity of life for the company, no matter what happens to any one owner. With other entities, an event involving a single owner can dissolve the company completely; these events include death, disability, insanity, retirement, resignation, and getting kicked out by the other owners.

Another ownership benefit is the ability to transfer interests freely (unless that's contrary to a shareholders' agreement). Basically, that means that any owner, no matter how large his ownership percentage, can give or sell his shares to someone else without needing the consent of his fellow owners.

Understanding the Disadvantages

After the last section, it may seem like corporations are the golden boys of business entities, but they don't come without some distinct disadvantages. These structures offer you a lot in terms of liability protection and tax-planning flexibility, not to mention very broad funding capabilities. But these solid benefits come at price, costing both money and time—two things many new or small-business owners do not have in abundance.

The primary financial downside to C corporations is double taxation, which means that the same income gets taxed twice: once to the corporation and once to the shareholder(s). That double taxation can be mitigated by revamping the way you take money out of the company. For example, you can take more in salary and less in dividends.

Corporations Can Be Small and Private

Many novice entrepreneurs avoid forming C corporations because they hold the common belief that it entails "going public." While it is true that many corporations are publicly held and traded on open exchanges, that is not a requirement. The overwhelming majority of corporations are actually privately held companies, meaning shares are not available to the general public.

The second common misconception concerns size. Many people believe that corporations must be very large companies. There is no limit on a corporation's size, in either direction. They range from the positively tiny to world-dominating giants. The entity is often, however, the best vehicle for transforming from tiny to gargantuan, from privately held to the next hot Wall Street stock.

The other financial drawbacks are mainly about fees: state filing fees, attorney's fees, and accounting fees. Even pass-through corporations have to pay annual fees to maintain their charters and file their reports. As for attorney's fees, they typically come in at the start-up phase, and they can run pretty high depending on your company's circumstances. Regardless of cost, this fee is not one to skip, as improper set-up can void all the benefits you gain from incorporation. Finally, there are the accounting fees. These may be higher than those for other entities due to extra filing and

Incorporating Wasn't Right for Brian's Business | Inside Track

Brian Sullivan was a professional career counselor who worked for a large head-hunting firm in the city. During his tenure there, the one thing that really stood out was how many people had truly horrible resumes and how spectacular he was at fixing them. For a while, he did some resume-writing work on the side. This side work quickly turned into a lucrative business, so Brian quit his job and started his own company.

Brian had just enough work to keep him busy and provide a nice living, but not so much that he had to hire help. He worked out of a home office and mainly met with clients over sandwiches during their lunch breaks; clients never came to his home. His resume packages were delivered via e-mail and UPS, after he received payment (which he deposited right in his personal checking account). The expenses were minimal, and mostly tacked on to customer invoices.

One of Brian's friends had just started a business, which he'd incorporated on the advice of his lawyer. So Brian met with that lawyer, who convinced Brian that his company should be incorporated as well. The lawyer charged Brian the "modest" fee of $1,500 for all of the incorporation paperwork, plus all of the state fees.

Brian didn't have an entrepreneurial background and didn't realize that he'd have a lot of ongoing paperwork to deal with now he owned a corporation. He neglected to file some state-required reports, and his corporation was dissolved for noncompliance. Though he had no legal problems to speak of, he did have some late filing fees to pay, and some official dissolution paperwork to file. At the end of it all, he went back to his sole proprietorship, a few thousand dollars poorer and a lot smarter.

reporting requirements. Again, this is not an expense to skip in favor of doing it yourself; this is another area where the pros can be most useful.

When it comes to precious time, corporations do require a lot of yours. In addition to the normal demands of running a business, you will have several corporate formalities to maintain. That includes having meetings, recording them, and maintaining specific corporate chronicles. If you meet the state requirements, form a close corporation; it will save you a lot of time, as the formality regulations are severely reduced.

Is It Time to Switch?

Should your company already be housed in another entity, you may want to consider incorporating. Even if the business structure you are using made sense at the time you first formed your company, it may not make sense any more. While you will consider the same factors as someone starting a new company, you must also take into account the impact on your current business—and there will be an impact.

For the most part, the decision to switch to the corporate form involves either liability protection or tax-planning flexibility. Whenever there has been a definitive change in either your business dealings or your personal financial situation, it may make sense to incorporate. Particularly change-worthy events include hiring your first employee, accumulating significant personal or company assets, and creating an expansion plan that needs outside funding to be realized.

If you're worried about the income-tax impact of such a switch, don't be. Most companies can be turned into corporations with no or very little income tax effect (more on this in Chapter 23). There are some exceptions, so talk to your accountant when you begin considering incorporation for your existing business. With careful planning, she can help you minimize or postpone any income taxes that could be generated by the transaction.

You have a lot of factors to weigh in your entity choice, and many of them focus on what's happening right now. To make the best decision for your company, imagine it three and five years from now. Do you see employees or additional business partners? Do you see sleek new office furniture and cutting-edge computers? Do you see more than one location, each with a lot of customer traffic? Even though some factors may point right now to an entity other than a corporation, if you expect them to change within the next five years, incorporation may still be the best structure for your company today.

"C" Means Regular

Every corporation starts its life as a C, or regular, corporation. Any company that doesn't elect to become another type of corporation (like an S corporation or a professional corporation) stays a C by default. C corporations have a set of characteristics in common; other forms share some of these traits but not others.

Every corporation has its own identity, essentially existing as a legal "person" created by state law. That means a corporation, like a person, has legal rights and responsibilities. For example, a corporation has the legal right to conduct business in its own name and enter into contracts. On the flip side, a corporation must meet its own contractual obligations and follow all necessary requirements under state law.

All corporations share the following characteristics:

- ➲ Limited liability
- ➲ Perpetual existence
- ➲ Easy equity transfers
- ➲ Centralized control
- ➲ Required legal formalities

As for unique qualities, C corporations are the only ones that pay federal taxes on their own income. While that sounds like a drawback, it may not be. Tax laws and tax rates are ever changing, and there have been (and again may be) times when corporate income tax rates were lower than the equivalent personal rates. Plus, because C corporations are separate income-tax-paying entities, these owner-shareholders enjoy the widest range of tax-advantaged fringe benefits.

Making the "S" Election

S corporations get their name from Subchapter S of the Internal Revenue Code section that defines them. The main purpose of this brand of corporation is to allow smaller companies to be taxed like partnerships, with pass-through taxation, and avoid double taxation.

In order to qualify for S status, your corporation must meet some specific conditions. The most stringent rules revolve around the owners themselves. There can be no more than 100 shareholders. Only certain entities are allowed to own shares: people, estates, some trusts and partnerships, tax-exempt charitable institutions, and another S corporation (if it owns 100 percent of the shares). Plus, the shareholders have to vote unanimously to choose the S election. If even one shareholder says no, your corporation gets stuck with C status.

Then come restrictions on the shares themselves. Unlike regular corporations, S corporations cannot have more than one class of stock. That means every share gets the exact same rights and privileges, like voting or dividend preference.

Applying for S Status

Once you decide that an S corporation better fits your needs, you need to fill out a special IRS form, Form 2553, to make that election. Form 2553 is a straightforward two-page form that you can find readily on the IRS Web site (*www.irs.gov*).

You will need to have some basic information about your company on hand as you get ready to complete your election. That includes things like the official name and address, date and state of incorporation, federal employer identification number, and the name and phone number of whomever you choose to represent the corporation to the IRS.

Timing Is Everything

To be valid, your S election has to be filed by the fifteenth day of the second month after the first day of the taxable year. That's the deadline in IRS lingo. Here's what that means to you. Suppose you form your corporation on April 1, 2006. For 2006, April 1 would be the first day of your taxable year. You would have until June 16, 2006, to file your S election. If your company's S election is not filed on time, you have to wait until the next tax year to make the change. That means the company would have to operate and pay taxes as a C corporation for its first taxable year.

States May Treat S Corporations Differently

Different states have different rules when it comes to S corporations, which is a federal designation. There are basically three ways your state may handle this:

1. Accept your federal election automatically and allow S status for state tax purposes
2. Force you to file a special state election form requesting S status there as well
3. Disregard the S corporation completely and treat the company as a regular corporation for all state tax purposes

When your state simply follows the federal track, everything will flow smoothly, at least from a tax perspective. However, if your state either does not recognize S corporations or disallows your state S election, you will have some extra work to do at tax time. In addition to the corporate and personal tax ramifications, you will also need to keep track of equity in two different ways (as you will learn in Chapter 22).

Small Corporations Get Close Status

The statutory close corporation is of special interest to small-business owners. Technically speaking, it is not really a distinct business form. Rather, it is a regular corporation that gets regulated under special state laws that supplement the standard corporate statutes.

Avoid This Common Error

It is common for people in the business community to refer to private corporations or those whose shares are not traded on public exchanges (like the NASDAQ or the NYSE) as close corporations; that's a mistake. Here, "close" refers to closely held shares, not a corporation formed under special statutory close corporation statutes. Merely having a closely held corporation does not afford your business the inherent benefits of the statutory variety.

The tremendous benefit offered by this body of regulations is that it makes life easier for owners of small corporations. Many of the usually cumbersome and time-consuming formalities normally required of corporations are toned down, allowing these corporations to be run almost as simply as LLCs. Though the exact rules vary from state to state, some common advantages of statutory close corporations include these:

- Elimination of the need for a board of directors
- Reduction or removal of the shareholders' meeting requirements
- The option to allow one vote per shareholder rather than votes per shares held
- Running the corporation via a shareholders' agreement

In exchange for these eased regulations, there are some statutory limitations placed on these corporations. For example, the number of total shareholders permitted is under thirty in some states, or under fifty in the rest. Plus, special restrictions on share transfers must be printed on the faces of the stock certificates themselves. Special, specific language must be included in the articles of organization when the corporation is formed (though in some cases a regular corporation may be allowed to convert after the fact).

So what's the big deal? Believing that you have a statutory close corporation when you actually do not can lead you to skip some of the more stringent requirements of regular corporations. That, in turn, can lead to an eventual loss of limited liability protection for you and your fellow business owners.

The True Benefit of Statutory Close Status

Most small-business owners choose the corporate entity for its innate personal limited liability protection. However, most of them do not realize just how easy it is to lose that protection.

The most common way to break that limited liability shield is to let corporate formalities lapse, something that happens all too frequently when small companies are doing everything in their power to simply survive. When that shield disappears, so does your personal protection, which puts your family's personal assets at risk. The easing of the formalities requirement serves to reduce the likelihood that a small corporation will lose its protective status. For most small-business owners who decide to incorporate, using state statutory close corporation regulations will offer the highest degree of protection.

The corollary (and more direct) benefit here is that you and your fellow shareholder-owners will have much less paperwork to file throughout the life of your corporation and won't have to hold nearly as many official meetings. That will allow you to focus your energies where they really belong: into making your company as successful as possible.

Which States Allow This Variation?

When forming your small corporation, if at all possible, do so under the statutory close corporation statutes of your home state. While there are some businesses for which this choice does not make sense (like those planning to launch a large-scale public securities offering) or for which it is not available (most states with the option limit total shareholders to either thirty or fifty), this is generally the best corporate option around for small companies.

That said, only sixteen states and the District of Columbia fully recognize the statutory close corporation option at present:

- Alabama
- Arizona
- Delaware
- Georgia
- Illinois
- Kansas
- Maryland
- Missouri
- Montana
- Nevada
- Pennsylvania
- South Carolina
- Texas
- Vermont
- Wisconsin
- Wyoming
- District of Columbia

Three additional states—Ohio, Maine, and California—offer an election for this status but do not have any specific statutes regulating it.

Should your home state not be listed above, you always have the option of forming your corporation in one of the states that does allow for statutory close status. However, you will then need to register your corporation in your home state in order to conduct business there. Yes, there will be some additional paperwork to fill out and more fees to pay, but the extra layer of protection for your limited liability shield may be well worth it.

Professional Corporations

When the owners of a corporation are state-licensed professionals, they must form a special type called a professional corporation. If you are planning to incorporate your personal-service business, you may have to form it as a professional corporation, so check with your state's corporate filing office. The following professionals are typically included under this umbrella:

- Doctors
- Lawyers
- Architects
- Engineers

- Accountants
- Acupuncturists
- Dentists
- Veterinarians

Other professionals may fall into the category as well.

For decades, professionals weren't allowed to form corporations at all, but increasing clamor from lobbying groups resulted in this special corporate form. The ban was mainly in place to protect the public from professional misconduct and malpractice, making sure people had the right to sue in appropriate circumstances. These corporations don't take away that right; rather, they protect the owners from personal responsibility from general business liabilities of the corporation. Professional corporations have the letters "PC" somewhere in their name ("Harmony Health Services, PC") to let customers know that the practice is incorporated.

Special Rules for Forming Professional Corporations

To set up this corporate form, you must use special articles of incorporation specifically designated for professional corporations. The basic forms for these are usually available at the Web site for your state corporate filing office or wherever else you would get forms for regular corporations. In addition to these special forms, there are specific rules that apply only to professional corporations.

The name of your company must include an entity indicator, like the initials "PC" or the words "Professional Corporation." If the state licensing board for your profession requires special naming conventions (like CPA or MD), that must be included in the corporate name as well. As for professional licensing, all shareholders may be required to show their current certifications along with the articles of incorporation, and only fully licensed members of the specific profession are allowed to be owners of professional corporations. The corporation can only be formed for one professional purpose, and all the shareholders have to belong to the same profession. In some states, like professions may be allowed to incorporate into a single practice. For example, two doctors with different specialties can form a single practice, like a licensed pediatrician and a licensed child psychiatrist.

Every shareholder has to comply with the legal requirements of the applicable state licensing board. (For example, each licensed professional has to carry the minimum liability insurance as prescribed by the state.) In addition, each owner must earn sufficient continuing education credits as required to maintain his license.

The Liability Factor

One of the main reasons to incorporate your business is personal liability protection from company debts. Professional corporations offer that limited liability, but with a twist. All owners are personally protected from the normal commercial debts of the business. They are not protected from full personal liability in cases of professional negligence or malpractice.

Here's the general rule. Licensed professional shareholders remain fully personally financially liable for both their own wrongful acts and those committed by people under their direct supervision. The different states vary on the issue of liability for acts of co-owners. In some states, professional corporations protect individual shareholders from wrongful acts of co-owners while in others, each shareholder is both jointly and severally personally liable for the acts of any other shareholder. That means if one professional commits malpractice, his co-owner colleagues could end up footing the bill.

Liability Climbs Up the Ladder

Dr. Ryan Smith is an internist in practice with two colleagues, both also internists; the three doctors formed a professional corporation to house their business. Their practice was quite successful, and the doctors were soon enjoying significant profits. To minimize the 35 percent flat federal income tax charged to all professional corporations, the company paid out virtually all of its profits to the doctors as salary bonuses. They kept just enough cash in the corporation to cover expenses.

One day, Dr. Smith was working with a just-graduated, newly hired nurse, Donna. A patient came in with clear signs of an extreme allergic reaction to a bee sting. Dr. Smith ordered Donna to administer a shot of allergy medication. Donna was flustered by the patient's extreme distress and accidentally gave him a shot of insulin. That erroneous injection put the patient into dire straits, and emergency medical services were required.

Though the drama ended well, the patient sued for a large sum of money to cover all of his medical costs, the lost salary from days he couldn't work, with some pain-and-suffering damages thrown in. Donna's own malpractice insurance covered a large chunk of those damages, and the corporation's insurance kicked in some more. There was still some money to be paid, and the only pocket with enough money to handle it was Dr. Smith's. Since Donna had been working under his orders, Dr. Smith was forced to pay $35,000 out of his personal holdings.

Not-for-Profit and Tax-Exempt

The primary purpose of a not-for-profit organization is, as the name implies, not to earn profits. Rather, these groups focus on doing good works, like feeding the hungry or providing medical care to those who cannot otherwise afford it. To help these companies achieve their humanitarian goals, federal and state governments excuse them from paying any income taxes, giving them tax-exempt status. That means they don't have to pay any corporate income tax on their revenues, which come mainly from donations. It also means that they can receive tax-deductible contributions from the general public and are eligible to get grant funding from other tax-exempt agencies.

Not-for-profit corporations are formed under special state laws that often follow a uniform model, the Nonprofit Corporation Act. These laws may mirror the regular rules of incorporation, but they come with some very important differences. The first is somewhat different articles of incorporation, specifically tagged as nonprofit articles. Forms for these are usually available at the Web site of the state corporate filing office or wherever else you would get forms for regular corporations. On the federal side, not-for-profit corporations apply for a federal 501(c)(3) nonprofit tax exemption once they've attained that status from the state. To do this, a founder of the corporation fills out IRS Form 1023, which is more like a pamphlet than a regular form. When that application is approved, the IRS will send out something called a favorable determination letter, which is retroactive up to fifteen months (since they can take a very long time to be processed).

The bylaws, while similar, also will have some unique twists. For example, many not-for-profit corporations create a central board of directors plus various special committees to deal with operations. Their directors also tend to meet much more frequently than those of regular business corporations. Plus, of course, there are no provisions to pay profits out to the members (similar to shareholders) as dividends. However, people who provide services to the organization, including officers and employees, can be paid reasonable salaries.

In addition to the different start-up paperwork, the laws governing not-for-profit corporations can be more intricate. ▶▶ **Your company must follow all requirements to the letter to maintain not-for-profit and tax-exempt status.** One slip could disqualify the corporation, and turn it into a fully taxable entity. Be careful to follow every rule to the letter, and make sure your corporation continually meets all of its tax-exemption requirements. Though tax-exempt corporations don't file actual income tax returns, they do have to file annual reports with the IRS to demonstrate their compliance with all the not-for-profit regulations.

State Law Rules

When it comes to the rules governing corporations, the states are in charge. The state decides what you need to do to form your corporation, keep it going, and dissolve it. Individual states may also choose to tax corporations as they see fit, as they are not required to follow the federal model (though many do choose this route).

Financial issues constitute the biggest differences among the states. They include things like income taxation as well as fee schedules and creation and maintenance costs. Other big differences include privacy protection, recognition of S status, the close corporation option, and court precedents. (Some states appear to favor corporate protections more than others based on the existing body of legal decisions.) As Chapter 10 explains, all of the factors come together to help you decide the state in which to form your corporation.

While many business owners simply incorporate in their home states, a great many seek a strategic advantage by forming their corporations elsewhere. Aside from home states and states in which a corporation will conduct most of its business, the two most popular states for corporate formation are Delaware and Nevada. This is largely due to their very favorable laws. Delaware, for example, can be very cost effective for both ongoing fees and taxes as well as for lawsuit settlement. Nevada offers the most stringent privacy laws, a benefit for corporate owners and board members who want to remain anonymous.

Foreign or Domestic Is a State Distinction

Sometimes, your corporation will have to deal with the laws of more than one state. That happens when your corporation is formed in one state and does business in another, or even several others, a very common occurrence. In the legal lingo, "domestic" refers to a corporation that's formed in its home state by filing articles with the appropriate state office. "Foreign" corporations are those doing business in a state they were not formed in, even if they have a strong physical presence and conduct a lot of business there. Basically, a domestic corporation is a hometown boy, while a foreign corporation is an out-of-state guest.

The foreign or domestic issue is not just a matter of semantics. For one thing, it changes the way the corporation will be taxed within the state. For another, the paperwork is different. A lot of states make foreign corporations jump through hoops before they will be allowed entry. This is both to make sure that domestic corporations keep the home-field advantage and to protect consumers in case a legal matter should arise.

If you want to operate your corporation in State A, though it was incorporated in State B, your corporation first has to qualify for acceptance. The qualifications are essentially that the company is a corporation and that it will be conducting business in State A. To qualify (which means virtually the same thing as "register," in this context), your corporation will have to go through almost the same process it did to come into existence.

The corporation must file its articles of incorporation in State A. On top of that, though, there is usually an extra set of papers to file that relates specifically to foreign state information. For example, that foreign information would include things like the name and contact information of the person (called a registered agent) who will represent the corporation in State A, and the address out of which the business primarily will be conducted (if it has a place of business in the state). In addition, once your corporation is accepted as a foreign player, it most likely will have to file periodic corporate reports and regular tax returns (depending on the laws of State A).

On top of the extra paperwork comes a bunch of taxes and fees. A lot of states make it expensive for foreign corporations to register, mainly to cushion the blow of added competition for domestic businesses. The filing fees to qualify as a foreign corporation will at least equal those charged to domestic corporations, but most states set them higher. As for taxes, most states require foreign corporations to file regular tax returns and pay accordingly. The rates may be different than those for domestic corporations. Finally, the foreign corporation has to have a local agent to accept service and other government or legal papers. These registered agents, when not already corporate employees, may charge hefty annual fees.

▶▶ TEST DRIVE

It's best to decide before you incorporate your business just what form of corporation best suits the circumstances (when you have a choice, that is). Consider these questions as you make your decision:

- ➲ How many shareholders will there be?
- ➲ Do you expect the business to incur losses for the first couple of years?
- ➲ Does the home state recognize S or close corporations?
- ➲ How good are you at keeping up with paperwork?
- ➲ Do you envision a public offering of shares in the future?

Limited Liability

Businesses run up debts, just as people do. Mistakes are made in the normal course of business: accidents happen, people get hurt, and property gets damaged. All of these things add up to liabilities for the business, obligations that must be paid out of company assets. Whether it's suppliers who are sending collection letters or a customer who slipped in the store and is suing for damages, they have a legal right to get paid what they are owed.

What happens, though, when the company does not have enough assets to cover its debts? The quick answer is "bankruptcy." That is a very common response to overwhelming obligations. Companies declare one form of bankruptcy or another, and they either fold or restructure. Creditors may go unpaid for long periods of time; in fact, they may never get paid . . . by the company, that is. Without the shield of a protective entity, business creditors can (and do) go after the assets of the business owners to satisfy any outstanding debts. That means that people or companies to whom your business owes money can sue you personally if your company can no longer pay its bills. They can drain your bank accounts, call for a personal asset sale, garnish wages, and take over your stock portfolio—unless, that is, your business has built-in limited liability protection, like that provided by every form of corporation.

▸▸ **Limited liability protection means that you do not have to worry about your personal assets being lost to business debts** (with a few specific exceptions, like your own acts of malpractice). It means that the wealth you and your family have worked so hard to build is shielded from creditors of your corporation. And it means that the most you could possibly lose if your business goes under is the amount you have invested. That's meant to be reassuring, given that the owners of an unincorporated business run the risk of losing much more than their capital investment.

Protection Goes Both Ways

Most people only consider the personal benefits of the limited liability shield, but that shield can protect the corporation as well, not against its own debts but against those of its owners. With other business entities, a company could be held financially responsible for the personal unpaid debts of one of its owners. Not so with a corporation. That business entity faces no liability for any outstanding debts of its shareholders, no matter how many shares they hold. As long as the corporation stands, personal debts and business debts will not mix.

There is one possible loophole that some personal creditors may use to get their hooks into the corporation. In some cases, a shareholder may be forced to turn his shares over to a personal creditor as payment for an outstanding obligation. Then, the creditor could use his voting power to try and get his money; for example, he could vote to distribute dividends or sell off assets.

Some Exceptions Apply

No matter how bulletproof your corporate shield, there are times when you can be held liable for business debts. Specific situations include these:

- ➲ A personal guarantee of a business debt
- ➲ A failure by the company to pay taxes (especially payroll taxes)
- ➲ Proven fraudulent transactions

Though these are not the only exceptions, they are the most common, and they are easy to avoid. If you don't cosign any corporate loans or promise any creditors that you'll personally pay any overdue bills, you won't be held liable for corporate obligations. If you make sure that all applicable taxes are paid, with a special emphasis on payroll taxes, you won't be forced to pay them. Finally, if you operate your corporation in an honest and legal manner, your shield should remain firmly in place.

Tax Advantages

At first glance, it may seem like forming a corporation will create more taxes. In a way that's true, as there will almost certainly be more tax forms to file. When it comes to the total federal income tax bill, though, incorporating gives you the most and best chances to minimize the overall amount that you and your company will end up paying.

The federal income-tax advantages you gain by incorporating your business depend in part on the type of corporation you form. Still, you can rest assured that regardless of which corporate variety houses your company, you will receive some very real federal tax benefits for your business and your family.

Some of the potential benefits of incorporation most commonly employed (again, which apply depends on which corporate form you've chosen) include tax-free fringe benefits and expanded retirement planning options and enhanced tax-planning capabilities.

State Income Tax Laws Vary Widely

Every corporation enjoys some income tax advantages on the federal level. State-level income taxes (and possibly even local-level taxes) may not offer the same, or even any, benefits. Though many states mimic federal guidelines, some veer fairly wide off the uniformity track, with laws wholly unique to their constituents.

For example, Arizona imposes income taxes on corporations based on their federal taxable income. Maine has its own graduated corporate income tax system. Michigan charges a tax on all business income, whether the company is incorporated or not. Ohio's corporate income tax is based on the total value of outstanding stock. Then there's Nevada, which imposes no income tax at all on corporations.

Fringe Benefits

Until recently, corporations were the only business entities that offered their owners totally tax-free health insurance; now, all small-business owners enjoy that advantage. However, health insurance is only one of many potential employee benefits, and many of the rest are only tax-advantaged for C corporation owners. Some restrictions may apply to some benefit offerings (as you'll learn in Chapter 20), but most of the advantages are truly that.

Group term-life insurance is one of those tax-advantaged fringe benefits. The premiums for up to $50,000 worth of coverage are deductible for every employee of the corporation, including you. Even better, you won't be personally taxed on those premiums, unlike other business owners. Along the same lines comes disability insurance, which is both tax-deductible to the company and tax-free to you as an owner-employee. Corporations also offer some of the best retirement plan options. Plus, they are the only entities that can offer any employee equity sharing plans, like stock options.

Better Tax-Planning Capabilities

Corporations are the only business entities where owners draw actual salaries, complete with withholding taxes, that are deductible as payroll expense to the company. All other forms of business require that the owner simply take nondeductible withdrawals. However, these entrepreneurs must pay tax on their complete share of business income whether or not they take any withdrawals.

Though S-corporation owners do pay tax on the income of the corporation, that income does not include whatever they took out in salary. C-corporation owners pay income tax on their salary and any dividends they pay themselves, but nothing directly based on the corporation's income. This salary capability offers an immense tax-planning tool to the owners of corporations, as they can shift income around in whichever way comes out best for tax purposes. One year they could take a lot of salary and no dividends; another year they could do the opposite, or even take only salary with no dividends. The final combination could depend on that year's tax laws.

This unique opportunity is commonly referred to as income splitting or income shifting, and only corporation owners can do it. As explained in Part 5, figuring out the balance involves some math and a thorough understanding of current tax law—and that usually means obtaining the advice of a qualified tax professional.

Access to Capital

When it comes to raising equity capital, it doesn't get much easier than selling shares of stock—once you get a handle on all of the legalities and registrations and filings, that is. When you form your corporation, you authorize the maximum number of shares the corporation can ever have outstanding. You might not issue all of these shares initially; in fact, you might never issue all of the shares. But you can, and that's what makes raising capital easier.

Different Shares for Different Folks

One of the biggest advantages of the corporate form is the built-in ability to allow for different types of ownership (a benefit is not available with S corporations). When you want to have different classes of owners, you can simply issue different classes of stock. Working owner-shareholders can hold the lion's share of the common voting stock, giving them control. Pure investors, those who won't be involved in the business side of business, can get preferred stock: no voting rights, but first in line for dividends. Employees can be given shares of nonvoting common stock, allowing them to share in the profits and growth (and thereby offering them a great incentive to work harder for the company) without giving them controlling interests.

Consider this scenario. You and your co-owners are completely tapped out when it comes to putting more personal cash into the company. The business already has some fairly substantial debt. The bank would probably approve another loan, but then virtually all of your profits would get eaten up by interest payments. You don't want to take on another true business partner. For all other business entities, taking on either undesirable debt or an undesired partner would be the only viable options. For a corporation, you have the golden option. You can sell off relatively small equity shares to raise cash without losing any control over your company.

Of course, selling shares means you're selling securities, and SEC regulations may apply to your offering. More often than not, though, small corporations will fit neatly into one of the SEC exemption piles, making it very simple to comply with these federal laws. In addition to these federal laws, you will also have to comply with any applicable state legislation before offering your securities for sale. You'll learn more about state and federal securities law in Chapter 8.

Funding Growth

When your company outgrows its normal pool of investors, corporations allow you to step outside that little box and offer shares to the general public. That gives your company the opportunity to bring in a large number of small investors, increasing your capital base while maintaining control of the corporation.

This scenario may bring in the SEC. Still, it's easier than ever before for small corporations to offer shares directly to the public (even over the Internet) without exhaustive red tape or prohibitive costs. At both the federal and state levels, securities laws have been eased for small annual public offerings. Of course, in the world of securities law, small is a relative term. Under these relaxed guidelines, your corporation can raise between $1 and $10 million every year through public offerings of stock. That can fund a lot of growth.

The "Serious" Factor

It's sad, but true. Many fledgling small businesses are not taken seriously by the surrounding business community. Once they've proven themselves, however, that changes. It can be difficult to prove yourself without the explicit and implicit support of the business community. It's like the old getting-a-job conundrum: You can't get a job without experience, and you can't get experience without a job. For your business, it's more like you can't succeed unless people take you seriously, and people may not take you seriously until you've demonstrated success.

An instant fix for that seriousness issue is for you to take your business seriously. Forming a definite entity by incorporating your business shows that you are not just giving entrepreneurship a whirl. Taking the time, trouble, and money to form a corporation adds a dimension of substance to your company. And, whether merited or not, incorporating brings with it a stronger impression of success than any other entity.

One of the easiest ways to boost your chances of obtaining a business loan or attracting investors is to add "Inc." to your company's name. The mere formality of incorporation is one factor, and the inherent corporate structure is another. That centralized management gives comfort that will continue seamlessly even when a key player drops out. Plus, nervous lenders or investors can request seats on the board of directors, allowing them a closer look and some involvement in the business to help protect their investment. Or they could request special powers, like the right to bar a major asset purchase or additional debt. Because of the extreme flexibility that is built in to corporations, investors and lenders can tailor their involvement in any number of ways.

In addition to attracting moneymen, corporations can also attract better employees. Corporations offer a sense of stability and a wider range of benefits, including employee stock incentives. That can help you draw a better pool of qualified employees and help you secure their loyalty.

Trouble-Free Transfers

Corporations have built in ease when it comes to transferring shares of ownership. All you really have to do is reassign a stock certificate and—presto!—you've transferred a share in the business. Assets and accounts are allocated proportionately with that share, in one fell swoop.

With sole proprietorships and partnerships, every asset must be transferred separately to the new owners. Each asset must be retitled in the name of the new company. Every account, every business license, and every permit must be transferred individually. Some items, like a valid taxpayer ID, will even need to be reapplied for. That's because when you transfer an ownership interest in one of these entities, the original company is liquidated and a new one is created. Not so for a corporation, which exists as-is no matter who owns it. Unlike these other entities, transferring ownership of a corporation does not have to affect its existence at all.

Crondall Plumbing, Inc., Gets a Loan

Robert Crondall is a plumber. For years, he worked side by side with his father, but then he got the itch to go off on his own. He had all the basic tools, an adequate work truck, decades of experience, and a good reputation. He was well known in the community as the plumber who came when he said he would and who charged a fair price for every job.

Robert realized he would have to spend money to get a new company going. After careful planning, he figured that he needed a better work vehicle, another full set of tools, and an ample supply of common plumbing parts. He wrote up a business plan and headed over to the bank he'd been using for almost twenty years to ask for a loan. Much to his surprise, they turned him down. When Robert asked for a reason, the loan officer told him that they just weren't sure he'd stick with it. While he was a great plumber, they didn't know whether he would make a good business owner or whether he would really commit to having his own business for the long haul.

Robert talked to his father, who suggested Robert incorporate his company. That would help take care of some liability issues and help convince the bank that Robert took this new enterprise very seriously. Robert listened to his father and created Crondall Plumbing, Inc. He revised his business plan accordingly, and went back to the bank—where they did approve his request for a business loan.

This ease of ownership transfers comes in especially handy for family businesses, one of the most common incarnations of small businesses. Corporations allow for simpler succession plans. All you have to do is gift shares to your children, and their ownership interests can grow as they get older. In addition, by owning shares jointly with your spouse, you can avoid probate. The corporation goes on, and your spouse has immediate access to the shares.

▶▶ **TEST DRIVE**

Since you've decided to incorporate your business, you can take full advantage of the personal benefits that go along with this entity. To get the most personal bang for your corporate buck, think about which of those benefits will offer the biggest benefits to you and your family. Your corporation may not be able to afford everything right away. You can take steps to implement them once you know which are most important to you right now:

⮕ Looking to build wealth? Consider a strategy to systematically transfer corporate profits into personal accounts, and look into retirement plan options.

⮕ Interested in protecting your family? Start pricing group health- and life-insurance plans.

⮕ Want to create a long-lasting business to pass down to your kids? Create multiple share classes, allowing you to bring in investors who can help your business grow faster and letting you start transferring ownership to your kids whenever you're ready.

PART **1**

Getting Started

Test Your Ideas with a Business Plan

Every business can benefit from a business plan, whether that business is still in the idea stages or is ready to expand to accommodate greater success. You may have big ideas about your business. Some of those ideas can translate into money in the bank, but there will be others that just don't make sense when you put the numbers together. Creating a business plan will help you see just which ideas may pack a profitable punch and which will get knocked out in the first round.

In addition to the very real insights you'll gain from creating a business plan, the plan is also a must-have when it comes to making business loan applications or proposals to attract equity investors. That's right. A solid business plan can draw outside money toward your corporation, and it's next to impossible to raise cash without one.

No matter the audience for your business plan, virtually every plan includes these basic elements:

- ➲ Standard front matter
- ➲ An executive summary
- ➲ A market analysis
- ➲ An in-depth look at the competition
- ➲ Descriptions of products and services
- ➲ The marketing plan
- ➲ The operations plan
- ➲ A lot of financial statements

Depending on the audience for your plan, you may include additional sections or choose to leave some out. For example, if you're using the plan for internal purposes, you may include proprietary research and development information that would not belong in a document that would be in outside circulation. On the other hand, if you were using the document as a sort of résumé for potential vendors, you might want to leave out the section that details your competitors, some of whom probably use the same vendors.

A Brief Look at Plan Elements

In the front of every business plan comes some standard front matter. This includes things like a title page, contact information, a confidentiality statement, and a table of contents. Next comes the executive summary, which is really a summary of the entire plan that focuses on the high points. **▸▸ The executive summary is considered the most important part of the plan, as bankers and investors often read this section to decide whether they'll bother to look at the rest.** A great impression here can turn the tide in favor of your company.

Now comes the real meat of the plan: the research, the numbers, and why and how you think it all translates into a profitable business venture. The market analysis includes information you've gathered about the industry and the target customer base, which when put together can help determine your company's potential market share. That will be followed by an in-depth analysis of your competition, from who else is out there to how you can snatch away some of their market share.

Plan readers will also want a solid idea of what you plan to sell, whether that's products, services, or some of each. Simply listing your offerings won't be enough, though. Your readers want to know why what you're selling is better than what everyone else is selling, and why customers will want to buy that product or service from you. That section segues directly into your marketing plan, which spells out how you plan to let the world know about your company and what it's offering.

The operations plan includes details about how your company will be run. In it, readers will find résumé-type information about the owners and key employees, along with an overview of the business structure, the chain of command, and other operational issues. If you're already in business, the business plan will conclude with a complete set of current financial statements; regardless of whether you're in business or just setting up, and you also have to include financial projections for the foreseeable future. Typically, prospective financial statements include projections for up to three years into the future, which is as far as anyone can realistically make reasonable profitability predictions.

Raise Money with Your Business Plan

It is virtually impossible to attract any kind of financial backers for your business without a complete business plan. The reason for that is simple: people putting money into your company want something in return. If they're lending money, they want to know that the company can pay it back, with interest, on time. If they're investing, they want assurance that they'll earn a reasonable return on that investment. The moneymen understand that new companies may need some time before they start turning a profit and maintaining a steady cash flow. At the same time, they want to know that those things have a high probability of occurring a little way down the road.

Many novice business-plan writers mistakenly assume that bankers and investors shy away from putting money into companies that have weak spots, but that's simply not the case. **▶ A successful business plan tells the truth, albeit with a shiny spin**. Rather than ignoring weaknesses and potential trouble spots, the best plans address those issues head on and describe a handy supply of workable solutions as well. In fact, if your business sounds too good to be true, potential lenders and investors will probably assume it is and place your request in their "no" pile.

Use Your Plan As a Guidepost

Once a business is underway, the business plan is usually filed somewhere and not looked at again—not until the company needs another outside source of funding, that is. That's a mistake. Your plan can be an extremely valuable reference guide, one that can help keep your company on a profitable track. In addition, should you be faced with any of the problems you foresaw while developing the plan, you have guidelines in place for the best ways of dealing with them.

Your plan is also an excellent yardstick for measuring the actual performance of your business against your expectations. Pitting your corporation's results against projections can help you improve profitability and cash flow going forward. It allows you to see where the company may be falling short of goals and provide a clear view of what areas can use improvement.

Transforming an Existing Business

Most small businesses do not start out as corporations. Many of them, though, go on to incorporate later, after they've been operating successfully for a while and want to start taking advantage of the inherent benefits of incorporation. When this transformation occurs, it involves a lot more than simply adding "Inc." to the end of the company name. There's a laundry list of steps to follow. Many are the same as those for brandnew businesses, but some are unique to the transformation situation.

At the most basic level, this switch to the corporate entity involves trading the net assets (the total assets minus the total liabilities) of your old company for shares in the new corporation. That's really all that happens on the strictly mechanical level. The assets and liabilities of the unincorporated business are transferred in to the brand-new corporation, then the new corporation issues shares of stock to the old company's owners in exchange.

The Mechanics

Once you've created your corporation, you still have some work to do to finalize the process. For example, your corporation will have to file its first annual report, get insurance, open a bank account, and perform several other administrative tasks, as described in Part 3 of this book. However, when your corporation is born out of a previously existing business, there are some extra steps you have to take.

First, the old company must be officially dissolved. Your state business office can provide the exact procedures you must follow, but most include the same basic tasks. You'll file the final sales tax and employment tax returns, including payment from the old company's checking account for any balance due. After that, close the old bank accounts, and open new ones in the name of the corporation (as laid out in the initial board meeting). Any business licenses or permits held in the name of the old company must be cancelled; the corporation must apply for its own versions of these documents. Finally, you must provide written notification to all parties who have been doing business with the old company that it has become a corporation. This is particularly critical in the case of creditors. (See Chapter 19 for more specific information about creditor notification.)

The Tax Impact

One of the most important issues is the potential tax consequence involved in making the change, but don't let that put you off from your decision. In many cases, there will be no tax payment necessary, but exceptions can apply depending on how the transformation takes place. The specifics can get a little murky, so call on the expert advice of a business-tax professional before you start transferring assets or issuing stock.

In most cases, a special IRS rule called IRS Section 351 kicks in. This rule allows people incorporating a business to defer any tax consequences until they sell off their shares in the new corporation. Without Section 351, you would have to treat the asset transfer as a sale and pay tax on any profits right now. The tax deferral allows you to put all of the old assets into the new company without worrying about tax consequences, a much better deal for the typical small business owner.

But this being the IRS, certain restrictions apply (of course). For example, shares being issued in exchange for services, rather than property, may count as immediate taxable income. Also, Section 351 only covers shares of common stock, so shares of preferred stock usually do not qualify. When liabilities are involved, as they often are, they can throw some gum into the Section 351 works. On top of all that, there may be some situations in which invoking a Section 351 tax-free exchange will not provide the best tax-planning option. Since there are so many potential sticking points, and since improper handling can result in a big tax bill, get advice from a qualified professional as you prepare to incorporate your existing business.

Required Notification

When you transform an existing business into a corporation, you have to notify everyone your old company did business with, from vendors to customers to bankers. These notifications are best made in writing, which provides you with proof that this task was completed.

In most circumstances, this is just another formality. As long as you keep paying the bills and fulfilling the company contracts, your creditors and customers probably won't care that your business has been incorporated. However, if your company had substantial outstanding debt before the transformation, and some or all of it was past due, you can expect some phone calls from those creditors. As long as you reassure them that they will be paid (or in the case of customers, that their contracts will be fulfilled), and actually do pay them, everything will continue as usual. If, however, those old obligations are not met, the corporate liability shield probably will not protect your personal assets against those claims.

The notification letters need not be formal or written in legalese. You can simply state that you've dissolved your old company, which is now doing business as this new corporation. Include the old company name and contact information right along with the new corporate name and contact information. You can add a brief note stating something about how much you've appreciated doing business with them in the past and how you hope to continue that mutually beneficial relationship in the future. Make sure to keep a copy of each notification letter you send, and place it in your permanent corporate records book.

Is Your Company Eligible for Regular Incorporation?

Some companies are simply not allowed to incorporate, ever, while some are prohibited from operating as regular, plain-vanilla corporations. ▸▸ **Certain licensed professions, such as lawyers and doctors, may be prohibited from incorporating or forming LLCs at all in some states**, though the tide has turned in favor of allowing them to form these entities. In the states that do allow these licensed professionals to incorporate, special corporate or LLC forms are usually required. At the federal level, professional corporations have a tax drawback: All profits are subject to a 35 percent flat income tax, relatively high compared to regular corporate and individual income tax rates.

These special corporate forms come with very strict guidelines about who can own shares. The basic rule (though, again, this varies a bit by state) is that every owner must be a fully and currently licensed member of the same profession. While these corporations do afford their owners a great deal of personal protection, their limited liability shield comes with one big gaping exception: malpractice.

The main idea behind this rule is to keep professionals who may face malpractice claims from hiding behind a limited liability shield. Malpractice involves mistakes made in the course of conducting professional business, and the legal standard ensures that the public has the right to sue in those cases. The corporate shield will never protect anyone from his own acts of malpractice, but it can provide protection from any claims resulting from a co-owner's malpractice, which is not the case in a general partnership.

The list of professions that must incorporate using this special entity varies somewhat by state. Check with your state business office to see if your professional services company falls under this umbrella.

Coming Up with a Name

Even the task of selecting a name for your corporation is governed by the corporate rule book. There are rules about words you must use in the name, as well as words you cannot use. And, as you may expect by now, the naming rules vary from state to state. That can make naming your business even trickier if you have a corporation that will operate in more than one state, as the name must meet the requirements for every state in which your corporation will do business. Though there is some variation, these are the standard naming conventions, one of which must be used in your corporate name:

➲ Corporation
➲ Incorporated
➲ Limited
➲ Inc.
➲ Corp.
➲ Ltd.

Randi Thompson's Almost-Fiasco

Randi Thompson had been a CPA for about ten years. She'd worked for a few firms and also did returns on the side during tax season. One day Randi met Jerry Katz at a professional seminar. Though Jerry was a CPA, he'd spent his career working for a private company, and now he wanted to start his own tax firm. He was looking for someone with strong tax experience to partner with, since he didn't have that background, and he started recruiting Randi for his firm.

At first Randi just laughed, but as he made it clear that she'd reap most of the rewards until he had more experience, she considered his offer to form a firm together. Randi insisted on a professional corporation, despite the extra outlay of money and time, with only the two of them as shareholders.

During their first tax season. Randi prepared the more complicated returns. Jerry handled the simpler filings, and Randi reviewed his work. But Randi had an emergency and had to take a week off. She told Jerry not to deliver any returns until she returned. Jerry intended to do that, but he got an "emergency" call from a client who needed a return done immediately, for a high rush fee. Relying heavily on his tax software, Jerry did his best to prepare the return accurately, and he never told Randi a thing about it.

A year later, the corporation got served; that rush client was suing for malpractice based on gross errors in his return. Their insurance paid the bulk of the claim, with a $20,000 deductible left over. The corporation had very few assets, as the shareholders took virtually all corporate earnings as salary. The client then turned to Randi and Jerry. Jerry was found responsible for his own malpractice and got charged with that $20,000. Randi was totally protected, thanks to her professional corporation entity.

There are also limits on the wording you can use, though these are much less specific. In most states, your corporate name must be easily distinguishable from other registered corporate names. That means your company's name cannot be the same as that of another corporation, and in some states it may also mean that the name cannot be so close to another that people cannot tell the difference between them.

Though these naming rules may seem like overkill, they do serve a specific purpose. The name of any corporation has to make it crystal clear to other parties that they are dealing with a liability-limiting entity. It must also not impede in any way on the business of a previously existing corporation simply by virtue of its name. Finally, if you use a company name that infringes on another company's trademark rights, there may be serious legal consequences to face.

Here's the bottom line. Before you get business cards and stationery printed up, before you order anything with your company's name on it, make sure you have chosen a name that you can use. Register that name right away, so no one else can claim it.

What's in a Name?

When you choose your corporate name, consider one that lets your potential customers know exactly what you do without limiting your company too much (after all, you may expand beyond the initial product or service line one day). This serves the dual purpose of providing an easy advertising tool and increasing the chances that the name will be available. For example, Bob Smith Incorporated doesn't give any clues about what your company does. On the other hand, going with Bob Smith's Baking Supplies, Inc., tackles both issues. There's no doubt about what kinds of products your company provides, and it's more likely that the name will be available in your state's registry.

Check Your State Filing Office

Before you fill out any paperwork, check with your state filing office to make sure you can use the name you want to use. If it's unavailable, the state won't accept your articles of incorporation, and you'll be back at square one. The state will reject your corporate name if it's exactly the same or close enough to confuse people. The "confusion rule" is kind of a gray area and somewhat subject to opinion. Basically, though, if the name would confuse someone reasonable—meaning that a reasonable person might call your company when she really meant to call the other one—resign yourself to picking something else.

There's an exception there (no surprise). Your corporate name usually won't be rejected when it includes your own name, even if that is already used or could cause confusion. So if your heart is really set on Bob Smith Incorporated, and the state already has another corporation with the exact same name on file, they'll likely approve yours anyway.

You can check whether your proposed corporation name already exists in the state's registry by calling your state filing office and asking. They'll usually let you check on up to three different names for free. You can also check the state's business office Web site, as many of them have a corporate-name search mechanism available.

Conduct a Trademark Search

As part of determining whether the name you want to give your corporation is available, you must perform a trademark search. This task can be challenging, as there are a lot of trademarks out there, and many smaller companies hire a professional firm to conduct the search for them. Fees often run into the $500 to $1,000 range. Or you can use the Internet and do it yourself, as long as you're prepared to devote a lot of time to the search. If that's the course you choose to take, start with the Web site of the U.S. Patent and Trademark Office, located at *www.uspto.gov/main/trademarks.htm.*

Once you're on the USPTO site, click on New User Form Search, and enter the proposed corporate name in the search window. If the name pops up, perform the search on your other choices until you find one that is free. You can't stop there, though, because potential legal complications can arise if the name you want to use comes very close to one that is already trademarked. Other ways to look up include spelling the name differently to cover sound-alike names. For example, if you want to call your company Zytech, you might also look up Zytek and Zitech.

Doing Business As

Many companies have more than one name, one for official purposes (like the name on your birth certificate) and one for actual business purposes (like your nickname). That corporate nickname is called the DBA name, where DBA means "doing business as," sometimes referred to as a fictitious business name. For example, a corporation registered as Bob Smith Incorporated could be doing business as Bob's Pizza Shack. In that case, the public would know the company as Bob's Pizza Shack, while government regulatory and tax agencies would know it as Bob Smith Incorporated DBA Bob's Pizza Shack.

Like your corporation's official name, **DBA names must be registered with the state**. It may be to your company's benefit for these two names to be as close as possible. Often, the DBA name is the same as the official name with the corporate designator (like "Incorporated") left off. The reason highly similar names are beneficial is that it strengthens your corporation's identity in the business community, such as among bank loan officers and suppliers.

You can find specific information regarding state procedures for filing a DBA name on the state business office Web site. Typically, this name registration can be completed for less than $100 and follows this three-step process:

1. File a DBA business name form with appropriate state and local authorities.
2. Put an ad in the local newspaper stating your corporation's intent to use that DBA name.
3. File an affidavit of publication with the appropriate state and local officials.

Filing your DBA registration form is fairly quick and painless. You can pick up the form from the state (and county, where applicable) business office, or download it from their Web site. You'll fill in information like the official name of your corporation, its primary address, any corporate ID numbers you've been assigned, and the DBA name you wish to use. When you're done with that, call at least one local newspaper that serves the county where your corporation is primarily located (usually its headquarters). The ad will normally need to be run for at least four weeks or maybe longer, depending on your state requirements. The state guidelines will let you know what specific language must be used in the ad, but it often involves simply stating your company's official name and the name you intend to use as the DBA name. Finally, you'll file an affidavit of publication wherever you filed that DBA registration. All that does is affirm that you've run the required advertisement, with the required wording, for the required time period.

This Is Tricky, So Use a Lawyer

The one huge (and pretty obvious) advantage to do-it-yourself incorporation is that it costs less, at least in the beginning. In the long run, though, bearing the costs of a professional to help you form your corporation could save both you and your corporation a lot of money.

If your corporation is not organized properly, you will be more susceptible to the attempts of creditors to pierce that corporate veil in order to reach your personal assets. In addition, improper formation could invalidate your corporation from the get-go, making your company a de facto sole proprietorship or partnership (depending on the number of owners).

Going the Discount Route

There are books out there with names like *Form Your Own Corporation in 60 Seconds* (no, that's not a real book) that offer cookie-cutter solutions, for all fifty states, focusing on keeping costs down above all else. While it is possible to form your own corporation using standard forms and basic legal language, that is not the best way to ensure your complete protection. After all, one of the reasons you have decided to incorporate your business is to shield your personal assets from business liabilities, so it only makes sense to use the strongest, least vulnerable shield you possibly can.

The next tier of solutions involve companies that specialize in mass incorporation. These guys know a lot of the ins and outs of getting the right papers filed in the right places at the right times. They can help you make sure that every *i* is dotted on every standard form. This will cost more than doing it on your own, but you'll spend much less than you would on a private attorney. Many of these companies will do a thoroughly serviceable job, but with that same cookie-cutter approach. Your corporation's paperwork will look exactly like everyone else's, regardless of any unique circumstances surrounding your company.

Before You Hire the Lawyer

Maybe you have a family attorney you have used for years to handle all of your personal legal needs, like wills or family trusts or custody agreements. You trust him with the most personal details of your life.

While trust is crucial to the attorney-client relationship, it is not enough to qualify someone to be your corporate lawyer.

To handle the legal needs of your company, you need a qualified business attorney. The bigger your corporation, the more owners it has, and the more complex its setup and maintenance will be. It takes someone who has experience in the field, who has set up complex corporations before, to make your liability shield airtight. Since that is really the whole point of your incorporation, it's nothing you want to hand over to an attorney who is winging his way through.

Beware of Incorporation Scams

The Internet makes a lot of things easier and more convenient, including the opportunity to take advantage of people. While you will find many legitimate incorporation services companies on the Web, you may also run across some that are not quite above board.

Before you offer any personal information to any unfamiliar company over the Internet, do some homework. Call any phone numbers they post to make sure they're actually in service. Try asking a question whose answer requires some thought, rather than an automatic reply. If you get a canned answer, or no response at all, take your business elsewhere. Contact an agency like the Better Business Bureau to make sure no complaints have been filed. Whichever steps you take, at least take some. Once your information is out there in the wrong hands, it can be hard to get things back on track.

Once you've found a competent attorney whom you like and trust, ask for a fee schedule right up front. Make sure you clearly understand how your company will be billed. For example, some attorneys bill in minimum ten-minute increments, while others bill by the half hour and still others have flat rates for particular services (like $50 per e-mail response). Find out whether you'll be billed in increments or must put down a sizable retainer before the work even starts. Don't be afraid to ask for an estimate of how much the entire job will cost, and don't be afraid to say it's too much if your business can't afford it. The attorney may agree to bring down his fees, or he may refer you to an associate. If you feel uncomfortable asking these questions, pick a lawyer you can talk to with ease.

Add an Accountant to the Mix

Extensive tax benefits have factored into your decision to incorporate, so make sure to preserve them by using an experienced accountant to handle your corporate tax returns. Sure, you could probably come up with an acceptable corporate tax return on your own. In fact, this move would likely be very popular with the government since the bottom-line tax calculations would probably be way too high. Doing this yourself could convert your tax benefits into a whopping tax bill, so resign yourself to going the professional route. Be sure to choose a professional with plenty of small business experience who lives and breathes the ins and outs of the tax code. His services may cost what seems like a lot of money, but the insights you gain and the tax savings you reap will be well worth every penny.

The federal tax code can be pretty convoluted at times, using pages of badly written text to explain the guidelines surrounding a single deduction. The rules are complex, and (to make things even harder to deal with) they change relatively frequently. Just understanding and keeping up with the latest incarnations is a full-time professional job.

In addition to the tax factor, your corporation's finances can benefit from the insights of an accountant. Every day, transactions will occur that can impact your company's future success. Dealing with these occurrences, maximizing profitable trends while minimizing negative ones, and keeping your corporation in the black takes a lot of work. While you (or one of your co-owners or employees) may be able to handle the basic bookkeeping tasks of the company, the more sophisticated statement preparation and business analysis may be best left in the hands of a qualified professional.

Consider your accountant to be a part of your management team, and choose one who fits in well with your vision and strategy. Remember, application and interpretation of tax laws is somewhat subjective. Many of the guidelines are sweeping, rather than pinpoint-specific, and can be applied differently in different situations. You want your accountant's strategies to reflect your own. For example, if you have a high tolerance for risk, and you want the most aggressive tax treatment possible, a conservative tax advisor won't be a good fit for your team. The final decisions will always be yours to make, but the options presented to you should correspond to your business philosophy.

Some Business Basics

When it comes to the business of doing business, there are some things that every company has to do, whether it is a sole proprietorship, an LLC, or a corporation. Most of these standard procedures come into play courtesy of state and local governments, and there can be a lot of them. Make sure that you meet every requirement, or you could find your company quickly out of business.

In almost every case, all it will take to fulfill your obligations is filling out forms and writing checks. Some cases may involve one-time or ongoing inspections, as those that are standard in the food-service industry. Other times, your business may be subjected to special non-tax audits to make sure you are in compliance with local law.

The most common business requirements your company will be asked to meet, depending on your industry, may include these:

- ➲ Local business license
- ➲ Professional licensing for all owners
- ➲ Sales tax registration
- ➲ Employer registration
- ➲ Fictitious name or DBA certificate (discussed in detail above)
- ➲ Industry-based registration

If you're not sure which apply to your company, contact your county administrator. That office will often have business start-up guides that detail all the steps you must take to keep your company in compliance.

In addition to regulation-related tasks, you will also perform dozens of business-related tasks for your corporation. There are accounting transactions to complete, books to keep, employees to pay, contracts to fulfill, customers to satisfy, and many other day-to-day tasks to keep up with.

 **TEST DRIVE**

Coming up with a great and available name for your corporation can be tough. You may even need to come up with three or four, in case your first choices are already taken. Use these tricks to come up with a unique name that can also serve as a free marketing tool.

- ➲ Include your name in the company name.
- ➲ Get specific about what your company does.
- ➲ Create a memorable fake word that captures the spirit of your business (like Xerox).
- ➲ Test the names on some people you know—then ask them a few days later if they can remember those names.

Understanding
Corporations

PART **2**

Corporations Are "People"

Legally speaking, a corporation is a person. That corporate person has certain legal rights and responsibilities, just as real live people do. A corporation has the right to enter into contracts, hire an attorney to represent it in court, file lawsuits, and conduct business in its own name. It also has the responsibility to pay taxes (whenever applicable), fulfill any contractual obligations, and comply with laws and regulations. Though a corporation is considered a person under the law, it is not a "natural person," and laws that specifically refer to natural persons do not apply to corporations.

Every state authorizes business corporations to engage in absolutely any business activity not specifically prohibited by law. Essentially, that gives corporations the power to do just about anything, including things like these:

- Open and maintain bank accounts
- Own assets
- Incur liabilities
- Lend money
- Make charitable donations
- Establish and maintain employee retirement plans
- Enter into joint ventures with other businesses
- Hire and fire employees

So, for legal and business purposes, corporations are people. However, they need actual people to take all of these actions and to be formed in the first place. Even though real people must be involved in order for a corporation to operate, the people don't have to stand in for the corporation when it comes to legal issues. Those are strictly the problems of the corporation itself, one of great benefits of incorporation.

Incorporators Get Things Going

If you want your business to be set up as a corporation, you have to incorporate it. The person responsible for doing that is called the incorporator. Basically, an incorporator signs the articles of incorporation and then files those articles with the state.

While many entrepreneurs serve as the incorporators for their own small businesses, there is no legal requirement that they do so. The incorporator doesn't have to be one of the directors or officers of the corporation; he doesn't even have to be one of the initial shareholders. In fact, the incorporator doesn't even have to be a resident of the state in which the corporation will be formed. All that's required legally in most states is that he be at least eighteen years old.

That said, it's a good idea to have one of your directors act as incorporator. This can be helpful because your board of directors has to carry the management ball just as soon as the corporation is formed. Plus, you know that any correspondence from the state will be sent directly to a director.

Beware of Entering Into Pre-incorporation Contracts

Contracts entered into before the incorporation process is complete will not be legally valid for the corporation. However, they may be enforceable against whomever signed them, typically the incorporator.

An exception kicks in if you (as the incorporator) sign the contracts in the name of the corporation only, without using your name, and explicitly inform the other party that the corporation doesn't actually exist yet. In fact, you must also inform them that the corporation may never come into existence and may not adopt the contract even if it does. The best protection, though, is to simply not engage in any legal or business transactions until your company is incorporated.

Remember, though, that your corporation doesn't exist until the incorporator's duties are complete. That means any business conducted before that point is not business of the corporation. Contracts signed before incorporation become valid only if the corporation officially ratifies them (a task performed by the directors) or begins to benefit from their provisions. For example, if you lease a computer in the name of the corporation before incorporation, having the corporation accept delivery and begin using that computer counts as the corporation itself accepting the contract.

Shareholders Are the Owners

The people who own corporations are called shareholders, whether there are two owners or 2 million. You can become an owner by purchasing or receiving shares of stock, and your percentage of ownership depends on how many shares you hold. There is no legal limit on how many shareholders can own pieces of any regular corporation; however, owners of privately held corporations may impose their own limits on how many shareholders there can be. Legal limits do exist for both close corporations (fewer than fifty, though it varies by state) and S corporations (no more than 100, according to federal mandate).

The role of shareholders often depends on the nature of the corporation itself, the total number of shareholders out there, and the stake each has in the business. As you'd expect, ownership of a larger percentage of shares comes with a keener interest in the inner workings of the company. Conversely, holding on to relatively few shares to collect dividends or as part of a retirement fund does not often lend itself to active involvement.

Shareholder Restrictions for S Corporations

In addition to the restriction on the allowed number of shareholders for S corporations, the federal government also imposes restrictions on just who may be a shareholder. First, the maximum number of shareholders is 100, but counting those shareholders comes with a minor twist. Thanks to newly enacted federal laws, an entire family can count as a single shareholder, not as several separate ones.

To figure out just who can be a shareholder, it is easiest to take a reverse approach and look at those who cannot be shareholders:

- People who are not U.S. citizens
- C corporations
- LLCs

➲ Most partnerships
➲ Other S corporations (unless it's the sole shareholder)
➲ Certain trusts

What Shareholders Do

By definition, shareholders do not run corporations. They do not oversee or manage operations, and they do not get involved in everyday business activities. In small companies, though, shareholders may hold multiple roles, such as directors or officers. It is in those other roles that shareholders take care of business, as you'll learn later in this chapter.

The primary role of shareholders is to vote on big-picture issues. Shareholders do not have the power to order directors or officers to do anything, but they can elect and get rid of directors, decide on major corporate changes (like mergers or dissolution), and influence the general course of business. There are five main ways that shareholders can affect corporate change:

1. Voting directors in and out is the most direct way shareholders can get things done. By choosing directors whose views most agree with their own, shareholders can indirectly impact the direction of the corporation. Conversely, they can remove directors seen as ineffective or acting improperly.

2. Approving changes in the articles of incorporation and sometimes the bylaws also falls under shareholder capabilities. These changes are proposed and adopted by the directors, but the shareholders have the final say.

3. Approving major changes also falls to the shareholders. Examples include large acquisitions, mergers, the sale of virtually any corporate asset, and complete dissolution of the corporation. None of these can occur without the explicit approval of the shareholders.

4. Voting on transactions where a conflict of interest is involved, such as one involving a director or officer with a major stake in the outcome of the transaction. Though votes like these are common, they are not legally required.

5. Shareholder resolutions circumvent all other channels and can directly propose specific corporate actions. Though these actions would need to be approved by the board of directors before taking effect, the will of the shareholders is generally followed.

The Reality of Small Corporations

S corporations have strict shareholder limits. The role of shareholders is primarily voting. These maxims are true, but do not always play a major part when it comes to owning and running a small, privately held corporation. The biggest shareholder-related difference between these and large publicly held corporations is the level of shareholder involvement.

In big business, shareholders typically take a passive role, rarely even voting their shares when significant issues come up. In the world of small business, though, shareholders usually play multiple parts, and they are directly involved in running the company on every level. Every state allows for this one-man-many-hats approach to owning and operating a small corporation. Almost all states will let you form a one-owner corporation, which makes you the sole shareholder. Along those lines, you'll probably also be the incorporator, a board member, and all of the officers. As long as you carry out all the tasks required of each specific job, your corporation should carry on just fine.

The Board Directs Everything

Shareholders do a lot of things, but they don't officially run their corporation. That job is left to the board of directors, which has both the responsibility and the authority to manage the company. Most states don't have any rules about how many directors your corporation must have; however, when your corporation has three or fewer owners, some require that you have at least as many directors as shareholders. So if you're the sole owner, you can also be the sole director, but if you have one or two co-owners, your corporation may have to have two or three directors, respectively.

Martha Benjamin Wears Many Hats

Martha Benjamin incorporated her one-woman knitting-supplies shop at the end of last year. Martha was the sole shareholder of Wool's Clothing, Inc. According to the corporation's home state laws, the company was required to have at least one director. In addition, the corporation was required to have at least two officers, a president and a secretary, though one person was permitted to fill both positions.

Martha had been part of the local business community for quite some time before incorporating, and she'd heard all the horror stories, probably exaggerated, about losing limited liability protection. Not one to take chances, she began fulfilling her formality requirements right away. As the incorporator, she named herself a director. As soon as her articles were approved, she held her first board meeting and officially issued herself shares of stock. She passed several corporate resolutions in her role as director. At the end of the meeting (in which she was the only participant), she compiled her notes and signed them, then placed them in the corporate records book.

Moments later, she held her first shareholders' meeting. She voted to confirm her position as director. Then she officially appointed herself corporate president and secretary. She also voted to affirm all decisions made at the first board meeting. Again, she kept notes during her one-woman meeting, and at the end of the meeting she signed and dated them. Finally, she entered those minutes into her corporate records book—her first official act as corporate secretary.

Directors are voted in each year at the annual shareholders' meeting. If you are the only shareholder, you do have to vote yourself in as a director. Most state laws allow for one-year terms for directors, meaning you have to re-elect your directors every year or vote in new ones. Once the directors are elected, they can hold their annual meeting.

The primary role of corporate directors is to meet periodically and make collective decisions, usually about major business issues facing the corporation. Day-to-day operational decisions are typically delegated to the corporate officers (though in small corporations that often means delegating to yourself). Directors reserve the broad, big-picture decisions for themselves, including things like these:

➲ Electing the corporate officers

➲ Issuing additional shares of stock

➲ Approving loans made to or by the corporation

➲ Authorizing major asset purchases

➲ Authorizing employee stock option plans

➲ Making major operational changes

➲ Choosing to expand into new business lines or locations

Like incorporators, directors don't need to meet a bunch of special requirements in order to serve. For example, state laws don't impose residency requirements, and directors need not be shareholders. Typically, the only formal requirement is that directors have to be real people, as opposed to other corporations, and at least eighteen years old.

In addition to all of the powers and responsibilities they are given, corporate directors may also receive compensation for their efforts if they choose. The board can vote to pay individual directors a reasonable compensation for governing the corporation, completely separate from any other pay they receive if they work in another capacity for the company. On top of that, directors can be reimbursed for travel and lodging expenses incurred while attending board meetings.

Meetings of the Board

One of the primary legal responsibilities of the board of directors is to conduct periodic formal meetings, at least once a year in most states. The main meeting typically takes place right after the annual shareholders' meeting, as that's when the directors get elected. At this meeting, each director formally accepts his election to the board. Then, the business of directing the business can get underway. Even if you are the only director, you must observe these formalities, and you must conduct and record these proceedings in order to preserve your company's corporate status.

The date, time, and location of the annual meetings are spelled out in the corporation's bylaws. Though most states don't force you to issue written invitations for the annual meeting to each director (after all, the information is included in the bylaws), it's still a good idea to provide notice of each meeting in writing. That way, directors are reminded to attend that year's annual meeting.

The rules regarding any other meetings of the board—any one that's not an annual meeting is considered a special meeting—vary by state. Generally, though, the legal requirement involves providing written notice to each director about meeting specifics, including time, location, and reason for the special meeting.

Responsibilities of the Directors

Under state laws, corporate directors must always act in the best interest of the corporation and exercise care as they make decisions that will impact the company. These are legal duties. Should a director be found to have violated these responsibilities, the courts may find him personally financially liable for any resultant losses suffered by the corporation or its shareholders.

Consider Adding an Outside Director

As the owner of a small corporation, whether you're the only one or one of a few, you will have to fill many roles. That doesn't mean, though, that you or your co-owners are necessarily expert in all of them. For that reason, you may want to add a sort of mentor to your board of directors, someone with specific professional expertise, like a small business attorney or an accountant, or someone who has extensive entrepreneurial experience.

This person does not have to own any shares (though you could offer a token number) or work for the corporation as an employee. He can merely get involved when major decisions are at stake and board meetings would necessarily be called.

First on the list is the legal duty of care. Essentially, directors must act in good faith and always in the best interests of the corporation and the shareholders. State statutes spell this out in fancier language, but the premise is the same. While the laws don't tell you exactly how to act or specifically what to do, the key is to have good and honest intent. The duty of care doesn't mean a director will be held personally liable for honest mistakes that are the best possible course of action given the information available at the time of a decision. Problems generally crop up only when severe negligence or actual fraud is uncovered by someone who has the legal standing to take action.

Next comes the duty of loyalty. Directors of a corporation have a legal duty to put the business interests of the corporation ahead of their own. In real terms, that means when the director happens upon a lucrative business opportunity while serving the corporation, he has to give the corporation first crack at it. If the corporation refuses the deal, then the director is free to pursue it. Also, if the deal would obviously be of no interest to the corporation (for example, a bean-bag chair supplier wouldn't normally be interested in buying a warehouse full of ice cream cones), the director can take advantage of the deal through other means. Basically, to comply with this standard, a director has to act fairly for the corporation when good business opportunities crop up.

Meet the Officers

Part of the corporate set up involves naming officers, each appointed by the reigning board of directors. Traditionally, corporations have four primary officers: president, vice president, treasurer, and secretary. Each office comes with a specific function, with specific responsibilities that must be carried out to meet corporate requirements. In many small corporations, all four roles are fulfilled by one or two people. That's fine, as long as none of the necessary formalities get skipped.

In some states, a corporation can have any number of officers, and the board members can confer any titles they choose. Some of these "optional" titles have become so commonplace that they are part of the standard corporate lingo: chief executive officer (CEO), for example, or chief financial officer (CFO). In these cases, the corporate bylaws set forth the title and responsibilities of each officer.

Anyone can become a corporate officer. In the case of big corporations, the people chosen for these roles usually come with plenty of knowledge and experience. In small corporations, the roles are typically filled by shareholders. To keep things simple, small corporations usually stick with the traditional officers, though sometimes multiple roles get mixed together.

Officer Compensation

While corporate officers are appointed by the board of directors, they are employees of the corporation and deserve compensation for their efforts. Federal tax laws allow corporations an expense deduction for that compensation, as long as it's reasonable. There is no exact definition of reasonable in the law, but you'll know it when you see it. Take into account the size of the company, its normal earnings level, and salaries paid to other people for similar jobs. That will give you a defendable definition of reasonable, should the IRS come asking.

Remember that officer compensation may include more than cash. Officers may also receive things like stock options and employee benefits. The IRS will take that total compensation package into account when determining whether it is reasonable.

The President

The president of a corporation carries the bulk of responsibility for putting procedures in place and overseeing corporate policies. He sets the direction of the corporation and is usually in charge of administering the day-to-day activities of the company. Typical tasks include negotiating and executing major contracts, signing stock certificates, and filing any other required legal documents. Though the president has the most authority within the corporation, he still must answer to the board of directors. In the case of a major undertaking, the president acts on behalf of the corporation, by order of a corporate resolution.

The Vice President

Small companies usually have a single vice president, if any at all. Large companies, though, may have dozens of them, each with more tailored duties (a vice president of marketing, for example). Where there is a vice president, he may step in for the president when he's unavailable. In addition, the board of directors may task a vice president with specific duties to fulfill, such as oversee particular divisions of the business. In states where not all the officer positions are required, this position is often left off the roster.

The Treasurer

The corporate treasurer is typically the company's chief financial officer (CFO), and he oversees all financial matters. With a small corporation, he may be charged with such things as managing the corporate cash and payroll, handling accounts receivable and collections, dealing with debt repayment, and maintaining a complete and current set of financial records. The treasurer is also responsible for preparing financial statements and presenting them to the board, the other officers, and the shareholders. Finally, the treasurer is in charge of corporate taxes and designing strategies to minimize those taxes (usually with a tax advisor).

The Secretary

The secretary may be the officer most critical to maintaining corporate status, and many states specifically require that this role be filled. When choosing a corporate secretary, look for someone reliable and meticulous.

As part of his duties, the secretary will be required to maintain records and minutes and attend all board, officer, and shareholder meetings.

▶▶ TEST DRIVE

Which corporate officer best matches with your unique skills and talents? Peek into their professional personalities to find out.

- ➲ If you generate a lot of big ideas, and have a great grasp of the big picture, you'll fit well in the role of president.
- ➲ If you like to roll up your sleeves and get down to business, vice president is the office for you.
- ➲ If you're proficient with financial analysis and interpretation, you would make a capable corporate treasurer.
- ➲ If you have an eye for detail, can manage lots of projects at once, and always complete tasks on schedule, go for the demanding role of Corporate Secretary.

PART **2**

Understanding Corporations

Articles of Incorporation

To create a corporation, you must first file articles of incorporation (also called articles of organization, certificate of formation, certification of organization, or charter) in the state in which you have chosen to form your entity. This does not have to be your home state, or even the state in which the majority of your company's transactions will be conducted; you can form your corporation in any state you choose. Once that state accepts the articles of incorporation, your corporation begins its official existence.

When you have decided on the state, you will have to file all paperwork according to its guidelines, which spell out exactly how to accomplish that task. Typically, this process involves contacting the secretary of state and requesting the necessary paperwork. In many cases, the simplest way to achieve that is to go to the state's business and commerce Web page and download the forms you need. (A list of appropriate state Web sites can be found in Appendix B.) ▸▸ **Though you can find incorporation kits at many stationery stores, these one-size-fits-all documents may not include specific requirements dictated by state law.**

Though articles of incorporation are of gigantic importance to your company, the document itself is rather small. In fact, your corporation's articles may not even take up one entire page (remember, contents vary by state law). At the very least, the articles of incorporation must include the following basic identifying information for your corporation:

- ⊃ The proposed corporate name (which you may have reserved when you came up with it)
- ⊃ The total number of authorized shares
- ⊃ The full address of the registered office
- ⊃ The full name of the registered agent
- ⊃ The name and address of the incorporator

Some states may require additional information, such as the intended par value of the authorized shares. When the articles of incorporation are completed, the incorporator must date and sign the document.

The next step is actually filing the document with your state corporate filing office. Here you may have a choice among electronic filing, mailing in your proposed articles, or walking them into the state office. Most entrepreneurs deliver their articles of incorporation by mail, along with a basic cover letter and a check to pay the filing fees. All the cover letter really needs to say is that you've enclosed a certain number of copies of your articles of incorporation for your corporation (use its name), followed by a request for the filing office to file those articles and mail you confirmation-stamped copies to a stated address. If your incorporator has reserved the name, include all pertinent information about the reservation in the cover letter. Finally, make sure your cover letter indicates that payment is enclosed.

Corporate Bylaws

Second in importance only to the articles of incorporation are the company bylaws. This crucial document does not get filed with the state office; instead, it's an internal document that sets out the rules for running the company. Rather than typical everyday business procedures, the bylaws cover big-ticket items, like the explicit powers of officers and directors.

The bylaws document can fill anywhere from one to one hundred pages, but most fall somewhere between five and twenty pages in length. Many of the items included in the bylaws have to fall in line with state statutes. For example, if your state says that directors have to be notified of special meetings at least ten days in advance, your bylaws can specify a notification period of fourteen days, but not one of five.

What to Include in Your Bylaws

When it comes to corporate bylaws, you can be as general or specific as you choose. After all, this document is for your corporation's eyes only. As long as you take care to conform with statutory requirements, what you put into your bylaws is wholly up to you. Along with any other issues you would like to define explicitly, the following issues are typically covered in a standard set of corporate bylaws:

- ➲ The number of directors who sit on the board
- ➲ The range of powers and duties for directors
- ➲ The date, time, and location of annual board meetings
- ➲ A description of how directors are elected and removed
- ➲ Procedures for appointing the corporate officers
- ➲ The range of powers and duties for officers
- ➲ The date, time, and location of annual shareholder meetings
- ➲ Voting rules for both directors and shareholders
- ➲ Proxy procedures

The Bylaws Process

The process of adopting corporate bylaws is a little more involved than simply writing up a set of rules. Once they're created, the bylaws must be formally adopted for the corporation by the incorporator, who can then appoint the initial directors. Remember, now that you're running a corporation, every major move you make is formalized in writing. When you are the only person involved in this process, you can approve the bylaws and approve yourself as a director all at once, though this action does require another piece of paper.

Fill-in-the-Blank Bylaws

Virtually all incorporation kits come with a generic set of bylaws, with blanks left open for you to fill in the specifics. This is one do-it-yourself area that makes sense. Many bylaws documents prepared by lawyers essentially recount state requirements. You can draft your bylaws with some flexibility, following state guidelines, while adding a provision to refer to those state requirements when necessary.

Remember, even when you use standardized forms, you can still tack on any specific provisions that you want to include. You are not limited by what shows up on the form. The only real limitations on your bylaws are the state laws, and those must be followed no matter who prepares this internal document.

This document, called something like "Action by the Incorporator to Adopt Bylaws and Appoint Directors," will be permanently included in your corporate records book. First, write that the corporation (use the name) has approved the bylaws per the incorporator and made them a permanent part of the corporate records. Next, include a passage that says you've appointed directors in accordance with those bylaws for a specific term, and name those directors. Affirm that you, as the incorporator, agree with this action. Then date and sign the document as the incorporator.

As you prepare this document, you can surf to your state business Web site and take a look at some sample language for this action. The language does not have to be formal or written in legalese to stand up. Just make sure the document is clear and that the necessary points are covered.

The Shareholders' Agreement

Whenever more than one person owns a company, there are bound to be disagreements. If your corporation has more than one shareholder, a formal shareholders' agreement is in order. Though it will take some time, money, and energy to iron out differences of opinion to create an agreement that all of you agree with, the long-run savings are countless. It's far better to come up with a plan about how to handle specific types of disputes now, when they're not actually happening and tempers are not running high. That way, when the inevitable disagreements occur, you'll have a piece of paper to consult to help you calmly sort things out.

A shareholders' agreement is designed to forestall potential problems and put in place procedures to fix them in a fair manner. It spells out exactly what will happen in the event of a difference of opinion among the parties to the agreement. This is especially critical in small, closely held corporations where it can be harder to get your money out when deal-breaking conflicts crop up. This is a particular problem for minority shareholders, who also have very little control over business operations.

No matter who your co-owners are, put a shareholders' agreement in place. Whether they're friends, family members, professional associates, colleagues, or just faceless investors, a shareholders' agreement can protect all of you from getting mired down in costly and protracted legal battles.

For S Corporations

Buy-sell provisions are not optional when your company is formed as an S corporation. Failing to maintain control over which and how many people hold shares can result in the loss of your corporate status. That can cause some disastrous consequences, not the least of which could be a huge personal-liability problem.

The rules about S corporation shareholders are very specific, and they must be followed to a tee in order to preserve the corporate status. Having just one too many shareholders or one disallowed shareholder for even one day can invalidate your corporate charter. In your buy-sell provisions, you can put procedures in place to avoid these problems.

What to Include in Your Shareholders' Agreement

Shareholders' agreements are common business documents. If you look at a bunch of them, much of the language will be similar, with a few personalized twists here and there. While you can really include anything you and your co-owners want to in this agreement, there are some points you should absolutely not leave out (as Chapter 14 describes in more detail). Every shareholders' agreement should contain at least the following provisions:

- Rights of minority shareholders
- How votes are won, by majority or unanimously
- The right of shareholders to serve as directors (even if they're not officially on the board)
- Salary caps
- When and how additional shares may be issued
- Obligatory arbitration
- Buy-sell provisions (typically the most important section of all)

A Word About Buy-Sell Provisions

When you have a small, closely held corporation, you want to maintain some control over who can be an owner. Should one of your fellow shareholders sell out, you could be stuck with a new business partner whom you don't know, don't like, or don't trust. For that reason alone, buy-sell provisions should be a key part of your shareholders' agreement, but there are plenty of other reasons these provisions are a must-have.

In addition to the "who" factor, another big issue when it comes to selling shares of a closely held corporation is "how much." It can be difficult to put a price tag on your corporation's stock; buy-sell provisions can offer a formula to follow that takes the guesswork and subjectivity out of the calculation.

Keeping the Minutes

Corporate formalities create a lot of paperwork, but none is so constant as keeping the minutes, which really means taking notes and including them in the permanent records. There are specific times and specific ways to keep the minutes, but all you're actually doing is keeping a written record of corporate happenings.

The bulkiest portion of your minute book (the permanent place to store all your minutes) will come from both annual and special meetings of both the directors and the shareholders. Every action that takes place during these meetings must be noted. The minutes need not be extensive or elaborate as long as they record what took place.

These are some of the items typically included in the minutes:

➲ What kind of meeting it is (for example, the annual shareholders' meeting)
➲ The meeting logistics (time and place)
➲ Whether the meeting was called by notice or notice was waived
➲ Who attended, including the person keeping the minutes
➲ Who chaired, or led, the meeting
➲ Any actions taken, like major asset purchases or elections, for example

| Inside Track | Minute Book Saves the Day |

Kathryn Smith was a certified massage therapist and aromatherapist. She had her own practice and a dedicated client list. As alternative-health treatments started to hit the news more, her small practice began to grow. Even with nothing more than a Yellow Pages ad, her business began to attract a lot of new customers.

Kathryn's dad advised her to incorporate her business. Kathryn followed that advice and incorporated her practice. She also remodeled her house, adding on a treatment room. She bought furnishings and a new massage table. She stocked up on essential oils and other supplies. Many of these purchases were made with a corporate credit card, and the oils were purchased on account from the vendor.

From the very beginning, Kathryn kept up with the corporate formalities meticulously. She held shareholder's and board meetings with just herself in attendance and carefully documented each. She kept records of every major decision, from the remodeling plan to the choice of corporate credit card, all filed in her corporate records book. She filed every piece of paperwork on time and kept copies of those in her corporate records book as well.

When the alternative "craze" slowed down, Kathryn was stuck with a lot of bills and a lot fewer clients. The corporation started losing money and was having trouble paying the bills. Her oils vendor threatened to take her to court personally, saying she wasn't really a corporation because she worked out of her home. At their initial conference, Kathryn whipped out her corporate records book along with her corporation's financial records. The vendor's lawyer conferred with his client, then told Kathryn's lawyer that they would not be suing her personally, since she clearly had a bona fide corporation. Instead, they'd have to deal with the corporation when it came to a repayment plan.

Whoever recorded the minutes must also sign and date them at the bottom.

Though it may seem ridiculous, you must keep minutes for annual meetings even if you meet only with yourself. (Yes, you have to hold the official meetings even when it's just you.) In fact, keeping the minutes for a one-owner corporation can help your entity stand up in court should it ever be called into question by someone looking to invalidate your limited liability shield.

Corporate Resolutions

Whenever directors or shareholders make major decisions for the corporation, the proposal must be documented and voted on by the appropriate parties. The document is called a resolution, and a resolution must be passed by a vote in order to be enacted.

Some activities that merit the filing of a formal corporate resolution may seem relatively unimportant in the scheme of things, like a resolution to choose the bank in which to open the corporate checking account. Others seem monumental, like resolving to sell off a portion of the business. What these actions have in common is that they were brought about by the directors or the shareholders, rather than the internal players of the corporation. With small, closely held corporations, these roles are often played by the same people: shareholders are directors are officers.

Writing up formal corporate resolutions, calling meetings, and holding votes to implement a plan may seem like overkill. However, doing this by the book helps to solidify your corporate entity and to fortify your limited liability shield. As such, whenever you plan to make a relatively significant business move (as compared to the usual everyday transactions of the corporation), go through these motions and file the documents away in your corporate records book.

Initial Resolutions

When your corporation is first created, only those directors named by the incorporator exist to run it. At their first meeting, the directors must adopt several resolutions to get the corporation up and running. From an organizational perspective, they must authorize the issuance of the initial shares, elect the officers, and accept the corporate bylaws. From a business perspective, they must choose a corporate accounting period, choose a bank to house the corporate accounts, enumerate the people who may sign corporate checks, and make any desired tax elections (like to apply for Subchapter S status).

All of these resolutions must be passed in order for the corporation to ever open its doors for business. Without officers, there would be no one to officially run the business. Until shares are issued and transferred, no one owns the business. Absent a bank account with authorized check signers, no one can pay the corporate bills. As for tax matters, without specific corporate action, the default rules would apply. For example, unless the corporation resolves to apply for S status, it will remain a C corporation.

Common Resolution Issues

Once the corporation is up and running, the officers make the primary business decisions. However, any shareholder (even a minority shareholder) or director can propose a resolution. When you are the one playing all three roles, you will make most decisions in your capacity as corporate officer. To fully protect your corporation and your personal assets, it's best to use resolutions for the bigger decisions. Documenting the decision-making process, from proposal to acceptance and implementation, follows the spirit of corporate formalities. These formalities can be especially critical to the preservation of small, closely held corporations.

While you don't need to issue a formal corporate resolution when you want to change the color of the corporate letterhead, there will be some situations where the formality is called for, such as these:

➲ Adopting a new DBA name
➲ Taking out a bank loan
➲ Leasing or purchasing major assets
➲ Opening a new corporate bank account
➲ Changing the fiscal year
➲ Hiring additional employees
➲ Engaging professionals (attorney, accountant, consultant)
➲ Selling off business assets
➲ Entering into or terminating a contract
➲ Dissolving the corporation

There aren't any specific language requirements in drafting corporate resolutions, but it's important to cover all of the important points of the action that will be taken. Most stationery stores supply fill-in-the-blank forms, as do corporate kits. You can also check online with your state's business office, many of which post sample documents for small-business use.

Stock Certificates

Once your corporation exists, it can issue shares to you, your cofounders, and any equity investors. To document this new ownership, each shareholder receives stock certificates. Though most states don't require those actual pieces of paper to acknowledge a shareholder, it's a good idea to have them anyway. That certificate provides physical, written proof of your ownership rights in the corporation.

As with most corporate documents, state law dictates the basic information that's required to appear on any stock certificates your corporation does issue. At the very least, the certificates will need to include the name of the corporation and its state of formation, the name of the shareholder and how many shares he holds, and the signatures of two corporate officers.

Beware Bearer Certificates

Bearer certificates are like cash. They belong to whoever is holding them, regardless of how they were acquired. Lose a certificate, and you've just lost however many shares of stock it represents; whoever finds that certificate technically owns those shares now. Most states do not allow bearer certificates, mainly because they're untraceable, but a few do. In theory, bearer certificates protect your privacy. Your name doesn't appear on them, and they don't have to be registered anywhere. In practice, they pose some personal financial risk. Should your bearer certificates be lost, stolen, or destroyed, you could have a very hard time claiming your ownership stake.

You can buy blank stock certificates at most stationery stores and simply fill in the blanks. Or you can go the more formal route and have your share certificates printed to your specifications—as you might expect, this option costs more. More than just fancy pieces of paper that often end up in the bottom of safe deposit boxes, stock certificates symbolize the underlying transfer of assets for ownership rights.

 **TEST DRIVE**

Start making notes about what provisions you would like to see included in your shareholders' agreement. Remember, anything you think is important to the successful management and maintenance of your corporation may be included (in addition to the standards, like buy-sell provisions). This can be especially important for small, closely held corporations. Here are some hints that may spark issues you may want covered in your agreement:

➲ Shareholders holding more than X% of shares must work at least XX hours per year for the company.

➲ At least X shareholders must approve expenditures over $X,XXX.

➲ At least X shareholders must approve replacing a major supplier (with "major" defined as purchases over $XX,XXX per year).

➲ At least X shareholders must approve the hiring of significant employees (for example, a site manager).

Corporate Capital Structure

In the business world, capital refers to ownership or equity. In corporations, every unit of ownership is represented by a single share of stock. The fact that corporate ownership can be divided into tiny little pieces gives it a distinct advantage over virtually every other form of business. You can get equity financing from a large number of people, making it the absolute easiest way to bring in outside investment, especially when you are looking for investors who will not want to participate actively in the business.

Especially when it comes to true investors, rather than active owners, smaller is easier. For example, you may be more easily able to persuade twenty people to contribute $2,500 than one person to pitch in $50,000. Corporations allow for this widespread ownership through the sale of stock shares.

Both the number and type of shares you wish to offer must be set forth in detail in your articles of incorporation. You have to know what you want the corporation to look like, at least in terms of equity structure, both now and in the distant future. At the very least, every corporation must have one class of stock that has voting rights; without this, the corporation would never be able to function.

Stock is only one part of the entire corporate capital structure, though that piece can come in several varieties (as the next section described). Other than stock, though, the structure may also include the following:

- Retained earnings
- Treasury stock
- Additional paid-in-capital

Retained Earnings

Retained earnings are really just what they sound like, earnings that the company holds onto for future use rather than distributing them to shareholders as dividends. Every time the company shows a profit, it must decide whether it wants to hold onto those earnings or hand them out. When the corporation has plans for expansion and growth, or when it is in the early stages of development, it is very common to keep the money in-house. On the other hand, most people started businesses because on some level they wanted more disposable income; with corporations, dividends are one way for them to get cash out of the company. Luckily, it does not have to be an all-or-nothing scenario. Your corporation can retain enough profits to begin building a nest egg for future use and distribute the rest to you and your co-owners as dividends.

When your company sustains a loss, that has an impact on the retained earnings account as well. It is not uncommon for new and small corporations to have negative retained earnings for the first year or two. Once the company starts turning a profit, that negative balance begins to turn toward the positive.

A Variety of Uses

You can think of retained earnings as a sort of corporate equity savings account. Those funds can be earmarked for things like major asset purchases, physical expansion of your store or factory, or even buying up another small business. In fact, you can have more than one retained earnings account, just as you may have a regular emergency savings account, a savings-investment account, and a vacation account. No matter how you decide to split the funds up, retained earnings is part of your overall corporate equity.

Treasury Stock

When a corporation buys back its own stock, the shares transform into something called treasury stock. Treasury stock is not the same as stock that has not yet been issued by the corporation. These are shares that someone has owned in the past and that are now held by the company itself.

In big corporations, a stock repurchase often revolves around resetting the market price of the stock. For small corporations, though, it can be a way to concentrate ownership without affecting the current balance of major shareholders. For example, if the three main shareholders each have 5,000 shares, they each have an equal interest in the company. Should one of the minor shareholders want to get rid of 1,000 shares, selling to one of the major shareholders would upset that equal balance; having the corporation buy the stock takes care of that problem. In addition, should the corporation wish to raise more cash in the future, it can sell off the treasury stock instead of having to issue new shares.

Additional Paid-In Capital

A share of stock comes with a predetermined value, called par value (as detailed in the next section). That value often has nothing to do with how much money is exchanged for the share, even by you; it's really just a number you choose to use when filling out paperwork.

Everything that gets exchanged for stock, whether it is money or other property, is considered paid-in capital because it got paid in to the corporation in exchange for a capital stake. The difference between the par value and the amount you paid for each share is considered additional paid-in capital, the excess over par, and it gets accounted for separately on the books. Additional paid-in capital is sometimes also referred to as capital surplus.

Different Types of Stock

When it comes to stock in a corporation, not all shares are necessarily created equal. The base version is voting common stock, and every corporation must have at least some of these shares. Common stock refers to shares that come with no preferential treatment when it comes to receiving dividends; every share earns the same amount at the same time.
▸▸ **Voting stock means that you get a vote for every share you own, to be used for things like electing a board of directors.** Regardless of how many classes of shares your corporation has, even if it is only one, the rights and privileges of each must be spelled out in your articles of incorporation.

Keep in mind that if your corporation is set up as an S corporation, it cannot have more than one class of shares. That means you cannot authorize or issue any preferred stock or any second class of common stock that comes with different rights and privileges. The single exception is that a single class can be divided into voting and nonvoting shares, as long as all other rights remain constant.

Common and Preferred Stock

Common stock is just what it sounds like: plain old bare-bones stock. This is the most basic stock of your corporation, the kind the true owners (as opposed to investors or employee-owners) will hold. Standard common stock comes with voting rights, and it is the people holding voting shares who play the most important part at shareholders' meetings. When dividends are declared, common stockholders will get their share of the pie—after the preferred shareholders are paid, that is.

Preferred stock is a class that usually gets no voting rights but that enjoys preferential treatment when it comes to dividend payouts. For that reason, these shares are often issued to investors. Preferred stock offers investors a more secure chance of return on their investment, without diluting the power core of the corporation. They get first crack at all declared dividends and may even get dividends when the common stock shareholders get none. In most cases, the preferred stock dividends are fixed, something that's stated right on their certificates. For example, preferred stockholders could be in line for $1 per share every time dividends are declared, with anything left over getting split among the common shareholders based on how much stock they hold.

Voting or Nonvoting Shares

The default version of common stock comes with voting privileges, one vote for one share. Your corporation may also have nonvoting common stock, where the holders cannot participate in any shareholder elections. Unlike preferred stock, holders of these take no priority when it comes to getting dividend payouts.

Nonvoting shares come in very handy in two specific cases: employee participation and family involvement. Company stock is a great employee motivator. When the corporation profits, employees get dividends. They don't, however, get a chance to vote you out as the president of the corporation. These shares also make good gifts for family members, especially those of the next generation. Owning stock lets them feel connected, helps them earn some dividends, but doesn't offer up any control over the company. You can also use these shares for family financial support of your corporation—they get an equity stake, and you don't have too many cooks in your voting kitchen.

When your corporation has investors, rather than shareholders who act as business owners and actively participate in running the company, they may request voting shares. Though they could get a steadier return with preferred shares, the class commonly issued to investors, many venture capitalists feel more comfortable having some control over the direction of the business. They won't necessarily participate in the day-to-day management, but they like to keep a hand in for major decisions. Since these investors will have the same class of shares as you and your co-owners, they will also have the same rights and responsibilities, just in smaller chunks.

Authorizing Shares

When you set out your corporate charter, you were required to authorize a total number of stock shares for your company. This number, the total authorized shares, normally includes how many shares you will need initially to fully capitalize the corporation and anticipates how many shares you may need in the future to raise even more capital. Your best bet is to overestimate. It's fine to have shares that are authorized, but not issued or outstanding, for the entire life of your corporation. Should you end up needing to authorize more shares, you would have to amend your corporate charter—no small undertaking, as Chapter 17 describes.

Why This Number Matters to Shareholders

Though it may seem like a trivial number at first glance, the total authorized shares can be quite important to shareholders, especially those who hold the stock purely for investment purposes. Although authorized shares are not necessarily outstanding, they could be, at any time. That additional issuance waters down the proportional ownership of existing shareholders, chipping away at their relative equity share. In the case of common stock, it reduces the per-share dividends they receive. Plus, a sudden influx of available shares can often decrease the current market value of the stock, an important factor for investors who may be looking to cash in their shares.

Family Feud

Daphne and Fred Lake had a small corporation for their bed and breakfast, At the Lakes. At first, the two were the only shareholders, each with 200 shares out of the total 1,000 authorized shares of common stock (the only class of shares). They owned and operated the inn for years and planned to hand it over to their four children one day. Fred and Daphne came up with a plan to keep the kids actively interested in the family business. Upon reaching the age of ten, each child started getting ten shares of stock every year in addition to their regular paychecks in exchange for helping out around the inn.

When their youngest children (twins, Alexa and Tommy) turned eighteen, they had a huge fight with their parents. The kids wanted to go on a cross-country trip for the summer, while their parents expected them to work at the inn during its busiest season. The twins had 180 shares between them; combined with their brothers' shares, though, the kids had 420 shares—and 420 votes—all told. The twins got their brothers' proxies, and called for a shareholder's resolution to close the inn for the summer. Since the kids' shares outnumbered Fred and Daphne's 400 shares, the resolution passed. The Lakes had no choice but to close the inn for the summer or to call for a second vote that their other sons would attend.

At the next shareholders' meeting just a few days later, Daphne and Fred explained to all of their children that closing the inn for the season could put them out of business. That loss could mean they wouldn't be able to fund college educations and might have to sell off the inn. They offered up a resolution to reopen the inn, and it passed (though not unanimously).

Authorizing shares merely allows for them to be used by the corporation. In itself, the authorization process is just paperwork. It does not mean these shares are activated or actually owned by shareholders; it just means they are available to be activated, sort of like inventory in the back room waiting to be put out on the shelves. The authorized shares number is an important one, though, especially to investors in your corporation. For that reason, you have to disclose your total number of authorized shares any time you prepare financial statements that someone not working within the corporation will see (like a pure investor or a banker). That disclosure will appear in the equity section of the corporation's balance sheet.

Deciding What to Authorize

When it comes to authorizing shares in your charter, you have two primary decisions to make. One is what kind of stock to authorize, the other is how many shares. Should you decide to authorize more than one type of stock (common and preferred, for example), you need to determine the number of shares for each.

Most small corporations, especially those of the single-owner variety, authorize only basic common stock. As for quantity, the normal range is between 1,000 and 1,000,000 shares. Entrepreneurs who expect to keep the business in the family or among friends typically go with a lower authorized share count. Those who plan to offer shares to the public at some point typically hit the higher end of the scale.

In addition to your own plans, keep abreast of your corporation's home state fee structure; it's just one more factor to consider. Some states set the filing fee for the articles based on the number of authorized shares. Therefore, authorizing more shares creates higher incorporation fees. That said, you should still authorize as many shares as you think you will realistically need over the entire life of your corporation. You may pay a slightly higher fee to incorporate, but you'll bypass the fee charged to amend your articles in the future.

A Look at Par Value

Shares of stock have value—once they are issued and outstanding, that is. In fact, they have two distinct values: par value and market value. Market value is the number you are probably most familiar with. It is the dollar amount you would have to pay for a single share of that stock on the open market. In the case of a small business, market value typically refers to the dollar value you assign to each share before transferring it. Market value is a floating number. It does not have to be the same for two days—or even two hours—in a row, as it reflects the overall market worth of the corporation and its assets.

Par value is a number set in stone. It refers to the face value of a single share, as indicated on each stock certificate. Essentially, it does not have any real market meaning. Par value is an artificial dollar amount assigned to the stock for legal, tax, and accounting purposes. On the legal front, par value has certain significance because it signifies the legal capital per share that has to be kept in the business as a safety net. That capital may not be withdrawn by shareholders.

On the accounting side, par value dictates the numbers that go in the bookkeeping entries whenever shares are issued and sold by the corporation. Regardless of how much is paid for the shares, the stock account gets credited only with the par value. The rest gets funneled to an account called additional paid-in capital, a procedure described in Chapter 18. As for taxes, many states levy a corporate tax based on the aggregate par value of outstanding shares. Where shares have no par value, there's still a per-share tax bill, and it's sometimes higher than if a par value had been set.

Setting the Par Value

Most corporations set the par value of their stock as low as legally allowable. The reason for this is that many states levy a corporate tax based on the par value of a company's stock. The lower the par value, then, the lower the tax bill. In addition, because of the legal capital issue, most states make corporations sell their shares for at least par value. If your corporation was formed in one of those states and you set a high par value, like $100 per share, you could not issue and sell new shares for less, even if the market value was substantially lower at the time.

▶▶ **The key point of par value is that it sets the minimum legal capitalization of the corporation, a level that must be maintained by the corporation or put its existence in jeopardy.** Your corporation is legally barred from making distributions to owners based on their equity interests, like dividends, that will put that minimum capital in jeopardy. For example, if the par value is set at $10 a share, with 100 shares issued and outstanding, the corporation's minimum capital is $1,000. Dividend or other such distributions cannot be made if they cause the overall equity to dip below that minimum. This is one of the main reasons par values are typically set very low.

No-Par Value Stock

When a corporation doesn't assign any value to its shares, those shares are considered no-par value stock. Many larger companies like to use this option to minimize confusion between par value and market value, which are usually extremely disparate. However, **some states charge higher taxes for no-par value shares, so check the rules in your corporation's home state before you choose this option.** With no-par value stock, the value of the entire proceeds received in exchange for shares becomes the minimum legal capital.

In some states, your corporation can have no-par value stock with an assigned stated value. Here, the board of directors can assign a stated value to the shares, and that value becomes the key number for determining minimum legal capital. The reason corporations do this is to segregate proceeds received for the no-par value stock, keeping some of it outside that legal minimum.

When corporations receive payment for no-par value shares, the entire proceeds from the sale get credited to the stock account. However, if the shares do have a stated value, that value determines how much of the proceeds goes to the stock account and how much to additional paid-in capital.

Issuing and Selling Shares

Though it seems like issuing stock would be the first thing to happen when you form a corporation, it actually comes a little further down the line. Before anyone can own a single share, several steps need to be completed. The first is filing the articles of incorporation, in which you authorize how many and what kind of shares your incorporation will issue. Then the board of directors, in its initial meeting, must resolve to issue shares. Next, the corporation has to actually receive payment for the shares, whether in cash or other property. In the absence of payment, the corporation has to at least get a signed IOU from the shareholder (if that's allowed by the home state law). Finally, shares can be transferred to their new owners.

How Owners Pay for Shares

Every state allows shares to be sold in exchange for any asset, including these:

- ⮑ Cash
- ⮑ Equipment
- ⮑ Real property
- ⮑ Vehicles
- ⮑ Trademarks
- ⮑ Copyrights
- ⮑ Inventory

In addition, a corporation can also accept as payment the cancellation of a debt owed by the corporation to the shareholder. This scenario comes up a lot when owners lend money to the business during its start-up phase and then settle that debt with shares.

Promises, however, are allowed only by some states. That includes promises to pay, like an IOU or more formal note, or to perform services for the corporation that fall outside the normal scope of duties as an employee. In states where this transaction is prohibited, shares cannot be sold unless the corporation receives something of current value in exchange.

Stock Certificates

As soon as an exchange is made—that is, some form of payment is traded for corporate stock—the transaction is considered complete. At that time, the shareholder's interest gets entered into the corporate records book. That's all you have to do legally, but from a traditional standpoint, there's still one more task to complete.

There's no obligation in most states to issue paper stock certificates, but most incorporators choose to take the traditional route and present them when shares are transferred. These certificates offer tangible proof of owner's equity, and most original shareholders like to have them in physical form.

Should you opt for stock certificates, check your state's business Web site to find out what content they require. In most cases, it will be basic information: the name of the corporation, its home state, the name of the shareholder, the number of shares issued, and the signatures of at least two corporate officers. You can find blank certificates at almost any stationery store.

What About Dividends?

When you think about dividends, it probably has to do with getting something like 22 cents a share from some big corporation stock, a little addition to your personal tax return. For small, privately owned corporations, though, dividends can look a lot different. In fact, the type of corporation you have, C or S, has a huge impact on what your company's dividends look like—or whether you have them at all.

The rules concerning dividend payments are set out in the corporate bylaws, in accordance with state statute. Under the laws of most states, dividend payouts can only be made from earnings. That means if there are no retained earnings, no dividends can be paid. Some states impose even tighter restrictions on dividend payouts, while some go easier. It's important to learn the rules of your corporation's home state before making any dividend payments as violating these rules can constitute a fraudulent transfer (which is as bad as it sounds).

Dividend Strategies

Dividend payouts fall under the financial strategies umbrella. In S corporations, they can be used to minimize the total taxes paid. Conversely, in C corporations, they are avoided in order to minimize the total taxes paid. The reasons for this are detailed in Part 5 of this book; for now, consider this difference a basic fact. S-corporation shareholders want to make their dividends as big as possible, while C-corporation shareholders (owners, as opposed to investors) don't want any. To that end, S-corporation shareholders try to minimize their salaries and maximize their dividends. C-corporation shareholders attempt the exact opposite.

This premise is the reason many C corporations choose to have multiple classes of stock. That allows them to pay dividends to pure investors, providing them a steady current return on their investments, without having to pay dividends to owners. The promise of dividends can help attract straight investors to your corporation; in fact, it's one of the best ways to appeal to small investors.

Different Kinds of Dividends

In most cases, there have to be earnings before dividends can be paid. Odd as it seems, however, there doesn't have to be cash. ▶▶ **Cash dividends are the most common type distributed, but even corporations short on funds can pay out dividends.**

Dividends can also be paid out to shareholders in the form of stock. Here, instead of getting a certain amount of cash per share, they receive some corporate stock. Each shareholder gets a proportional increase in equity holdings by shifting some of the corporate earnings into the contributed-capital arena (counting as additional paid-in capital on the books). Most stock dividends offer a piece of a new share for each old share held. For example, if you declared a 10-percent stock dividend, each shareholder would receive an additional one-tenth share for each share already owned.

Keep in mind that regardless of the form, all dividends count as taxable income. It is therefore not possible to avoid the C-corporation double-taxation issue by declaring a stock dividend instead of a cash dividend.

Navigating the Dividend Process

As with many other corporate activities, there are a few formalities that must be followed to declare a dividend. First, the board of directors must take a vote and decide how much to pay out as dividends. Then, they make a formal declaration, announcing this decision to the shareholders. Once the dividend is declared, it is a legally binding commitment, and the dividends must be paid as specified.

The next step is setting the record date. This date helps determine exactly who is entitled to the dividend. In small, closely held corporations, this issue may not seem too important, but in corporations with outside investors, the distinction can be significant. Dividends can only be paid to the person who actually owned the shares on the record date, even if he no longer owns those shares. Once that item is settled, the dividends can be paid, with a check (for cash dividends) or certificate (for stock dividends) mailed out to each shareholder.

▶▶ TEST DRIVE

Figuring out how many and what kind of shares to authorize requires some forward thinking. As you make this decision, picture your corporation five or ten years from now. At that point, it may be ready for expansion, or you may be ready to spread the responsibilities. Authorize at least voting and nonvoting shares and up to double the number of shares that you want to own if your future company may involve any of the following:

- ➲ Gifts of shares to family members
- ➲ Making shares an employee incentive
- ➲ Seeking out investors to fund expansion
- ➲ Bringing in additional owners

Meet the SEC

The U.S. Securities and Exchange Commission, commonly known as the SEC, is a federal agency assigned the task of regulating securities. Here, "security" basically means any instrument, such as a debt or equity interest in a company, that a person can buy in the expectation of profit potential based on the efforts of other people. A lot of regulations apply to anything that has been declared a security. On the federal level, that means complying with SEC rulings.

Accredited Investors

The SEC is in place for the protection of average investors, to keep them from being taken in by scams. There are some people, though, that the SEC regards as more sophisticated than average when it comes to making investment decisions, and these people are called accredited investors.

To qualify as an accredited investor, the person must have a minimum net worth of $1 million, or a minimum annual income of $200,000. Directors and officers of the corporation also qualify for accredited-investor status, even if they don't meet the financial guidelines. When you limit your offering to accredited investors only, your corporation may be eligible for a much simpler set of securities registration requirements.

The U.S. Congress initially created the SEC with the Securities Exchange Act of 1934 after the big stock market crash of 1929. The primary purpose of this legislation is to protect investors from fraud by requiring companies that seek to raise capital from the public to publish a lot of disclosure information. Though it may appear at first glance to be impersonal and overwhelming, the SEC is quite friendly to small-business owners. Its Web site keeps getting easier to navigate, and it offers a lot of documents in plain English to help the average business owner understand specific registration requirements.

Securities Registration

One of the key functions of the SEC is to review and accept the disclosure statements of companies that wish to offer securities to the general public. That function helps accomplish the primary goals of the agency, which are to provide investors with significant information about securities up for sale and to help prevent lies and misrepresentations made with the intent to defraud investors. The agency accomplishes these goals through the securities registration process.

Any securities sold in the United States have to be registered with the SEC (unless they qualify for special exemptions, described in the section beginning on page 101). Registration forms are comprehensive and ask for a standard menu of essential facts from the companies hoping to sell their securities. At the same time, the SEC tries to make compliance as burden-free in terms of both time and money as possible for those companies. The goal is to elicit full disclosure of virtually any issue that could influence a potential investor's decision to invest. And while the SEC requires that all the information provided be accurate, the agency itself does not guarantee the accuracy of registration documents.

Every registered public offering requires a prospectus, which is basically a sales document. In the prospectus, your company (a.k.a. the issuer) must include at least the following information:

- A business description
- A listing of properties owned or run by the company
- A detailed description of the security being offered
- A statement about the intended use of offering proceeds
- Pertinent information about the company's management team
- Important facts about ongoing operations
- Information about any ongoing material legal proceedings
- Certified financial statements, audited and signed off on by independent accountants

Now all of this information must be registered electronically. In turn, the SEC quickly makes the offering information (including a prospectus) available to the public via access to EDGAR, a huge corporate database.

The SEC Forms

Big corporations have to complete Form S-1 to register their public securities offerings, an exhaustive and detailed document. Qualified small-business issuers get a little break here, as they can file a more simplified registration document when they want to offer their securities to the public. To count as a small-business issuer, a company can't have earned more than $25 million in revenues during the last fiscal year and it can't have outstanding publicly held stock that's worth more than $25 million.

When your company qualifies here, two pared-down registration forms apply: Form SB-1 for offerings to raise no more than $10 million, and Form SB-2 to raise unlimited capital. These filings require substantially less narrative information than the standard Form S-1. However, both of these small-business versions do still require audited financial statements.

Federal Securities Laws

Federal securities laws were put in place to protect investors. After a crushing number of Americans lost everything in the 1929 stock market crash, many to swindlers, the federal government stepped in. To make it much harder for scams to succeed, and in part to weed out the serious businessmen from the charlatans, the U.S. government put a lot of strict and demanding regulations in place. Unfortunately, the procedures they implemented were so tough that it also became harder for honest businessmen to raise capital for enterprises—especially small businesses.

The aim of federal securities laws is full disclosure of all the risk inherent in a particular investment, with the goal of ensuring that an investor can make an informed decision before taking any risk at all. To accomplish that goal, companies that will offer securities first must undergo a complex, lengthy registration process with the SEC or the applicable state authority, one that involves a lot of comprehensive documents and disclosure statements.

It's virtually impossible for a novice entrepreneur to navigate federal securities regulations alone, and the cost of a professional field guide can be prohibitive to the small business owner. However, the full-blown version of federal securities laws, even those already modified for small business issuers, can sometimes be pared down even further. These are called exemptions, and they are designed to help small companies raise capital.

State Securities Laws

When it comes to the legalities surrounding securities offerings, people tend to focus on the federal laws and the SEC and overlook their state law responsibilities, at least at first. However, state law is just as vigorous, and compliance is just as critical.

Each state has its own body of laws regarding the offering and sale of securities. When you offer shares in more than one state, you must comply with all laws of each state. So if, for example, your corporation was formed in Massachusetts, and you plan to offer securities there and in New York, the New York sales must be conducted according to New York standards while the home-state sales must follow the laws of Massachusetts.

Though the securities laws for each state do vary quite a bit, they do all have some basic premises in common:

1. Compliance is voluntary when it comes to private sales. The state won't hunt you down if you offer shares of your corporation privately; however, laws surrounding those issues are in place to protect both the corporation and the investors.

2. Disclosure requirements are all pretty much the same. You must disclose everything, or at least all pertinent material information that would sway someone who was considering investing in your corporation. That typically includes things like thorough historical and prospective financial statements and other critical business or financial information.

3. Registration procedures must be followed, which really just means that you must file all required registration paperwork with the state before you start selling shares. Once that registration is accepted and approved by the state, you'll get a permit that lets you start issuing shares.

4. If you fail to comply with state laws, the state will likely charge you and your corporation with some financial penalties.

Exemption from State Securities Laws

Just as with federal regulations, many small corporations are exempt from at least some of the exhaustive state securities registration procedures. There are many different types of exemptions available, most leaning toward giving a break to small-business owners. Only a few, though, are pertinent for the majority of small corporation offerings. Though specific details may vary by state, here's the substance of each possible exemption:

➲ Exempt issuer transactions apply to your corporation's initial stock offering.

➲ Incorporation exemptions cover newly formed corporations with ten or fewer shareholders.

➲ Small-offering exemptions kick in when you offer shares to more than ten but less than thirty-five people within a one-year period.

➲ Limited-offering exemptions apply when shares are sold directly and privately to thirty-five or less investors, with a special nod to accredited investors.

➲ Regulation D exemptions may automatically kick in if your state follows the federal Regulation D model (as described on page 104).

The SCOR Process

Thanks to the North American Securities Administration Association (NASAA), some states allow for a simplified process under a special process known as SCOR (Small Company Offering Registration). The SCOR standardized procedure has been adopted by a lot of states (forty-five at the time of this writing), making it even easier for small corporations to raise capital. The limit is generous, as your corporation can raise up to $1 million from the general public as long as those people live in one of the SCOR states.

The paperwork is streamlined. There's an easy-to-deal-with questionnaire (fifty questions) that fills in for a comprehensive prospectus. The costs are lower than the standard registration, especially when it comes to legal and accounting fees. Some states may even allow you to make your prospectus available online, while others forbid it. Check the applicable state guidelines before you involve the Internet in your offering. To find out more about SCOR, visit the NASAA Web site at *www.nasaa.org.*

Selling Shares on the Internet

Don't think you can skirt either state or federal securities laws and requirements by selling shares on the Internet. All securities laws apply on the Web just as much as they do anywhere else, and authorities have gotten serious about cracking down on issuers who try to circumvent the registration process.

In fact, many states have issued cease-and-desist orders to stock promoters who fail to register their offerings in the state before broadcasting them on the Web. Since current laws insist that stock issues be registered in a state before sales can be made to residents of that state, Internet promoters must either decline any offers to buy from any state in which their stocks are not registered or face severe legal and financial consequences.

The Basics of Exemptions

Preparing SEC filings can be an onerous process. It's one part intimidating, three parts complicated, and two parts expensive. Together, those features could scare away a lot of small-business owners looking to incorporate. Fortunately, the folks in Washington, D.C., want to encourage entrepreneurship, so they created some special exemptions just for small-business owners to streamline the process and make it enormously easier.

On the federal level, there are three major categories of exemptions. One covers intrastate or single state offerings; one covers private offerings; and one, known as Regulation D, covers small offerings. Most small businesses that are looking to raise some capital fall into at least one of these categories, allowing them a much simpler securities offering process on the federal level at least, if indeed they have to deal with the federal government at all.

The simplest of these exemptions is the one involving intrastate sales. When you offer shares of your corporation to residents of a single state, chances are that your offering will be exempt from federal registration requirements. That's because federal laws typically only kick in when more than one state is involved; otherwise, the issue is left to the home state. SEC Rule 147 covers these intrastate sales, and if your offering follows the specific guidelines, you may not have to deal with federal registration at all.

If your corporation is locally owned and operated, it will probably qualify for this exemption. Here are the basic requirements:

➲ At least 80 percent of the company's assets must be in your state
➲ 80 percent or more of the revenues must be earned in state
➲ The main office is located in the home state
➲ The securities are only offered and sold to residents of your state
➲ At least 80 percent of the proceeds from the issuance must be used for business operations in the state

To learn about all of its specific provisions of Rule 147 and get it in print, visit the SEC Web site at *www.sec.gov*.

The point is that most small, closely held corporations will land in one of these categories, even if they do take on investors outside the core group of owners. Don't be afraid to consider a small public offering because you're afraid of all the compliance requirements—they probably won't apply to your very small offering. Even if you think you are absolutely sure that your corporation qualifies for an exemption, though, talk with a qualified attorney. A small mistake here can create massive consequences down the line.

Private Offerings

Private offerings are just what they sound like. You offer to sell shares of your company directly to people you know, with absolutely no advertising to the public. Though the rules give no specific number, the group of people must be limited. All potential investors must either be accredited investors, involved in the company, or considered financially astute,

A Small Corporation Lands a Big Investor   Inside Track

Ethan Sullivan and Spencer Flanagan owned a bike sales and repair shop. The company, S & F Bicycles Unlimited, Inc., was incorporated. The guys wanted to open a second shop, just for new and used bike sales, in a busier shopping area. They needed a hefty cash infusion to put their plans into action, but the corporation was really in no position to take on additional debt. They had already tapped most of their friends and family for cash, some in exchange for notes and some in exchange for nonvoting shares. The total shareholder count stood at eleven.

Ethan and Spencer talked to their accountant and their lawyer, both of whom sat on their board of directors and were minor shareholders, about finding new investors. The corporation had 2,000 nonvoting shares yet to be issued, each with a par value of $5 and a fair market value of about $20. The lawyer had a wealthy friend who was looking to invest in a local business, so he passed along S & F's business plan. Jordan Radison (the investor-friend) was impressed with the existing shop and with the plans for expansion. He agreed to invest $40,000 in the corporation in exchange for the 2,000 shares.

Ethan was concerned that bringing on an outside investor would bring all kinds of securities laws into play, as well as forms to file and fees to pay. The attorney assured him that this stock sale was exempt on two counts: Jordan had a close relationship with a corporate insider, and he qualified as a sophisticated investor. Those two facts exempted the offering under state securities law. In addition, the sale was exempt from SEC rules under the private-offering exemption.

meaning they have financial investment experience. All the shares bought have to be for the buyers themselves and not resold immediately. Plus, every potential investor must have been given or have easy access to pertinent information that would allow them to make a fully informed decision before buying their shares.

Though these rules don't contain a lot of details, following some basic guidelines should keep your offering in the clear. For example, telling virtually everyone you know about the stock, hoping that at least some of them will bite, does not count as a private offering. Even if you don't do any official advertising, selling shares to anyone other than a specific small circle of people will lose this exemption for your corporation.

Make sure that the people you sell shares to will not turn around and sell them the next day. That kind of turnover can also kill the exemption for your corporation, as it will appear to effectively be a public offering. One way to handle this is to ask the people to whom you offer shares to sign a statement saying they plan to buy and hold the shares and are not buying them for the purpose of reselling them.

Finally, there's one more unwritten rule to keep in mind. Though there's no specific maximum dollar amount listed in the private offering rules, don't go overboard with your offering. Too big a sale can knock your offering right back into the nonexempt camp, even if that sale only includes a limited number of sophisticated insiders. As long as your total haul is reasonable—and you can figure that out with your accountant—it will probably meet that hidden guideline.

Regulation D Is Your Friend

The main purpose of Regulation D, a special section of federal securities law, is to smooth the path for small corporations looking to raise some private capital. ▸▸ **Regulation D comprises three rules, Rules 504, 505, and 506, each of which offers distinct exemption circumstances.** Though each of these rules has unique features, they do share federal Form D, and each requires it to be filed. As an added bonus, there's no filing fee.

What does vary among these three rules is how much money your corporation can get in exchange for shares, how many people you can sell shares to, and exactly who is eligible to buy those shares. All three rules highlight accredited investors. When you limit your offering to only people meeting those qualifications, the rules may be relaxed even further.

Even though the purpose of these rules is to make things easier for small corporations to raise capital, they are complex and subject to some interpretation. For that reason, it is in your corporation's best interest to hire a small-business attorney who is well versed in SEC regulations and exemptions to guide you through the offering process. An experienced lawyer will understand all the regulatory intricacies and technicalities and can help your corporation use the exemption best suited for it.

Rule 504

Under the provisions of Rule 504, offerings of up to $1 million (in shares) made within a one-year period are exempt from the full-blown offerings rules. In some circumstances, you may even be able to publicly advertise your shares and sell them, sort of a highly limited public offering. Whether your corporation qualifies for this treatment depends on a few factors:

➲ Whether you registered this issuance with your state securities agency

➲ If you're selling to only accredited investors

➲ Whether you complied with state rules on delivering disclosure documents to your shareholders

Here, there's no limit to the number of potential investors you can contact, as long as you stick to the $1 million maximum sale.

Rule 505

This rule gives you a wider berth when it comes to raising capital for your corporation, as it caps out the total shares sales at $5 million within a twelve-month period. The catch is that you can't sell shares to more than thirty-five nonaccredited investors. As for accredited investors, though, you can sell to as many of them as you want.

Also on the "don't" list is advertising; absolutely no general advertising is allowed. In addition, shares cannot be resold for at least one year unless the offering gets officially registered. The restricted stock information should appear explicitly, right on the stock certificate. On the to-do list is paperwork, as there is specific information (all of a business or financial nature) that must be disclosed to all the nonaccredited investors you offer shares to.

Rule 506

Unlike the previous rules, there is no dollar limit imposed on offerings eligible for exemption under Rule 506. Advertising remains against the rules, and shares cannot be sold to more than thirty-five nonaccredited investors.

Rule 506 does have some unique special requirements that must be met in order to qualify for exemption from full registration. First, all non-accredited investors must be sophisticated investors. That means that they (or their financial advisors) must have enough knowledge and experience to be able to effectively evaluate the risks involved in making this investment. Second, your corporation has to give prospective nonaccredited investors particular financial and business information. Plus, these investors must get the chance to ask any questions—and receive prompt answers—about anything they want to know about offering terms and conditions or information they need to verify the financial disclosures they've received.

Finally, these shares are restricted. They cannot be resold unless the offering is registered or qualifies for exemption under existing securities laws, and each stock certificate must spell out this condition.

Will your corporation be exempt from formal federal and state securities law? That depends on just how many and what type of investors your corporation will have. Grab your business plan. Look at your company's present and future cash requirements. Review how you've planned to acquire that financing and where you could turn if the company needed significantly more funding than you expected. Make a list of potential investors that you and your co-owners know, no matter how distant the relationship. If you don't think you will be able to raise enough capital within that circle, a public offering may be in the cards.

PART **2**

Understanding Corporations

What Is Limited Liability?

Liability is debt, whether that debt is money, services, or something else of value owed to someone else. Virtually every business, virtually every person, in the world owes someone something, and your corporation will be no different. What is different is the legal treatment of business liabilities between corporations and partnerships of sole proprietorships.

When sole proprietorship or general partnership is the entity of choice, the debts of the business are also debts of its owners—personal debts. That means if there isn't enough money in the company cash box to pay the bills, the owners have to settle up using their personal funds.

Corporations, on the other hand, offer a protective shield against personal responsibility for business debts. This shield is called limited liability, and it limits the financial obligation of shareholders to their ownership interest in the business. They can never lose more than their investment when it comes to liabilities of the corporation. If the corporation runs out of assets and creditors aren't getting paid, they can't come knocking on your door as a corporate shareholder. Only the corporation is legally responsible for its outstanding debts.

The Goal Is to Protect Yourself

One of the reasons you own a business is to create a solid foundation of wealth for your family. In addition to building up your nest egg, you also want to make sure to preserve and protect it from losses, fees, taxes, and lawsuits. One of the biggest benefits you'll get from your corporation will be protection, especially when it comes to lawsuits.

The world, especially the United States, is in a litigious phase. People will sue for almost anything they or their lawyers think they can get away with: because they burned their mouths when their hot coffee was really hot or because they ate at a fast-food joint too often and gained weight. If you can imagine a scenario, someone can make it a court case, and businesses (especially) are prime targets. Not just for frivolous lawsuits, although those may come up, but for real incidents where the company just may bear some responsibility. The beauty of incorporation is that whatever happens in the business, stays in the business.

Your corporation is like shining armor, protecting your personal assets against the lances of lawsuits that seek to pierce that protective veil. The burden to do that piercing is on the party bringing legal action against you, which he can't do if you've run your corporation with adequate care. While that shield remains firmly in place, your private wealth can't be touched by creditors of your corporation, no matter what.

A Very Common Misconception

Many novice entrepreneurs mistakenly believe that their corporation also has limited liability for business debts. They believe that the corporation's assets, everything owned within the corporation, are shielded. This is simply not true. Your corporation is fully personally liable for all of its debts. Should any debts go unpaid, creditors can sue for satisfaction, and the corporation may be forced to surrender any or all of its assets to fulfill its obligations. It can lose every asset it owns, and that includes your investment in the business.

That's where your limited liability kicks in, as your losses are limited to your investment in the business. Whereas the corporation may lose all of its assets to satisfy debts, your personal assets are protected.

Minimizing Your Exposure

Incorporating your company, and thereby erecting a wall of limited liability protection, is a great first step toward preserving your personal assets. One of your personal assets, though, will not be protected, and that is your investment in the corporation. That asset may be lost should the company incur more debt than it can possibly repay or if it is sued and charged with enormous damages. On top of that, losing your business and all of its assets can cause a serious personal financial crisis.

There are definite steps you can take to keep losses to a minimum. Some of these steps involve removing vulnerable assets (like cash) from the business on a regular basis. Use caution here, though, as removing too much can result in the piercing of the corporate veil. The trick is to walk that fine line between asset protection and sufficient capitalization.

Withdrawal Strategies

You and your corporation are two separate legal entities, and you, in your role as shareholder, enjoy limited liability protection because of that distinction. That's the legal view. In real life, though, that corporation is yours, and your shares in it make up a big portion of your personal financial holdings. So when that corporation is hit with liability claims, those may not spill over on to your other personal financial holdings, but they do substantially impact what may be your primary personal asset—your corporation.

You can protect your corporation with your personal limited liability shield by shifting assets from the business to your personal holdings. That's not to say you should drain every ounce of cash and earned equity out of your business. That strategy would have a long-term negative impact on your company's success and growth potential. Implementing a reasonable and systematic fund-withdrawal plan, though, protects your nest egg better than simply leaving assets in the corporation, where they would be vulnerable to creditor's claims. Should your company need an infusion of funds for any reason, you can then lend money to the corporation, making you a creditor for that transaction.

Common withdrawal strategies include two you already know about (salaries and dividends). You can also achieve this goal by leasing space or equipment to your corporation, or by lending money to the corporation and setting up a repayment schedule that includes interest. These regular, steady withdrawals get cash out of the business in a way unrelated to your ownership interest in the business. **▶▶ Loan and lease payments are considered usual and necessary business expenses, regardless to whom payments are made.** The courts generally deem these distributions valid, even when the corporation is having financial difficulties.

Remember to back up these withdrawals with approved corporate resolutions, filed in the records book. Properly drawn up loan or lease papers should also be signed by you and an officer of the corporation (which can also be you, but your corporate role must be included; see Chapter 12 for advice on how to sign in the name of the corporation).

More Liability Than You Realize

When you think about business liabilities, you probably think about every-day creditors like vendors, utility companies, and landlords. Those can stack up to a formidable pile of liabilities, to be sure, but they make up only a small portion of the total potential liabilities of your corporation.

The minute you add certain factors into your business mix, your corporation's liability risk goes up astronomically. These factors include the following:

- ➲ Employees
- ➲ Customers on site
- ➲ Physical products
- ➲ Delivery services
- ➲ Food and beverages
- ➲ Personal services

Those items are just the tip of the potential liability iceberg, and you'd be hard-pressed to run any business without at least one of these factors in play.

You may be wondering whether there's any kind of business that doesn't invite liability? The quick answer is no. Even freelance writers, who work strictly on their own, who never see clients, and who work out of their own basements face some potential business liabilities—just fewer than most other businesses.

Everyday Business Liabilities

Just as people can end up mired in debt, so can corporations, especially new and still-struggling companies. It's very easy to pay the bills with a corporate credit card and to get vendors to extend just a little more credit. It's hard to make sure customers pay on time or to even make enough sales to keep things flowing smoothly. Many small businesses crash and burn because they have cash problems, meaning they have to send out more cash than is coming in.

Just like personal creditors, corporate creditors want to get paid. They want their money in full and on time. When the government doesn't get paid, tax penalties and interest start piling up, and that's the best that can happen. When leasing companies don't get paid, they'll repossess your equipment, from computers to heavy machinery. When vendors don't get paid, they won't continue to supply your corporation, and that cuts off part of your company's main source of future cash. Before you know it, your corporation is dealing with bankruptcy court.

These types of liabilities issues are easily anticipated with a solid business plan. Most new and small businesses experience periods of cash crunch. Talk to your accountant, your business mentor, and your accountant about ways to avoid this problem before it crops up. Preparation is key, as this is one kind of business liability that you can keep from sneaking up on you and sinking your corporation.

The Employee Factor

Employees add at least two new dimensions of potential liability to your corporation: injury to them, and injury by them. The minute you add an employee to the picture, you've opened your corporation up to dozens of potential lawsuits.

Here are just some of the more common internal employee-driven liabilities to keep in mind:

- Sexual harassment lawsuits
- Wrongful termination claims
- Discrimination suits
- On-the-job injury damage claims

Add to those the possibility that your employee could make a mistake (or do something intentional) while on the job that hurts someone else, like a customer or an innocent bystander. Traffic accidents alone cause a great number of employee-caused lawsuits. Sure, in these cases, the employee himself bears responsibility for the consequences of his actions, but so does your corporation.

The Business Itself

Some industries are obviously inherently dangerous: the use of hazardous chemicals, blasting (like at quarries), and bridge building all pose very clear risks. Other businesses may seem harmless, at least in comparison, but bear very large potential liability risk. Virtually every time a company deals with the general public, it opens itself up to the possibility of lawsuits.

What Can You Lose?

Suppose your personal net worth is $100,000, plus a $10,000 investment in your company. Business is great, until your biggest customer goes belly up. You learn that this customer owes your company $75,000. Not only does your company need that money to pay its bills, but the future revenue loss constitutes a severe financial setback. Now your company can't pay its bills, and creditors bring lawsuits amounting to $150,000. Your corporation can't cover that $150,000, so the creditors come after you.

If your business was structured as a sole proprietorship, you'd stand to lose your entire personal net worth plus your investment in the business. However, with a corporation, your personal loss is limited to your $10,000 investment in the business, and your $100,000 nest egg remains intact.

When customers come to your facilities, they can slip and fall. If your corporation is in the food-and-beverage service industry, there's a risk of food poisoning, contamination, choking hazards. Personal services, like massage and manicure, can cause unintentional injury. But even unintentional injuries come with the threat of lawsuits hanging over them. The courts are jam-packed with suits brought on by unsatisfied, or slightly (really slightly, like a Band-Aid fixes the problem) injured, or truly but unintentionally injured customers.

Corporations Provide a Shield

Some entities leave your personal assets hanging out for everyone to claim should your company be unable to meet all of its debts or fulfill all of its obligations. Sole proprietorships and general partnerships provide the

Inside Track	Michael Stern Drops the Ball

Michael Stern is the sole shareholder of Bowling World, Inc., a bowling alley and snack bar. In addition, he is the corporation's only director and only officer. To get the initial funding for his bowling alley business, Michael had to sign the bank's loan paperwork as the corporate president, as well as personally guarantee the business loan.

The company was doing well until an accident occurred. Michael was helping a customer select a bowling ball. As the customer picked up balls and tested them, she kept handing the ones she did not like back to Michael until finally he had three bowling balls in his arms. Another customer bumped into Michael, and he dropped one of those bowling balls. The ball landed on the ball-testing customer's foot, breaking three of her toes.

The customer sued Bowling World, Inc., and won a judgment against the business. Insurance picked up a big portion of the tab, but the corporation was still on the hook for $5,000, virtually all the cash the company had. The next few months were very difficult for Bowling World in terms of cash flow, and several vendors went unpaid. On top of that, Bowling World was unable to make payments on its bank loan.

The bank then sued and scored a judgment against the corporation for the balance of outstanding principal plus accrued interest. Coming on the heels of the broken toe lawsuit, Bowling World simply didn't have the funds to satisfy that judgment. However, since Michael personally guaranteed that business loan, the bank went after his personal assets as well and prevailed in court. Michael ended up dipping into his retirement funds (getting hit with a big tax penalty in the process), and paying off the corporation's bank loan.

least protection—none at all. Corporations, on the other hand, offer more than a century's worth of proven personal protection. In fact, it's the very reason they were created in the first place. In order to attract money to underfunded business ventures, legislators came up with the idea of incorporating, which allowed investors to contribute capital without risking the remainder of their wealth should the business fail. The idea of limiting liability to the amount of investment went over very well, and its popularity among investors has kept the corporation around for centuries.

That's the key to limited liability: It protects the investors, not the corporation itself. As the name implies, it does have limits. This premise grants protection against liability greater than the investment, but the investment itself could be lost to corporate creditors. The shield protects only assets owned by shareholders outside the corporation. In most cases, these personal assets cannot be attacked by creditors of the corporation should the company be unable to meet its obligations.

Some Things Are Not Covered

Even with the strongest corporation protections in place, and a virtually indestructible limited liability shield, there may be times when you will be held personally liable for matters related to your corporation's operations. As mentioned earlier, any time you personally commit malpractice, or an act of negligence, you will be held responsible under the law. You may also be held personally responsible for the misconduct, malpractice, or negligence of the people who report directly to you.

In addition to tortious acts, corporate shareholders may be liable for specific contract obligations. These situations can crop up when a contract is signed improperly, or when a shareholder personally guarantees provisions in a contract, as in cosigning for a loan. It can also happen when you sign contracts before the corporation legally exists, like signing a lease for office space before your business is actually incorporated.

These circumstances present a double whammy, as both you and the corporation can be held liable for the same action, whether tortious or contractual. Whichever party has the funds to pay up will be the one to end up paying, and in some cases both parties will be forced to pay.

There are some steps you can take to avoid these liability-inducing situations. One is to make sure you always sign corporate contracts as an agent of the corporation, using your title as part of the signature. Another is to use extreme diligence in hiring employees, including things like verifying references and confirming active licenses (for driving and professional purposes). In some cases, you'll need to take that diligence up a notch and require drug testing (for pilots, for example) and criminal background checks (such as for preschool employees).

Piercing the Veil

One of the worst things that can happen in corporation land is the piercing of the veil of limited liability. When that occurs, it means that a court has determined that you and your corporation should not be treated as wholly separate entities. In turn, liabilities can cross over between you and your company. You are fully responsible for its debts and obligations, and it is fully responsible for yours.

To avoid this dreadful state, you must know what can cause it and take steps to ensure the causes do not exist in your corporation. As the owner of this company, you must stay on top of recordkeeping, in both the accounting and corporate formality senses, and you must make sure that your corporation is adequately capitalized (according to state law) from the very beginning. The most common cause of judicial veil-piercing is the failure to meet one of those essential requirements.

In fact, this issue is the most common reason small-business owners get called into court. This is more likely to happen when a business doesn't have a lot of capital and a particular debt can't be satisfied using corporate assets. That's when the creditor's eyes turn to the owners of the corporation, to see if it is possible to get satisfaction from them.

In order for your corporate liability veil to be pierced, a creditor of the corporation must initiate a lawsuit against the owner(s), asking the court to impose personal liability. In his complaint, the creditor has to plead the specific doctrine of piercing the veil as well as prove to the court that the law applies in this case.

To do that, the creditor can choose between two legal theories. One is called the alter-ego theory, the other is called the undercapitalization theory. The alter ego theory holds that the shareholder did not treat the corporation like a separate entity—for example, corporate funds were mixed with personal funds, like when a shareholder uses the corporate checking account to write personal checks. The undercapitalization theory states that the corporation was intentionally underfunded from the get-to for the very purpose of defrauding creditors.

Your Best Defenses

The alter-ego theory is used much more frequently than its counterpart. Many small-business owners do shuffle money back and forth, paying for business items with personal money and personal items with corporate funds. The best way to make sure this particular allegation won't work against your corporation is to be scrupulous in the separation.

Always maintain separate bank accounts for your business and personal money. If you need extra money from the corporation, give yourself a salary advance or declare a dividend. Make sure to carefully document these decisions, as documentation can go a long way toward saving your hide. When you make business connections, always refer to yourself as an officer or other representative of the corporation. If a company thinks they're doing business with you, rather than your corporation, they can invoke that alter-ego theory.

It's crucial to adequately capitalize your corporation, and not just as future protection against creditors attempting to pierce the veil. For your corporation to have any real chance of succeeding, it must have sufficient funding. This is another spot where a complete business plan can provide a lot of guidance. Many novice entrepreneurs underestimate how much cash they'll need to get their companies up and running before they can support themselves.

▶▶ **TEST DRIVE**

Employees can add a great deal of liability to your corporation, but there's a lot you can do to minimize the company's exposure. As you begin interviewing employees for a position, consider these issues:

- ➲ Is this person truly capable of doing this job properly?
- ➲ Has this candidate brought on problems for past employers?
- ➲ Does this person have the disposition to follow instructions?
- ➲ Will existing in-house training programs be sufficient to teach this person how to do the job at hand?
- ➲ Does the applicant have a proven safe driving record?

Creating Your Corporation

PART 3

Why "Where" Matters

Incorporation is strictly a state gig. The process is dominated by fifty separate and distinct, though often similar, bodies of law. Each state has its own rules about creating, maintaining, and dissolving corporations, along with its own twists on taxation. It often makes the most sense to form your corporation in the state where most business will be conducted. However, there are some scenarios in which your home state gives you no advantage, in which case other options should be considered. For example, corporations that will operate in multiple states may choose the one that provides the best tax picture.

Before you decide which state your corporation will call home, consider these factors:

- Exactly where your company will be doing business
- All state-level taxes
- The option to form a close corporation
- Treatment of S corporations
- Initial filing and ongoing fees
- Minimum capital requirements (where applicable)
- Annual reporting requirements

Corporations in industries that bear higher-than-average liability risks, such as hazardous chemical companies, may also want to check into the prevailing body of legal decisions, as some courts are more business-friendly than others. In addition, specialized state legislation governing privacy or securities can also be an important factor.

Some states, particularly Delaware and Nevada, have structured their corporate laws in order to attract more businesses. Many corporations make those states home, even if they conduct little or no business there. While there are some unique advantages available to corporations in those states, those advantages may not outweigh the benefits of forming your corporation close to home.

The Single-State Solution

Small corporations operating in only one state usually fare best by incorporating in that state. This choice keeps fees to a minimum, even if your home state fees run on the high side. That's because if you incorporated in another state but still did business locally, you would have to register and pay fees and taxes as a foreign corporation in your home state. On top of that, you would have to comply with all the laws of both states, instead of focusing solely on the ones that truly affected your everyday business transactions.

There's one key exception. If you have big expansion plans for your corporation, and all indications point to eventual multistate operations, consider other options. Even if you're starting out in just one state, jump ahead to where you realistically expect your corporation to be a few years from now. With multiple states to consider, a different one may make the best home state for your corporation.

Crossing State Lines

When your corporation will be conducting business in at least two states, you have an expanded set of factors to consider. Since you will be required to register your company as a foreign corporation somewhere, incorporating out of state won't really add more paperwork and fees.

Now you can use state differences to your corporation's advantage. The factors here are mainly objective: fees, filing requirements, income tax structure, recognition of S or close corporations. By ranking these factors in order of their importance to you, you'll be able to determine which state's rules are most beneficial for your business. You can then incorporate your business in your chosen locale and register as a foreign corporation in every other state where your corporation will be conducting business.

The Home-State Advantage

For most small, local companies, incorporating close to home is the most efficient way to go. Regardless of how your home state ranks on the scale of corporate law, from "great" to "poor," creating your entity there will save you money, time, and trouble. Unless your company operates in more than one state, or you think that will be the case in the future, stick with your home state for incorporation.

Incorporating in the home state offers some distinct advantages. First, as described in Chapter 8, you'll be able to use the intrastate securities law exemption should you need to raise capital. That allows you to offer shares to the local general public without going through the full-blown (and quite harrowing) SEC registration process. Second, you and your corporate lawyer only need to deal with the laws of one state, and you can count on local attorneys to know the local laws inside and out. Third, when you'll be conducting business primarily in the home state, you won't have to pay two sets of state fees or file two sets of state tax returns. This alone can save your corporation thousands of dollars in state fees, accounting fees, and taxes over the years.

When and if circumstances change—for example, if you decide to branch out into other states—you can always form a new corporation in a more advantageous state and fold the existing corporation into it. For example, suppose you have a small graphic design firm incorporated in your home state of Pennsylvania. Over the years, you've picked up a lot of clients in New York and New Jersey, and you decide to open branch offices in both states. Should one of those states' statutes be more advantageous for your corporation, you can reform it there and merge your Pennsylvania corporation into the new one. Or, since you are now running a multistate operation, you may decide that Delaware or Nevada will provide the best home for your corporation. Either way, you'll still have to register this new corporation in Pennsylvania and the other not-home states in which your company conducts business under their foreign corporation rules.

Setting Up in Delaware

For decades, Delaware has been the favorite formation state among incorporators. The small state is big on bringing in business and has a very friendly corporate environment, in addition to very low corporate taxes. Because of its popularity, a booming corporate services industry has also developed in Delaware to serve the outside companies that choose to incorporate there.

On the plus side, incorporating in Delaware is a snap. That's partly due to the state office's vast experience in working with outside companies seeking to incorporate. The state offers competitive standard fees, low taxes (most companies get away with just the annual $35 corporate franchise tax), and a special separate court system that deals only with corporate litigation. Delaware corporations are free to operate with a great deal of anonymity, and corporate directors face lower risk of personal liability should actions taken in their roles as directors land them in hot water. Other benefits of incorporating in Delaware include no minimum initial capital investment requirement (meaning you can form your corporation with as little capital as you like); immediate incorporation within a few hours (for an extra fee); and a very well-staffed and easy-to-deal-with Division of Corporations. Finally, Delaware corporations tend to carry an air of prestige, which can boost the first impression your corporation makes to investors and lenders.

There are some drawbacks to incorporating in Delaware, albeit relatively minor ones. First, even though the state corporate franchise tax is easy to swallow, the form is hard to follow. You can solve this problem easily by having a qualified tax preparer do the job for you, though that can lessen the low-tax benefit. Second, the state office is very helpful and professional, but the state Web site (at *www.state.de.us/corp/*) leaves something to be desired. It does not allow for an online corporate name search, and it can be a little tricky to navigate.

Extra Benefits

Delaware's body of corporate law may be the most flexible in the nation, placing the vast majority of power in the corporate founders themselves. ▶▶ **Many states impose a lot of restrictions on corporate governance, telling corporations how to do things. But not Delaware.** There, the shareholders are given a very long leash when it comes to defining their own corporate bylaws.

The state also allows one person to hold every corporate office and serve as the corporation's sole director. That person doesn't have to be a Delaware resident. Thanks to the privacy laws, that name can be kept out of the articles of incorporation. Thanks to its liberal tax laws, nonresidents who own shares of Delaware corporations don't face any Delaware state taxes, no matter how many shares they own.

The Court of Chancery

The Court of Chancery is a Delaware creation, designed to expedite actions involving corporations. This special court is particularly well versed in the intricacies of business law and is well known for its advantageous settlements of internal corporate disputes (though these are more common in corporations with outside investors).

Because the Court of Chancery hears only corporate and business-related cases, the entire system is geared toward accommodating the business community. Because they hear no other kinds of cases there, all members of the court are intimately familiar with this single body of law. Plus, this system doesn't use juries, who may not truly understand the ins and outs of complex business matters, to settle cases. All cases are decided by judges who have been appointed based on their experience and knowledge of corporate law. Finally, with its long history of being a favored corporate home state, Delaware's Court of Chancery has decades of precedents on which to base its decisions.

Setting Up in Nevada

After years of looking on, Nevada decided to follow Delaware's example and make itself a corporation-friendly state, and it has done so with much success. Rather than compete on the same playing field, this state carved out its own specialized corporate niche. Here, the big draws are privacy and anonymity. ▸▸ **If you own a corporation housed in Nevada, you'll get an extra layer of personal protection**. When keeping your name out of things is a priority, Nevada incorporation merits consideration.

On the tax front, Nevada scores big points as well. For one thing, its corporate taxes are among the lowest—of the taxes it even levies, that is. There is no corporate income tax, franchise tax, or tax on shares. It also gets high marks on protection, for both directors and officers, from personal liability for corporation-related actions. Corporations are afforded a lot of anonymity and privacy, as are shareholders. Unlike most other states, for example, the state does not have an information-sharing agreement with the IRS. Nevada has also proven itself a strong protector of the corporate veil. Creditors manage the tough job of piercing the corporate veil in only the most extreme of circumstances, such as a clearly proven fraud case. Finally, the state's corporate customer service rates very high, including its extremely user-friendly Web site.

Nevada incorporation is not, however, too good to be true. There are definite potential downsides to forming your corporation here, the first being relatively high incorporation fees. There's also an $85 annual corporate fee due along with the annual report. Plus, while privacy is a key word in this corporate haven, the original directors must be explicitly named right in the articles of incorporation. Last, Nevada incorporation may come with a slight air of shadiness, as if incorporators chose that state because they had something to hide—whether it's true or not.

Bearer Shares

Along with Wyoming, Nevada is the only state that allows bearer shares. Bearer shares offer complete privacy to their holders, as their names need not be registered. The shares can be bought, held, and sold completely anonymously. Whoever is holding the shares owns the shares, kind of like cash.

In all other states, stock certificates are registered to their owners by name in a stock ledger. Every time shares are transferred, that transfer information gets recorded in the ledger. This recording does offer some distinct benefits. For example, stolen shares cannot be traded, and shareholders of record can receive dividends.

In most cases, bearer shares aren't worth their inherent risk. Loss of the physical certificates, such as through theft or fire, can result in loss of equity in the corporation. In addition, regardless of your legitimate reasons for wanting to use bearer shares (like to cut down on record keeping or to protect your privacy), their ability to be used illegally often casts them in a disreputable light.

An Extreme Tax Advantage

It bears repeating: Nevada is like a corporate tax haven within the United States. Check out this list of taxes it doesn't impose:

- Corporate income tax
- Tax on corporate shares
- Franchise tax (a.k.a. general business tax)
- Personal income tax

That saves your corporation a bunch of money in taxes as well as in tax-return preparation fees. This benefit also comes with an advantageous side effect, especially in this day of rampant identity theft. When you don't have to file any state tax returns, there's a lot less paper out there with your personal information on it, affording you an extra layer of privacy protection.

Interstate Business

When your company's transactions extend across state lines, you have an interstate business. Since corporations are created under state law, you will have to register your corporation as such in every single state in which your corporation does business. Failure to do so in any state will result in your operating an unincorporated business in that state, which among other things means no personal limited liability shield.

Conducting business in multiple states can have a substantial impact on your company. In addition to foreign corporation registration (explained in the section beginning on page 128), your corporation may have to pay state income and payroll taxes as well as collect and remit sales tax. That means preparing, or paying someone to prepare, at least two states' worth of tax returns and possibly local returns as well.

Crossing state lines can also change where you'll have to go to defend your corporation against lawsuits. In some instances, the state in which the suit was brought will hear the case. In others, the home state of the corporation will prevail. Which jurisdiction rules depends on the laws of both, as well as the particular situation.

What Constitutes Interstate Business?

It's nearly impossible to have a company that doesn't have at least some transactions that cross state lines. Not all of these transactions, however, make your company an interstate business, and not all of them result in the need to deal with foreign corporation registration. For example, getting your office supplies from a shop right across the state line may literally constitute interstate business, but it has no legal impact on your company. Nor is a one-time job for a single customer in a different state enough to trigger the need for foreign registration.

There are some very gray areas when it comes to conducting business in more than one state, and it can get pretty confusing at times. The general rule goes something like this: if your company has significant business activities within a state, it must register to do business in that state. The definition of "significant business activities" varies by state, but some activities qualify almost everywhere:

➲ Incorporating in one state but conducting business in another
➲ Conducting a significant amount of ordinary business within a state
➲ Having an active office (or shop) in the state
➲ Manufacturing goods in the state
➲ Conducting a lot of business over the phone, the Web, or by mail

Essentially, if you have significant operations or a lot of customers in a state that's not your corporation's home state, your corporation is conducting interstate business.

Keep Abreast of Different State Regulations

In addition to business filings, fees, and taxes, your company must also adhere to the laws of each state in which it does business. For example, if you have employees in two different states, your branches will have to abide by the laws of the states they're in. That can influence things like the minimum wage, overtime pay, and company-provided benefits.

Contract laws also vary among states, as do other types of business legislation. Each state in which your corporation may have different licensing requirements, such as those for professional corporation shareholders. Not all states recognize S corporations or allow for statutory close corporations, meaning you could have one type of corporation in State A and another in State B. In addition, the name of your corporation may not be available in each state where it conducts business, requiring you to choose different corporate names in different states.

Operating As a Foreign Corporation

Anywhere your corporation conducts business outside of its home state is foreign territory, at least under corporate law. Every other state considers your company to be a foreign corporation and requires it to be registered and operated as such.

Registering as a foreign corporation lets the state know that your corporation will be operating there. It sets the corporation up as a taxpayer. In exchange, it allows your corporation access to the state legal system and affords it the rights and protections afforded thereunder. Without that formal registration, the state in question may not recognize your company's status as a corporation. In fact, conducting business in a state without first registering your corporation could be illegal. At the least, it is likely to result in the levy of hefty fines.

The consequences for not registering range from minimal (register and pay the fee) to monumental (not recognizing the business entity). On the minimal side, it's all about cash. Simply pay the fines, penalties, and fees and move on. On the monumental consequence side, you and your corporation face possibly disastrous outcomes. For you, the disaster is loss of limited liability protection, leaving your personal assets vulnerable to creditors with whom the corporation has conducted business in that state. The disaster for the business is that the state may not enforce the contracts your corporation entered into while it was not legally registered.

Registering as a foreign corporation is pretty simple. You just fill out and file a foreign registration certificate with the state (the one that's not your corporation's home state) and pay the required fee. The certificate

Donna's Pasta Crosses the Line

Donna Lindsey opened her first Donna's Pasta, Inc., a medium-priced Italian restaurant, in State A, her home state. Donna and her Uncle Lou were the only two shareholders of the corporation. For the time being, they planned to keep things simple and local. On the other hand, the two had dreams of opening up more restaurants as Donna's Pasta gained popularity.

After a couple of years, they had five restaurants, all in Donna's home state. Donna's Pasta had become so popular that Donna and Uncle Lou decided to open a sixth restaurant. After much discussion, they settled on a spot in neighboring State B. Since many of their customers already traveled across the state line to dine at Donna's, they had a ready customer base. Unfortunately, they ran across a snag when they started the foreign corporation application process: their business name, Donna's Pasta, Inc., was already in use, and therefore unavailable. To operate in State B, they'd have to come up with a different name. That would cost them more money, as they'd have to do a lot of advertising to let people know who they were, rather than just using the name customers already knew.

Before closing the deal, Donna and Lou sat down with their accountant and crunched some numbers. The marketing hurdle, combined with the extra expenses of maintaining a corporation in two states, worried the pair. But when they compared the potential to that of another spot back in State A, where there were already five restaurants, they found that it made sense to open in State B—name change, fees, and all. They finally settled on Donna & Lou's Pasta, Inc., for a new name, and opened the doors to their first "foreign" restaurant.

asks for basic information, like the corporation's name and home state, the address of the main office in the home state and this state, and complete contact information for the registered office and registered agent. It must be signed by a corporate officer. The fees are sometimes nominal, but sometimes they are even higher than if you'd formed your corporation in that state; there's a lot of variation in the fee structures among the states. You may also need to obtain a certificate of good standing (or similarly named document) from the state of incorporation to submit along with your foreign registration paperwork. This document serves as proof that your corporation officially exists and is authorized to conduct business in the home state.

▶▶ TEST DRIVE

When your corporation will do business in more than one state, use these questions to help figure out which makes the best choice for your home state:

1. Which state allows for the type of corporation you want to form?
2. Which state has lower incorporation fees?
3. Which state has lower annual filing fees?
4. Which state has more advantageous tax laws?
5. In which state will your corporation have its main office?
6. Which state allows you to run things completely on your own (sole officer, sole director, sole shareholder)?

Visit Your Secretary of State

As you prepare to form your corporation, you will find yourself getting very familiar with the secretary of state's office, particularly its Web site. (In about a dozen states, a different office controls incorporation, but you can still find that office through the state's official Web site.) This office will provide you with many resources, including these:

- ⮂ Requirements for forming a corporation
- ⮂ Rules for registering a foreign corporation
- ⮂ Conducting your corporate name search
- ⮂ Reserving the name you want
- ⮂ Filing your articles of incorporation
- ⮂ Stock issuance or transfer tax information
- ⮂ The required annual report form
- ⮂ Guidelines for maintaining your corporation
- ⮂ Instructions for dissolving your corporation

Contact the secretary of state's business division as soon as you decide to start your own business. Knowing the steps can save you both time and money by keeping you from taking the wrong steps or from taking the right ones but in the wrong order,.

The Internet has streamlined the incorporation process. Now you can obtain forms and even file some forms right online. You'll find downloadable instruction manuals that go with the forms to help you fill them out properly. In addition to specific business-related paperwork, your state's official Web site will likely provide links to the offices of taxation, business licensing (for particular industries), and employment. Many states also include a "frequently asked questions" (or FAQ) section on their Web sites to help walk you through the incorporation process. Should the information you're seeking not be available on the site, the quickest way to get a response is via e-mail. Most state sites contain a direct email link, usually found at the bottom of the home page or on the "Contact Us" page.

Getting the Name Right

The name you select for your business can be one of your most important marketing tools. It alone can draw business and encourage repeat business. An easy, descriptive name attracts customers, and it makes it simpler for them to remember who to call when they need your products or services again. You want your corporation's name to stand out and to stick in people's minds. For that reason, it should be easy to say and spell and should bring to mind what your company actually does.

At the same time, as discussed in Chapter 4, you shouldn't pigeonhole your company by making the name too specific. For example, Baltimore Strawberry Ice Cream Shop, Inc., limits you both product-wise and geographically, and that can make expansion a little trickier. Especially if you plan to do some sales over the Web, try to stay away from making location part of the name. Once you've come up with some names that you like, test them. Ask potential clients or vendors what they do and don't like about the name.►► **Consider feedback and suggestions.** People may respond differently than you expect, and their ideas can help you craft a better name for your corporation.

Remember that state law also dictates what words must or must not be included in the name of your corporation, so know and follow their guidelines. For example, you will need to include some kind of corporate identifier in the name, like "Inc." or "Corp." Other words, on the other hand, are sometimes forbidden by state law: Assurance, Insurance, or Trust, for example.

Before you start filling out any paperwork for your company, thoroughly research the name you want to use to make sure it's not already in use by another business. If it is, you will probably have to move down your list and pick one of your backup names. When there's any doubt about name availability, go with an alternative. There have been plenty of horror stories about small businesses that sunk thousands of dollars into promoting their new businesses only to be forced to stop using their names. That loss can be avoided easily by simply making sure the name you want to use comes free and clear.

Performing the State Search

As was also discussed in Chapter 4, the first stop in your name search will be the state filing office. They can let you know if the name you want is already in use by an existing corporation within the state. Some state offices will answer written requests and even those made by phone. These requests can take a while to fulfill, so don't expect an instant answer. If you're the do-it-yourself type, check your state's business Web site to see if you can conduct your own search of corporate records. Most states post a database of current and dissolved corporations online for just that purpose.

Do the Same for a Fictitious Name

Many corporations have two names, one official sounding name for the records and one easily recognizable name for the customers. That second name is known as the company's fictitious (or DBA) name, and it merits the same level of investigation as the company's official name.

The rules for fictitious names are a little different. In some states, these names are registered with the Secretary of State, right along with the formal name. In others, DBA names are registered at the county level. Also, there may be no requirement at all to formally register a fictitious name, so another company could be using the name you want without your knowing it. They still have a firmer right to the name than you, so consider searching other alternatives as well, such as the phone books.

The state will not let your corporation form with a name that's the same as an already registered business. In fact, they probably won't let you use a name that's "confusingly similar" to an existing name (though there's definitely some wiggle room there). For example, if you want to call your corporation Greater Supplies when a corporation called Great Supplies already exists, you probably won't be allowed to use that name. If in doing your search you come across a name that is similar—like Greater Supplies and Grate Supplies—call the state filing office and ask them if you can use the name you want. Of course, there are always exceptions, the primary one being your name; even if there are fifteen other corporations called Tom Jones, Inc., you can still use it (if your name is Tom Jones, that is).

Check Trademarks, Too

Once the state hurdle is cleared, conduct a trademark search. This step is necessary because a name doesn't have to have been filed with the secretary of state to be in use; it just means it's not a registered corporate name. Another company could still have a stronger prior claim to the name and prevent your corporation from using it.

The rules about trademarks and trade names can take precedence, no matter how thorough you are in your name registration. It's really a matter of who got there first. So if a company has been using a name for thirty years, even if they haven't bothered to register that name, they get to use it and your corporation may not. The courts will get to decide whether you can use the name, even when what you're selling isn't remotely the same as what they're selling. If a court determines that your use of the name hurts theirs, you will have to choose a different name.

There are some readily available registries you can search to get this part of the job done. The first is your state's trademark registry, which you can usually find on your state's business office Web site. Next, check the name you want to use in the federal database. You can conduct a free search on the U.S. Patent and Trademark Office Web site, at *www.uspto.gov.*

Don't Forget the Internet

Even if you don't think your corporation will be selling products or services over the Internet, having a company Web page still makes sense. Potential customers will be able to find you more easily, particularly since a lot of people now use Internet searches in a similar way to the Yellow Pages when they're looking for a business to contact. On your Web site, you can include things like a full listing of products and services offered by your company, directions to all of your locations, and contact information.

While your corporate name should be easy to deal with, your Web site address should be even more so. Most people won't bother typing in a complicated Web address, so try to keep it short and simple. Register your

Web name as soon as you come up with it, and don't be surprised if it takes a few tries to come up with a name that's still available on the Web.

Reserve the Name

Once you've chosen a name and made sure it's not being used by someone with a better claim, reserve it immediately. By taking this step, you guarantee that the state will hold that name for your corporation exclusively until you have filed your articles of incorporation. The hold won't be indefinite. Most states give you a sixty-day window, but this time frame varies, so check with your state office to see how long you have.

You can do this simply by filling out a name reservation form. The forms are usually available on your state's filing office Web site. If not, call the office and ask for one by fax or regular mail. Fill out the form, which will ask for a little basic information, and submit it. The state will send you back a receipt confirming your reservation. Keep this where you can find it easily, as you'll need the information when you file your formal articles.

Information to Include

As you prepare the paperwork that will give life to your corporation, you'll walk a fine line between what to include and what to leave out. At a bare minimum, you will have to include anything your home state requires. At the other end of the spectrum, you can include a lot more detail than the law requires, but this is not advisable. The more you include in that original paperwork, the more you tie yourself down. In any business, all kinds of details have the potential to change. With a corporation, every change requires the filing of amended paperwork, which takes up more of your corporation's money and your time. Anything you want to expand on, put in the corporate by-laws instead, and include only requirements in the paperwork that will be officially filed with the state. While you can use the state's fill-in form, or a similar form from a generic incorporation kit, you can also draft your own—no special paper is required.

The basic information you will likely present in your original articles of incorporation includes these items:

- ⮂ The name of your corporation
- ⮂ The street address of its primary location
- ⮂ A mailing address (if different)
- ⮂ Business purpose
- ⮂ The number of authorized shares
- ⮂ A listing of stock classes (if more than one)
- ⮂ The name of the registered agent
- ⮂ The address of the registered office
- ⮂ The incorporator's name and address

In some cases, other information may be required. For example, if your corporation is not intended to have a perpetual life, that must be spelled out in the articles. The intended duration must be specified. Also, if your corporation's effective date (like a "born on" date) will not be the same as the filing date, the chosen effective date must be listed in the articles.

Declaring a Purpose

Since you want to include only constant items in the articles of organization, stating a business purpose can seem troubling. After all, the corporation you form today may have very little in common with the thriving business you imagine down the road. Putting in a specific business definition can lock your corporation into a box or force you to amend your articles every time you change direction.

To overcome this hurdle, be as vague here as your corporation's home state statutes allow. For example, rather than repeat the mission statement laid out in your business plan, you can write something like this: "This corporation's purpose is to engage in any lawful activities for which corporations may be formed, according to the laws of this state."

Choosing a Registered Office and Agent

Every corporation must have a registered office and a registered agent. If you are forming a one-man, local corporation, you will still have to include these officially in your articles of incorporation, even if the agent is you and the office is your house.

A registered agent is simply a person authorized to accept legal papers on your corporation's behalf. The agent can simply be someone hired to perform this function without being connected to your corporation at all. Typically, though, the registered agent will be someone linked to your company, like a board member, director, or shareholder. When your corporation's home state is not where the corporate headquarters are, though, you will have to have someone local to receive legal service and other official documents. The registered agent also has to be regularly available and reachable at the registered office during business hours.

The registered office has to be located in the corporation's home state. It can be the corporation's main office, its attorney's office, or that of the registered agent. The only real requirement is that it be a physical address, not a post office box. Although the registered office cannot be a residence (according to most state's laws), having a corporate office in a home transforms the address to one that can be used for legal purposes.

When your corporation operates in multiple states, it must have a registered agent and registered office in each state. There are companies that specialize in providing this service to foreign corporations for a fee. You can do a online search, or check the local phone book listings to find the appropriate professional; or you can simply ask your local attorney to act as the registered agent.

Should your corporation's registered office or agent change, you will have to fill out and file some standard paperwork. Most state Web sites have a downloadable form readily available for you to print out. The same form can be used to change either or both; when you're changing only one, use the current information in both the "old" and "new" spaces. When it's complete, the form gets sent to the Secretary of State's office, along with the required fee.

Have Your Attorney Cross the T's

Corporations are legal entities. Some are quite complex, others fairly simple. One primary purpose for incorporation is legal protection for the company's owners. To ensure that you are protected with an ironclad shield, involve an attorney as you form your corporation.

Close Doesn't Always Count

Greg Mariano liked to do things himself. In fact, he was about to transform his successful sole proprietorship into a corporation. He surfed the secretary of state's Web site and downloaded the forms for articles of incorporation. He read the instructions and filled in every blank accordingly. Then he stuck the completed articles in an envelope, along with the requisite fee, and mailed the package to the secretary of state's office.

Five weeks later, he got his paperwork and his check back, along with a form letter stating that the articles couldn't be accepted as filed. So Greg went back to square one. He downloaded the forms and instructions again. As he reread the instructions, he realized that he had forgotten to include the name of the registered agent. He made that change, then mailed the new form along with the same check to the same state address.

Four weeks later, he got his the whole package back, including that same form letter. By now, Greg was getting pretty frustrated, as he was eager for the new corporation to take effect. He finally decided to talk with a small business attorney. He brought all of the paperwork to the lawyer's office and asked why his articles kept getting rejected. The lawyer looked over his paperwork and smiled. He told Greg that he had done a lot of it correctly but missed a few tricks. Most important, though, he had enclosed a check for the wrong fee. His check covered the fee for a nonprofit rather than a for-profit corporation.

Greg made all the suggested changes, paid the lawyer, and sent in the revised paperwork and the new check. Four weeks later, he got his approval paperwork back, and his corporation was finally in business.

The main obstacle here for many small businesses is cash. Attorneys demand it, and new small businesses often don't have it (at least not in abundance). For that reason, a lot of fledgling entrepreneurs take the DIY route and leave out a trip to the lawyer's office. That will save money right now, but it can cost you dearly in the long run. That said, there are ways to limit attorney involvement, saving the majority of their participation to the really important issues, like the shareholders' agreement.

When it comes to preparing and filing the articles of incorporation, you can do most of the work yourself. Most states have very straightforward filing requirements and post very clear step-by-step instructions. Most state Web sites contain easy to download, fill-in-the-blanks forms you can use for your company's articles. Unless you have some complex issues (like several classes of stock, for example), you can feel confident preparing them.

Even with the simplest corporations, though, have your attorney just look over what you've prepared. The fee here should be nominal, but the assistance can be priceless. One small mistake in your articles can cause the state to kick them back, keeping your company from becoming a corporation. Worse, you can create your corporation but leave yourself open to trouble down the line by adding in or leaving out something that makes a legal difference.

Filing Your Articles

Once the articles of incorporation have been created and reviewed, it's time to execute them. The incorporator signs and dates the articles. The registered agent signs a brief statement accepting her duties and attaches that to the articles. (This statement can also be part of the state articles form.)

While You're Waiting

Technically, your corporation doesn't exist until its articles have been processed by the state. That can take several weeks, during which time you may be itching to get things moving. However, you can't start doing business in the name of the corporation—not exactly, at least.

What you can do is prepare contracts (such as leases) with language stating that the corporation is yet to be formed and that execution depends upon the approval of the new corporation's board. That way, if the corporation is never formed, you're not stuck. Should the other involved party be opposed to this, insisting that you sign in your name, you can insist on a clause that authorizes you to assign the contract to the corporation once it's formed.

Your next step is to file your articles of incorporation with the secretary of state. You can do this by mailing the document, along with the required filing fee, to that office. Enclose an extra copy of the articles and ask that the office stamp them with the filing date and return them to you in the self-addressed stamped envelope that you've enclosed. Alternatively, some states allow you to file articles electronically, along with credit card payment of the fees. If you want a certified copy of the articles returned to you, you can request that, but be prepared to pay an extra fee.

Typically, the turn-around time for articles of incorporation is seven to ten business days. Should you need them back more quickly, you can request that they be returned by delivery service. Again, there will probably be an extra fee for expedited articles, as well as the delivery charges.

▶▶ TEST DRIVE

Get together the information you need to prepare your corporation's articles of incorporation. You'll need your corporate name reservation and DBA name certificate. Along with that, have the name, address, and phone number for the registered agent and registered office you've chosen to represent your corporation. Collect the names and addresses of all of the initial corporate directors, and make sure they're available to sign off on the articles if necessary. Make sure you have the right mailing address (which may be different than the physical address or the expedited service address) for new corporation formation. Double-check that the check you've enclosed is made out to the correct party and is issued in the correct amount. Remember, any errors can result in your articles being returned unaccepted.

PART **3**

Creating Your Corporation

Signing in the Corporate Name

As soon as your corporation is legally formed, get into the habit of signing in the corporate name rather than your own. Though this may seem like an unimportant detail, it's really quite the opposite. Signing incorrectly can leave you personally liable for contractual obligations.

Any time a document needs to be signed, remember you are signing it as an agent of the corporation. Every single time you put your signature on any piece of corporate paper, make sure you include the full name of the corporation, along with your position (vice president, for example). As part of that full corporate name, remember to include the corporate designator (like Corp. or Inc., whichever is part of your company's official name). Leaving out any part of this total signature package can result in personal liability issues for you, so make sure to sign properly and fully every time you sign.

Here's what your new signature will look like:

> ABC Corporation
>
> By: *Amanda Matthews*
>
> Amanda Matthews, Vice President

By omitting either the name of the corporation or your position as a representative of the corporation, the other party to the contract could sue you for completion. Unless you make it crystal clear that you are merely an agent of the corporation through your signature, the courts could hold that you, personally, entered into this contract. Should that happen, it moves you perilously close to having the corporate veil pierced under the alter-ego theory (see Chapter 9). That means you and the corporation act interchangeably, rather than as two separate entities, leaving your personal assets vulnerable to corporate liabilities.

Licenses, Permits, and More

As you establish your new business, you will probably have to apply for various licenses, permits, and identification numbers from various government offices, from federal all the way down to town. Among the most important, and probably the first ones your corporation will need, are tax identification numbers. Once you're armed with these, you can begin applying for whatever other licenses and permits are required, which depends largely on the type of business you have.

State laws (which vary widely) are chockful of hoops for businesses to jump through. From occupational licensing to standard business permits, it's a rare business that doesn't need any licenses or permits. Regulations often require that companies meet certain specific qualifications before they can be granted business permits or licenses or certificates of registration. Local area laws also may require business permits be obtained before your corporation can start engaging in trade in that jurisdiction. Be aware that many home-based businesses are subject to special zoning laws; it could be illegal for you to conduct business out of your home under specific circumstances.

In addition to the usual business fare, federal and state laws require special licenses or permits for particular industries, typically based on the products to be sold. Products that fall into this category include these:

- ➲ Firearms
- ➲ Alcoholic beverages
- ➲ Tobacco
- ➲ Food
- ➲ Securities (like stocks and mutual funds)
- ➲ Gasoline
- ➲ Lottery tickets

If you are not sure which licenses and permits your corporation needs in order to be operating on the right side of the law, contact your state business office and ask. Other good sources of information include your local chamber of commerce, a SCORE office (that's the Service Corps of Retired Executives), the Department of Labor, and the trade association for your industry. ▶▶ **If you live in a condominium, co-op, or other home that's regulated by association guidelines, make sure you understand exactly what types of business, if any, may be conducted from your home.** Should you be in violation of their rules, you will be breaching a contract, and your business could be shut down.

　　　　Home-Based Business Gets Kicked Out

Brad Jarrett ran his professional corporation, a small tax practice, out of his three-bedroom townhouse in Baltimore. He had skimmed through the county zoning laws and figured he was on solid legal ground for operating out of his home. After all, the local zoning laws allowed homes to be used for professional purposes, as long as the home was used mainly as a residence. In fact, the law explicitly included accounting work as one such allowable occupation, so Brad thought he had nothing to worry about.

At first, he met clients at their homes or offices. Pick-up and delivery was part of his value-added service, and he added a great number of clients to his roster. He prepared tax returns from the office, otherwise known as the third bedroom, essentially doing only paperwork in the house. As his practice grew, he transformed his living room into a client waiting area, and his dining room into a meeting room. The living room still looked like a living room, but the dining room now housed a conference table and a reception desk, complete with the part-time receptionist he had hired. Brad also turned the guest room into a second office, to be used by the part-time associate he hired during the busy season.

When word got out, the zoning board came to investigate and issued a summons. Their position: Brad had pushed the limits of the zoning law by transforming his residence into a business, as the house was now primarily used for his business. The judge agreed with the zoning board, ruling that while it was allowable for Brad to conduct business out of his home, he could not make the business the main user of the property. The court ordered Brad to scale back the business or close up shop.

Get Your Corporation's Federal Tax Identification Number

Your corporation is an entity all on its own, and the law requires it to have a federal employer identification number (the EIN). You can get your corporation's EIN by filling out IRS Form SS-4 (available for download from the IRS Web site, at *www.irs.gov*). You can either print out and mail in the form, fax it to the IRS, or file your application right online.

When you go the traditional mail route, it can take up to six weeks to get back your EIN. Faxing the form to the IRS typically reduces the return time to about five business days. Filing online can cut even more time off that waiting period, giving you a response within minutes. You also have the option of applying by phone to the appropriate IRS Service Center (based on the state of incorporation) when you need that EIN right away.

Professional Licensing

Many states require certain professionals to be licensed in their fields. These fields run the gamut from dentists to exterminators to private investigators to acupuncturists. If your corporation will be providing services that require the attainment of professional licenses, you must make sure that everyone performing such services is duly licensed by the state.

In some instances, particular professionals are only allowed to form a special type of corporation called a personal services, or professional, corporation. Every owner of these corporations must be licensed in the applicable field. Professions that commonly fall under this umbrella include architects, accountants, doctors, and lawyers.

Applying by Phone

Before you start dialing, fill out your SS-4 completely. In the instructions that print along with the form, you'll find the right phone number to call based on the state of incorporation. If you don't have the form ready, the agent will instruct you to call back when it's completed.

When you are ready, the agent will ask you to read the information from the form so he can enter it into the system; this takes ten to fifteen minutes. When that's done, he'll tell you the EIN and ask you to fax over the form.

Be aware that some IRS offices will not give out EINs over the phone. In that case, you can expect to receive it via regular mail within five business days.

Retitling Assets

When you first formed your company, you did it by trading some of your personal assets for shares of the corporation. Most of the time the asset in question is cash, but in many circumstances it's fixed assets that are contributed to get the business up and running. Just letting the business use your assets, though, isn't enough to make them count as assets of the corporation. You must go through the formal process of retitling those assets in the name of the corporation. Otherwise, you may find the corporation's depreciation and other asset-related expenses being disallowed by the IRS. Worse, commingling personal and corporate assets can threaten your limited liability protection. By failing to keep personal assets out of the corporation, you run the risk of having the corporate veil pierced by the courts.

In some cases, transferring title for an asset is as easy as simply signing it over on the back of the original title document, as you would with a car. Other times, as in the case of assets like mutual funds, you may need to fill out special, but still simple, paperwork. Still other times, it may be sufficient to write up and sign a document stating that you are transferring an asset into the corporation. When real estate is involved, take special care to make sure that the new legal title to the property has been effectively executed and recorded per state and local regulations. For more complicated transactions, or for missing title documents, you may want to bring your lawyer into the loop. Finally, don't forget that some states impose transfer taxes every time an asset changes hands.

Don't Get Put Off by KYC Rules

As part of the original Patriot Act, banks were required to collect more information when opening new customer accounts. These requirements are known as the "know your customer" (KYC) rules. Before any bank can let your new corporation open a bank account, it will have to collect quite a bit of data from you.

Keep in mind that these rules apply to everyone, so expect to fill out lots of forms and answer lots of questions. Don't take it personally when the banker asks you to answer some seemingly senseless or unrelated questions. The banks have to gather all the information required by the federal government to remain in compliance with these rules, and they face some stiff penalties when they don't.

On the business side, in order to properly transfer assets into the corporation, you'll need some pertinent information for the records. That starts with when and how the asset was acquired and its original purchase price. If any depreciation deductions have been taken for the asset (for example, if it was used in a previous business), that information must transfer over as well. Keep a file for transferred assets, including this information plus the newly transferred title paperwork. This documentation cements the corporate ownership of the assets.

Set Up the Corporate Bank Account

One of the simplest formalities to follow—but one that many small corporation owners neglect, causing trouble down the line—is heading over to the bank and setting up a corporate account. Assigning a new bank account exclusively for the use of the corporation is crucial to maintaining that separate corporate identity. In addition, federal law prohibits shareholders from cashing checks made out to their corporation, so you'll need a corporate account in order to be able to process payments made to the business.

Before you can take this step, though, you must already have received your corporation's new federal employer identification number (also called its tax ID number). The bank needs this number before it can open your business bank account. That's because there is some information that must be reported to the government using that ID number, such as interest income. Other documents you'll need to bring along with you may include a certificate of incorporation (or stamped articles of incorporation), the business license, a copy of the corporate resolution approving the new bank account, a document stating exactly who has signatory power over the corporate bank accounts, and a personal photo ID. Requirements vary by state and by bank, so call ahead to find out exactly what you need to bring with you.

Be prepared to pay business banking fees, which are often higher than those for personal accounts. A lot of banks will give small businesses a break for using special accounts. These usually come with strict minimum balance requirements, ranging anywhere from $500 to $5,000. Unless you already have a strong relationship with a particular bank or loan officer, it pays to do some comparison shopping. Corporate account fees can easily add up to hundreds of dollars every year, so it pays to find a bank that offers no-fee accounts, even if those do come with hefty minimum balance requirements.

The Corporate Records Book

Every corporation must have a corporate records book, and establishing this crucial document is a necessary step in forming your corporation. This records book provides a central file in which you'll keep important corporate paperwork, including such things as these:

➲ Articles of incorporation
➲ Corporate bylaws
➲ Minutes of the initial meeting of the board
➲ Minutes of all director and shareholder meetings
➲ Stock certificates and stubs
➲ Shareholder receipts
➲ Corporate resolutions
➲ Amendments to the original articles or bylaws

Due to the critical nature of the records book, keep it close at hand at your primary corporate location.

Should you and your fellow shareholders ever be hauled into court for a case where the liability shield is in question, having a complete corporate records book for an exhibit will serve you in good stead. Keeping this book is one of the formalities required by state law. If you don't have one, your corporation could be dissolved by the courts.

How to Create the Bylaws

Once the secretary of state has accepted your articles of incorporation, and you have duly placed the stamped articles into the corporate records book, you are ready to create your corporate bylaws. These were discussed in Chapter 6 as part of the paperwork needed to set up a corporation. Basically, this document is like the constitution for your corporation. It sets out the rules and guidelines you and your fellow owners and employees will adhere to in carrying out the daily business of the corporation.

The bylaws are solely for internal use, so there's no state filing here, but you still must prepare them in order to solidify your corporate status. **▸▸ In addition to setting the ground rules for officers, directors, and shareholders, the process of adopting bylaws indicates that you take your corporation seriously.** Along those lines, outside parties may ask for a copy of the bylaws. This is a relatively common request among bankers, vendors, and IRS agents. In this role, your bylaws provide an air of legitimacy to your company—even if you are the sole shareholder, director, and officer.

That said, this is a strictly internal document, and there's no need for it to be over the top. You don't need a lawyer to prepare your bylaws, and you don't need to use specific legal language or phrasing. To make them most useful to you, your bylaws should contain clear language, specific procedures, and a big dose of common sense. While it's easy to go overboard here, it's far wiser to keep your bylaws short and sweet, with references to state law dictates (which may change frequently) as needed.

How to Use Your Bylaws

In addition to meeting just one of many corporate administrative requirements, your corporate bylaws serve as an operating manual and reference guide. Whenever you have a question about procedures, such as how to hold a shareholders' meeting, simply refer to your bylaws. In this role, your bylaws may become the most important corporate document to you when it comes to the continuing life of your corporation. They will remind you of the formalities you need to carry out to preserve your entity's status and help you unfailingly adhere to state law.

In fact, for many small corporations, the bylaws act as an operating agreement, spelling out how the corporation will be run, as well as what it can and cannot do. When you are the sole owner of your corporation, the bylaws will contain mainly functional information. When there are two or more owners, though, you should consider adding some buy-sell provisions. Yes, these provisions will be thoroughly detailed in a complete shareholders' agreement, but having a reference to such provisions in your bylaws can strengthen both documents.

Specific Provisions to Include in Your Bylaws

One of the most important areas to cover in your corporate bylaws is meetings, both for shareholders and for directors. Set out the guidelines for the annual meetings, such as invitation and notice protocols, time and place (though you may want to include provision for flexibility here), and voting procedures. As for special meetings, the state rules surrounding these may vary. For that reason, you may want to include a provision that authorizes specific personnel to call for special meetings and that directs them to the state laws for the particulars of doing so.

Another important set of guidelines to cover is rights and responsibilities for shareholders, directors, and officers. This section can include things like the absolute right of directors and shareholders to see corporate records on demand, specific powers of the directors, compensation for directors and officers, what to do when an officer or director leaves a vacancy, and the role of each officer and particular tasks that role encompasses.

Other items to write into the bylaws include the following:

- ➲ Indemnification of and insurance for officers and directors
- ➲ Stock issuance procedures
- ➲ Setting record dates (for the purposes of identifying shareholders)
- ➲ Procedures for amending the bylaws
- ➲ Information to be included in the annual report

Most fill-in-the-blank corporate forms include generic language covering all of these points. You just have to fill in a few blanks to make the bylaws specific to your company. A good form includes several references to the Business Corporation Act (BCA), rather than merely repeating its provisions. This saves you the trouble of amending your bylaws every time your state makes changes to its BCA, a fairly frequent occurrence.

 **TEST DRIVE**

Choosing a bank seems like an easy task, as easy as point and click. For the long-term health of your corporation, though, shop around until you find the bank that gives you the best deal. Here are some questions you can ask while comparison shopping:

- ➲ Does the bank have special fee rates for small businesses?
- ➲ Is the bank part of the SBA-approved network?
- ➲ Are corporate credit cards available?
- ➲ What are the minimum and maximum monthly fees?
- ➲ Are there penalties for writing too many checks or using teller services too frequently?
- ➲ Do existing bank customers receive preferred loan rates?

The First Board Meeting

Once your corporation exists, you're ready to hold the first meeting of the board of directors. Like all of the meetings that will follow, this meeting must be memorialized in your corporate records book. All actions taken by the board during this meeting are recorded in the minutes.

Though each board meeting is unique, some common items covered in every corporation's first board meeting. Even if you are running a one-man show, you must take care of these issues in your initial board meeting. These items include the following:

- Formal adoption of the corporate bylaws
- Approval of the issuance of shares to the original shareholders
- Appointment of the corporate officers
- Identification of the primary corporate location
- Selection of the company's fiscal year (for accounting and tax purposes)
- Completion of any remaining corporation set-up tasks (these may vary by state)

Even if you are the only director, you must hold and document this meeting. The actions called for in this meeting, though, may take a lot of time to complete. It may take weeks to order and receive printed stock certificates, open a corporate bank account, and complete other immediate post-incorporation tasks. In many cases, those initial meeting minutes may be added to during this period. For example, you can't name the corporate bank until you've chosen one and opened an account. For that reason, the initial board meeting minutes may float around for a couple of weeks before they are finalized and the directors sign off on them.

Issuing Shares

Now that your corporation is up and running, it needs owners. To accomplish that, stock must be issued and sold to the initial shareholders. Your articles of incorporation put an upper limit on the total number of shares you can issue, which cannot be greater than the number of shares authorized. You may, however, issue fewer shares. Under that circumstance, the board of directors must determine exactly how many shares will be issued, then vote and approve the issuance of the shares.

Name Your Directors

In order for the board of directors to hold its first meeting, directors must have been appointed. Often, this occurs in the articles of incorporation. However, some states don't require this information, and some incorporators may choose not to include it there for privacy purposes. Unlike the articles, the document naming the directors goes straight into the corporate records book.

If the directors are not named in the articles, the incorporator prepares a formal statement specifically naming those initial board members prior to the first board meeting. That document is called an incorporator statement. It must include a short paragraph stating its purpose: to name the people chosen to serve as the initial directors until the first shareholders' meeting, when directors will be duly elected. List the names, and have the incorporator sign and date the document.

Once the directors have passed the resolution detailing how many shares will be issued, to whom, and for what, the transaction can take place. Though state law typically does not require actual physical certificates, shares are issued by handing over stock certificates to shareholders. At the same time, those shareholders have to pay for their shares, in full. Payment does not necessarily have to be made in cash, though that's pretty common with start-up corporations. For existing businesses that are being incorporated, asset transfers are almost always involved at stock issuance time.

The Corporation Receives Payment

Your corporation must receive payment in exchange for its stock, and that payment must equal at least the par value of the shares. (Par value, as explained in Chapter 7, is set forth in the articles of incorporation.) Though some states place restrictions on what counts as payment for shares, all allow payment to be made in the following forms:

➲ Cash
➲ Real property
➲ Personal property
➲ Intangible assets
➲ Previously performed services

When the exchange is not for cash, make certain that the fair market value of the payment equals the fair value of the shares. For example, paying your corporation with a used car with a book value of $500 in exchange for $5,000 in shares could cause some legal, tax, and accounting problems. In addition, when any type of property is used as payment, make sure to transfer title to the corporation and to prepare a detailed bill of sale as proof of the exchange.

Tax or No Tax?

Traditionally, trading property for something of value constitutes a sale, and that can trigger a tax liability. The federal tax code gives small-business owners a break here, though. When the person (or people) trading that property for stock end up with at least 80 percent of the total outstanding shares, the IRS gives them a temporary pass on paying any resultant taxes. Translation: you don't have to pay until you sell the shares. Of course, this being the IRS, the full-blown rule (called IRC Section 351) contains a lot of exceptions and exclusions. For more about the fine print, check out Chapter 23.

State Variations

Even about something as seemingly straightforward as stock issuance, there are a lot of differences within state law. The three main areas of disparity are the forms of payment that are acceptable, whether physical stock certificates must be issued, and the existence of par value rules.

First, take a quick look at par value rules. When your corporation is formed in a state that requires par value, shares cannot be issued for less than that. In states that allow for no par value, the full amount paid for shares goes into the stated capital stock account—unless, that is, your state allows for some of that payment to be segregated as capital surplus. For a further look at par value rules, go to Chapter 7.

Second, your corporation may or may not be legally required to print and distribute stock certificates to shareholders. Most states give you the option by not mandating the need for physical documentation. Nonetheless, most corporations prefer to go the traditional route and distribute certificates. Even the states that don't require certificates may have requirements about what must be printed on them should you decide to issue them. (See Chapter 6 for some common language requirements.)

Finally, get to know your state's payment restrictions. While all states allow shares to be traded for cash and property, that's where the similarity ends. Many states do not allow promises to be exchanged for shares, a pretty frequent occurrence among new small-business owners. That may include things like promissory notes or future service contracts. To learn whether or not your state will allow specific promises as payment for shares, check with the secretary of state's office.

The First Shareholders' Meeting

Shareholders have many responsibilities, but perhaps none is as important as their very first: electing the directors of the corporation. While initial directors were appointed before the first share was issued, those roles were temporary until and unless the shareholders vote to keep those directors in place. The first board meeting occurred before there were any shareholders; now that there are shareholders, they have to officially elect board members. This vote will take place at the first shareholders' meeting, and its importance underlines the necessity of holding that meeting as soon as possible after the corporation has been formed. Also in that meeting, the shareholders must vote to affirm all of the actions taken by the board of directors at their organizational meeting.

Before you can hold that meeting, though, it must be officially called. That means each shareholder must be given notice of the meeting in writing, even if there are only one or two of you. This constitutes a formal notice, and as such requires formal documentation by the corporate secretary.

Though electing directors and affirming their decisions will be among the first orders of business, many other items will appear on the agenda of the first shareholders' meeting. This is basically the kick-off meeting for your corporation, and it sets the tone for everything that's to follow. Even if you are the sole director and the sole shareholder, take the time to go through this process. This is a good idea not just to satisfy state formality requirements but to start your corporation properly and make sure nothing important gets overlooked.

Finally, like every other shareholders' meeting to come, this meeting must be formally memorialized in your corporate records book. If you've prepared a written agenda, attach that to the meeting minutes, as well as any other written evidence of the meeting.

Call the Meeting

All corporate actions must be documented by the corporate secretary. Calling the initial meeting of the shareholders fits into that category. To document this action, an affidavit of meeting notice can be prepared. You may be able to find this form in a stationery store (probably as part of a corporate kit), or you can simply draft your own. Either way, the corporate secretary must sign and date the document, remembering to attach all required documentation.

Basically, the affidavit says something like this: "I, [your name], acting as the secretary of [your corporation's name] have personally mailed copies of the attached notice announcing the initial meeting of the shareholders to each person whose name appears on the attached list."

In small corporations, especially those with very few shareholders, it's common for formal notice of meetings to be waived by the shareholders. Instead, the shareholders simply decide on a place and time to hold their meeting, and just do it. Then they document that choice in a waiver of meeting notice, which reads something like this: "We, the shareholders of [your corporation], incorporated in the state of [the corporation's home state] waive notice of the initial shareholder's meeting. We do fix [date and time] for this meeting which will be held at [the meeting place]. We waive the requirements of [name of state] statutes as to meeting notice."

Each shareholder must sign and date the waiver. The fully executed document must then be placed permanently into the corporate records book.

Hold the Meeting

Here's the most important thing you will read about this meeting: ▸▸ **Hold it.** Especially if your corporation has fewer than three shareholders, holding formal shareholders' meetings—particularly this critical first meeting—is essential to maintaining your corporate status. Even if the entire meeting takes place inside your head, go through all the formal steps of holding it, including selection of a distinct time and place where you will consider all the items on the agenda.

At all shareholders' meetings, the first thing you'll do is take a roll call, ensuring that a quorum is present. After that, as you read earlier, the first matters up for discussion and vote will be the election of directors to the board. Other items typically included on the agenda of an initial shareholders' meeting include these:

➲ Approving the articles of incorporation
➲ Approving corporate bylaws
➲ Affirming corporate officers
➲ Receiving stock certificates
➲ Approving any other items decided in the initial board meeting

When all matters have been discussed and decided, the meeting will be officially adjourned.

Document the Meeting

The corporate secretary is tasked with keeping the minutes of this initial shareholders' meeting. This task is very important to preserving the corporate entity, as keeping the minutes of shareholders' meetings is a formality that every state requires. Though the importance of this task is enormous, the task itself is fairly simple. All your corporate secretary really has to do is take notes during the meeting.

The minutes will include some basic identifying data: corporate name, time and date of the meeting, meeting location, and attendees. In addition, the secretary will write up the details of all discussions and votes held, as well as all decisions made. When there are pertinent documents involved, like the approved articles of incorporation, those will be attached to the minutes. Finally, the minutes (with attachments) are entered into the corporate records book.

Applying for "S" Status

Every for-profit corporation begins its life as a regular (or C) corporation. That's the default setting. When it makes more sense for your corporation to become an S corporation, and all the extra criteria are met, you'll have to take some extra steps to accomplish that goal. (S corporations are discussed in Chapter 2; if you're considering making this change in status, be sure to read that chapter as well as the following sections to learn about the particular characteristics of S corporations.)

The State Challenge

S status is strictly a federal gig. However, some states go along with federal treatment of these corporations and allow the same sort of pass-through taxation. Other states don't recognize this corporate form at all, and they treat your S corporation just like a regular corporation, with its own corporate income tax liabilities. This can make tax time pretty confusing. Income passes through to the shareholders' returns for federal tax purposes, but the corporation pays its own income taxes for state purposes.

In states where the S corporation is recognized, you may have to file an application for S status, similar to what you would file under federal law.

S-corporation status is mainly a taxation issue. S-corporation shareholders enjoy all of the same legal protections as regular corporation owners, and the overwhelming majority of corporate formalities are exactly the same. The business itself won't be run any differently whether your

Tom and Ed's First Shareholders' Meeting

Tom Knight and Ed Kingsley owned a fencing academy. As they began to attract more students, the two men decided to incorporate their business. They would be the only two shareholders, directors, and officers of the corporation, called En Garde!, Inc.

Once their articles of incorporation were accepted by the state, Ed and Tom held their first board meeting and passed over a dozen resolutions. They issued shares to each other. Then it was time to hold their first shareholders' meeting. Tom didn't want to bother holding the second meeting; the two had been together all morning in their board meeting. Ed insisted, Tom caved, and they ordered in lunch while their official shareholders' meeting began.

Ed called the meeting to order, and began proceedings. The first order of business was for both men to sign a waiver of notice for the meeting. Then, they handed each other stock certificates. As the meeting progressed, Tom took notes, acting in his role as corporate secretary. The two reviewed all the resolutions they had made in the earlier meeting (as directors) to make sure they still agreed with those decisions. They voted each other in as directors, approved the articles of incorporation and the corporate bylaws, and affirmed all the votes they had held as board members.

After the meeting wrapped up (with Ed banging his fork to signal the official adjournment), Tom typed up his notes. He printed a copy for Ed to review, then both shareholders signed and dated those notes. Tom stuck the paperwork in the corporate records book, turned off his computer, and called it a day.

corporation applies for S status or sticks with the default. The only major difference is its tax status and the extra compliance requirements that go along with that.

When you elect S corporation status, it shifts the income tax burden from the corporation to its shareholders. That phenomenon is called pass-through taxation. It works by acting like the corporation is invisible, so that its income items show up directly on the shareholders' personal income tax returns. For example, if the corporation earns interest income, the shareholders report interest income on their Form 1040.

The Benefits of S Status

Pass-through taxation works especially well in the early years of a company, when it's most common for losses to be sustained. With regular corporate taxation, those losses just hang around, waiting for future income against which they can be deducted. With pass-through taxation, though, the shareholders may be able to deduct those losses against their other income, reducing their personal taxable income and their income tax liability in the present.

In addition, when personal income tax rates are lower than corporate income tax rates, the company-owner combination taxes are lower with pass-through treatment. S corporations offer an added advantage over other pass-through entities: Owners typically do not have to pay self-employment taxes on their shares of the profits, and those additional taxes knock another 15.3 percent off of income. Since S-corporation owners are usually also salaried employees, their payroll tax obligations get taken care of there, and other income derived from the company isn't considered payroll.

S corporations also avoid the double-taxation issue. The corporation pays no federal income taxes. The shareholders pay federal income tax on 100 percent of corporate income, whether they pay themselves dividends or not. There's no extra tax imposed when they do take cash out of the company in the form of dividends.

Meeting the Requirements

In order to be eligible for S status, your corporation must meet some very strict requirements, not only at the time of election but forever forward. Any deviation from these rules can result in termination of S status.

In order to qualify for S status, your corporation must have the following characteristics:

- ➲ May not have more than 100 shareholders
- ➲ Can only have shareholders who are individuals, estates, and some trusts
- ➲ Can't have any nonresident alien shareholders
- ➲ Can only have one class of stock

On top of all that, every single shareholder must agree, in writing, to make the election for S-corporation status. If even one shareholder doesn't, the corporation is not eligible to apply.

Fortunately, the American Jobs Creation Act of 2004 (AJCA) made some of the federal S-corporation rules much easier to deal with, mainly by easing up shareholder restrictions. For example, the shareholder limit used to be seventy-five, and members of the same family were each counted as separate shareholders; now the limit is 100, and all family members (as defined by the AJCA) count together as a single shareholder.

The Application Process

As soon as you and all of your fellow shareholders agree to create an S corporation, you should start the application process right away. ▶▶ **The due dates are a little tricky, and if they pass before your corporation applies, the application has to wait until next year.** Then it actually has to convert from an existing C corporation to an S corporation, and that's a little more complicated.

The process actually begins with a different application, IRS Form SS-4, for a federal employer identification number (EIN), which is required for all corporations (as described in Chapter 12). Once you've done that, you can complete IRS Form 2553, Election by a Small Business Corporation. (If you don't have your EIN back yet, you can simply write "Applied For" in the space.)

Form 2553 must be filed by the fifteenth day of the third month of the tax year in which you want the election to take effect. Any later than that, and it won't take effect until the next tax year. That means if your corporation follows the calendar for its tax year, the election must be made by March 15 to be effective for the current year. The exception is for newly formed corporations. For them, the activation date of the corporation is the start point, which is the earliest of three possible dates: when the corporation first got shareholders, acquired assets, or began conducting business. Now the deadline shifts to the fifteenth day of the third month, starting with the activation date. For example, an activation date of April 11 requires an S election to be filed by June 15.

The form itself is much easier than figuring out the filing deadline. It's a simple, fill-in-the-blanks form, and starts with pretty basic information: corporate name and address, EIN, incorporation address, state of incorporation. Next comes the year you want the election to take effect, usually the current year. That's followed by the name and phone number of a corporate officer whom the IRS can contact with questions.

Along with all of that, each shareholder must sign a "consent to election" statement. They can either sign directly on Form 2553, or you can attach extra sheets if necessary. Along with their signatures, shareholders must disclose their full names and addresses, the number of shares they own, the date they got the shares, their social security numbers, and the month and day on which their personal tax year ends (usually December 31).

The Case for Close Corporation Status

Keeping up with all the formalities of a corporation can be tough, especially when you've got a business to run and profits to earn. If you're a small business owner, it's very easy to let some of the seemingly less important requirements slide, like holding and recording meetings with yourself. However, **failure to maintain your corporation strictly according to the rules can result in the loss of your corporate protections.**

To help small-business owners stay in compliance, most states allow for a special form called a close corporation. Don't confuse this with a closely held corporation, though your corporation may be that as well. The statutory close corporation is one governed by special state laws rather than merely a corporation with very few shareholders. Essentially, close corporation laws relax the formalities normally required of corporations. For example, your corporation may forego a board of directors—that means no board meetings, votes, minutes—which can save you and your co-owners a good deal of time and paperwork.

Special Requirements for the Articles

In order to properly form your statutory close corporation, there are certain items that must be included in your articles of incorporation. Though some of the details may vary by state (as noted), make sure your articles specify these three things:

1. The corporation may not offer its stock to the public.
2. Ownership is limited to a specific number of shareholders (either thirty or fifty, based on the rules of the home state).
3. Ownership interests must be subject to the terms of a buy-sell agreement.

In the states that offer this business choice, you'll find a separate set of forms to use for your articles of incorporation. The provisions listed above will be contained within those specialized forms.

How It Works

With a close corporation, even shareholders don't have to hold formal meetings (or at least not in most cases). Instead, they can use a shareholders' agreement like an operating agreement and run their corporation according to its provisions. They can even switch the voting protocols to one vote for each shareholder rather than one vote for each share.

While the formality rules are relaxed, the shares themselves may face more restrictions than normal. Share transfers are subject not only to provisions in the shareholders' agreement, but may also be restricted under state law. Buy-sell provisions in the agreements of close corporation shareholders are among the most strict, usually requiring that existing shareholders be given first right of refusal. State law typically dictates that close corporation shares cannot be sold through a public offering. These restrictions can make it tough to sell your shares when it's time for you to move on. To protect yourself and your fellow shareholders, make sure you include fair-valuation procedures that kick in any time one of you wants to sell your shares.

▶▶ TEST DRIVE

For people who own small, closely held corporations, one of the special forms often makes the best entity choice. See if your corporation is eligible for either S or close status by answering these questions:

1. Does the home state offer either of these options?
2. How many shareholders does the corporation have now?
3. Do you envision a public offering (even a small one) in the future?
4. Do you have enough time and determination to complete a long list of corporate formalities?
5. Are your fellow shareholders amenable to a special corporate form?
6. Are all shareholders U.S. residents or citizens?

Agreement Now Avoids Problems Later

Any time you have more than one person in a room, you'll also find more than one opinion. That is doubly true when a business—or, more specifically, when money—is involved. When your corporation will have more than one shareholder, particularly when more than one person will hold sizeable stakes, disagreements are bound to occur. Some will be small, settled by compromise or convincing arguments; others will be monumental, and threaten the very existence of your corporation. Thinking ahead about problems that have not yet happened and coming up with reasonable solutions to be implemented should those problems ever occur can be your corporation's saving grace. That's where the shareholders' agreement comes into play. It uncovers potential problems and offers workable solutions to keep your corporation going strong in periods of disharmony among its owners.

Shareholders' agreements are often likened to prenuptial contracts, offering defined steps to follow when things don't work out. They can, however, be much more than that. ▸▸ **A strong shareholders' agreement can act as a guidebook for operating your corporation in accordance with state law.** It can help preserve S-corporation status by forbidding anything that would place that preferred tax status in jeopardy. A thorough agreement can also provide ways to help you and your co-owners work things out amicably when hard-to-settle issues crop up as well as help you avoid deadlocked situations that can prevent your corporation from moving forward. These contracts can cover virtually anything you and your fellow shareholders want included, even what to do when one of you wants to (or has to) withdraw from the company.

Here are the items most commonly included in shareholders' agreements:

- ➲ Voting procedures, including definitions for quorums and majorities
- ➲ Buy-sell provisions
- ➲ Required arbitration
- ➲ Restrictions on share transfers

➲ What happens should a shareholder become incapacitated

➲ Why and how to dissolve the corporation

Though you can find boilerplate versions of shareholders' agreements in most stationery stores, this is one document best prepared by an attorney. Shareholders' agreements are binding contracts, and special language may be required to make sure they mesh with state corporate regulations. Having a lawyer draw up these papers will cost the corporation some money, usually in the $1,000 to $5,000 range depending on how intricate the provisions get, but that cost is nothing in comparison to the cost of protracted litigation when you don't have an agreement to turn to.

Remember S-Corporation Restrictions

S corporations have a more precarious existence than their regular cousins. The rules of share ownership are substantially more restrictive, and bending those rules for even a single day can result in the loss of S status. For this reason, S-corporation owners must take special care to spell out transfer constraints explicitly in their shareholders' agreements.

Though the AJCA made these restrictions a little more livable, especially for corporations that are largely family-owned, the rules are still strict, and they must be followed to the letter. To make sure your corporation remains in compliance at all times, include these two rules explicitly inside your shareholders' agreement:

1. No transfer can be made that may result in the number of shareholders exceeding the legal limit (currently 100 shareholders).

2. Shares may be owned only by U.S. citizens or residents.

Detailing these restrictions within your shareholders' agreement can help ensure that accidental disallowed transfers do not occur.

In addition, you want to make sure that your agreement specifically prohibits the authorization and issuance of a second class of stock, as S corporations are allowed to have only one.

What Could Go Wrong?

At the outset, it seems as if the shareholder restrictions could never impact your small corporation. But it's easier to violate the rules than you might think. In the absence of restrictive buy-sell provisions in your shareholders' agreement, situations could arise to put your corporation's S status in jeopardy.

Consider this example. One of your co-owners (who is a U.S. citizen) marries a Canadian and moves to Canada, where the new couple sets up house. The spouse cannot own any of the S-corporation shares. Those shares cannot be given to the spouse as a gift, and they cannot be jointly owned by the couple. In fact, in some cases, even the act of filing a joint U.S. tax return (as opposed to married, filing separate) could imply that the shares are jointly held; talk with a tax advisor to see if this might apply in your situation. If the Canadian spouse, living in Canada, ever owns those shares, the S-corporation status may be revoked.

The New Family Rules

Before the AJCA, every family member counted as a separate shareholder. That made it tougher for many S corporations to stay within shareholder limits. Now, families may elect to be considered as a single shareholder, no matter who actually owns the shares. However, the definition of family here isn't the same as the dictionary definition. After all, this is the federal government and, as always, confusing language may apply.

Here's what the law considers to be a qualified family member: "the common ancestor, lineal descendants of the common ancestor, and the spouses (or former spouses) of lineal descendants or common ancestor." Common ancestors cannot be more than six generations removed from the youngest shareholders (of the same family).

Here's what this means to you: from great-great grandparents on down to your grandkids, all of you who hold shares can elect to count as a single shareholder for counting purposes. It doesn't matter if you are the sole actual shareholder, or if sixty-five of you each hold shares separately. This will not impact any one person's personal income tax liabilities, just the recorded number of shareholders of the corporation.

Now, imagine this scenario. Your S corporation starts out with twenty-five shareholders, each of whom holds 100 shares. One of them turns right around and sells five shares each to each of his five fraternity brothers. Now you have thirty shareholders. During the year, you all agree that the corporation needs a cash infusion, and you vote to issue an additional 1,000 shares; you find fifty investors each willing to put up the cash for twenty shares. Now the corporation has eighty shareholders. Over time, ten of those investors sell half their shares to outside parties. Now you're up to ninety shareholders. Add in an ESOP (a retirement plan where employees get shares of the company; see Chapter 24), and your corporation could easily end up exceeding the shareholder limit.

Different Regulations Govern Close Corporations

In the states that allow this option, close corporations are regular corporations that get special dispensations under state law. (For a complete listing of states that offer this option, see Chapter 2.) Forming a small corporation under the statutory close corporation statutes is almost always a good idea, as they help your corporation stay in compliance. By easing up on a large portion of the normally required corporate formalities, these rules reduce the risk that you and your fellow shareholders will do or skip something that can put your entity in jeopardy.

There are two reasons a thorough shareholders' agreement is even more important for close corporations than regular corporations:

1. You don't want to risk losing the benefits of these special relaxed regulations.

2. This agreement acts like an operating agreement, a legal contractual manual for running the corporation.

Though the rules may vary somewhat among the states, the biggest exceptions to standard corporate law usually include making directors optional (and everything that goes along with those directors, like board meetings) and eliminating the meeting requirement for shareholders. That significantly cuts down on the chances of noncompliance with corporate formalities as a threat to ongoing corporate status. Now you can run your corporation like an LLC, where everything is decided by the owners whenever they feel like deciding things. Plus, when it comes to decision-making, you and your fellow shareholders may decide to go with the one person-one vote rule (rather than voting on a per-share basis) to give each owner an equal say regardless of ownership percentage.

To make sure that the business is run smoothly, even in the absence of required meetings, the shareholders' agreement in a close corporation maps out policies and procedures for making decisions and taking actions. Your shareholders' agreement may require particular decisions to be subject to votes, like capital expenditures in excess of $5,000 or the hiring of management staff. It can also require votes for things like raising the salaries of owner-employees, paying dividends, or approving loans to or from individual shareholders.

As for remaining in compliance with the governing statutes, your agreement should also include any share-transfer restrictions required by law. All states that allow the close-corporation option limit the number of shareholders, usually to thirty or fifty. Here, those special new S corporation rules regarding family members don't apply—one person counts as one shareholder, no matter who he is. In addition, state statutes typically restrict transfers (for example, public offerings are strictly prohibited), and those restrictions may be required to be included right on the face of stock certificates. All of those restrictions should also be specifically spelled out in your shareholders' agreement.

Voting Rules

In corporations, every major decision (and some less-than-major ones as well) is decided by vote. ▸▸ **According to the standard rule of thumb, one share equals one vote—one voting share, that is, as your corporation may have classes of nonvoting stock.** Whenever you and your fellow shareholders want to get together to make decisions by holding votes, you have to hold a meeting, complete with a quorum and someone to record the minutes. While state law dictates some of the procedures involved in voting, others are based on the preferences of you and your fellow shareholders, documented in your corporate bylaws and emphasized in your shareholders' agreement.

Your corporation's voting rules must be in compliance with state statute. Most state laws have similar regulations; check your state's rules for any specific requirements. Some of the more common statutory provisions include the following:

➲ The ability for shareholders to waive notice
➲ A quorum presence when a vote is held
➲ The ability to use cumulative voting procedures for director elections
➲ The authority to call special shareholders meetings (usually at least 10 percent of shareholders must together call for the meeting)
➲ Only items specified in the meeting notice may be approved during that meeting
➲ Majority rule for vote decisions
➲ The allowance of proxy votes

As long as your rules are at least as stringent as the state rules, they will be in compliance with the law. For example, your corporation can require unanimous votes for certain actions rather than simple majorities. You can also make rules for issues not explicitly covered by state law, such as a rule that votes will be expressed by ballot rather than voice.

The Basics of Buy-Sell Provisions

When you and your co-owners started a business together, you probably already knew each other; maybe you'd even worked together before. In small companies with only a handful of owners, who you're working with is one of the most important facets of your business. It's imperative that you and your fellow owners share a vision of the company, know where and how to compromise, and trust each other. That's the most important reason you need to include buy-sell provisions in your shareholders' agreement. If you suddenly find yourself in business with people you don't like or trust, it can wreak havoc on your corporation.

▸▸ **The very purpose of buy-sell provisions is to help you control changes in ownership.** This is accomplished by detailing all the ways in which a shareholder may and may not transfer his shares. You can include things like first-buying rights for other shareholders, restrictions on transfers (like at least two other owners must approve the buyer), and how to value shares (beginning on page 179).

Most states mandate that owners of statutory close corporations agree to and sign off on buy-sell provisions. Even if your corporation doesn't face this requirement under state statutes, it just makes good business sense whenever a corporation has more than one owner. Once the agreement has been entered into, each physical share certificate must come complete with a notice of restrictions on transfers. Some states require particular language, while others let you choose your own. Before you draw up any language, check your state statutes thoroughly to make sure you include any required language exactly.

Two-and-a-Half Ways to Manage Stock Sales

The underlying purpose of buy-sell provisions is to make sure no owner can sell his shares to an outsider without the consent of his co-owners. That, however, can put the shareholder who wants (or is forced) out in quite a bind. So buy-sell provisions, in addition to protecting the interests of the remaining owners, also include inherent protection for the would-be seller.

There are two ways to accomplish this, as well as a third that combines the first two. First is what's known in legal circles as a cross-purchase agreement, the simplest and most common form of buy-sell provisions for small corporations. This states that the selling shareholder will sell his shares to the remaining owners. Next up is the entity purchase agreement, in which the corporation itself buys back its own shares and either holds them as treasury stock or retires them. The final method is a hybrid, combining the other two forms. Here, the corporation has first dibs on the shares. However, if the company doesn't want to or can't buy them, the shares have to be offered to the other shareholders.

Circumstances May Dictate Transfers

The name of this section of the agreement, buy-sell provisions, immediately puts you in mind of a shareholder who simply wants out of the business and wants to sell off his shares. That's not the only situation that can set off a share transfer, though, and it's not even the most common. Other circumstances that can put buy-sell provisions into effect include these:

- ➲ Death
- ➲ Disability
- ➲ Bankruptcy (of a shareholder)
- ➲ Divorce
- ➲ Irresolvable internal disputes

Consider this. You and your long-time friend Frank formed a corporation together fifteen years ago. Frank dies suddenly, and you find out that he's left his shares equally to his three kids. One day, your corporation has two shareholders who've been working together easily for years; the next, your corporation has four shareholders, two of whom have no business experience, but lots of big ideas. Now four people are involved in major business decisions, three of whom are siblings who may just band together during votes.

Now imagine the same situation, but with comprehensive buy-sell provisions in place. Your agreement could state that in the event of the death of one owner, the other owners or the corporation itself have the first right to purchase his shares. Here, instead of being forced to work with someone else's heirs, you have a choice and some control over what comes next.

Choose Arbitration and Mediation

Face it: Court battles are divisive and acrimonious by nature. You and your former associates will be pitted against each other, true adversaries with no room for compromise. The personal costs here can be high, especially if your fellow shareholders are family members or friends. Now add on the financial costs, which can be staggering for a drawn-out legal battle.

If that picture didn't appeal to you, consider adding an arbitration-and-mediation clause to your shareholders' agreement. These methods cost less, on both the financial and the personal level, and make the best first shot at reaching an agreement.

Mediation is more flexible. Here, a trained professional recommends various ways your dispute can be settled. He can't force a decision but merely suggests options and helps all involved parties communicate effectively with one another. When an agreement is reached, and all parties sign off on it, that agreement will be legally binding.

Arbitration, on the other hand, is automatically binding. With this method, all parties waive their right to trial and agree to reach a decision privately, and not through the court system. The arbitrator holds a hearing, then makes a decision. When the decision is for the plaintiff, the arbitrator determines an award. This decision is final and binding on all parties. Its biggest advantage is cost, as arbitration can cost a mere fraction of a trial in the court system.

Situations in Which Shareholders Must Withdraw

There are situations in which shareholders will be forced to withdraw from the corporation. Some of these situations involve personal tragedy, like death or disability. Others may involve situations in which the shareholders might want one of their members to bow out (like in the case of personal bankruptcy, where there's a fear that the shareholder's shares could come into play during creditor proceedings). A thorough shareholders' agreement must address these possible circumstances, as unpleasant as they are to consider, making sure that the withdrawing owner's shares are handled fairly. At the same time, these occurrences may be unexpected and sudden, and the corporation and remaining shareholders may not have the immediate cash on hand to buy out those shares at the price stipulated by their agreement.

The best time to solve these potential problems is before they happen, when it's just a business exercise and not an emotionally charged event. This is a good spot to get the corporate attorney involved, as she has probably seen these situations before and has learned some of the best ways to handle them. Pre-emptive actions (as in the case of a shareholder about to declare personal bankruptcy) and emergency payment plans (as in the case of a shareholder's sudden death) can keep your corporation afloat when even terrible situations occur.

The Life Insurance Plan

Death can come unexpectedly, leaving grieving families and business partners to deal with business matters in a time of loss. The family may want (or need) to sell corporate shares right away. The corporation or other shareholders may not have enough cash at the ready. The solution: life insurance.

With a cross-purchase agreement, the primary shareholders of the corporation hold life insurance policies on each other. With an entity purchase agreement, the corporation itself holds life insurance policies on the owner-shareholders, with the corporation as the beneficiary. Either of these plans can be worked into the buy-sell provisions of your shareholders' agreement, giving everyone one less thing to worry about when the worst happens.

How Much Are Your Shares Worth?

Normally, when you think about buying stock, you start by checking the price (on the Internet, in the paper, on the TV ticker). That's how it works for big, publicly traded companies—you look up the price, and place an order with your broker. Not so for small, closely held corporations. Here, the price is not a single number you can find in sixty seconds. Here, you first have to agree on how the share price will be figured before you can even begin a transaction based on your buy-sell provisions.

Spelling out exactly how equity interests will be valued is a critical part of any thorough shareholders' agreement. Otherwise, you face deep disagreement at a time of turmoil, and things can get pretty ugly. To avoid such an extremely unpleasant circumstance (piggybacked on to the withdrawal of one of your business partners), deciding on a formula at the outset, when no one is actually trying to sell his shares, is the only way to go.

Here, you have three choices. You can use book value, fair market value, or a pre-set formula. Each method has its merits and shortcomings. The formula approach, in particular, can be a dangerous choice; this price is essentially set in stone.

Book Value

Setting share price equal to book value is the simplest way to come up with a share price. Book value is just what it sounds like: the value of the shares on the books, a number that's already there. There's no math, no appraisal, no fuss—just a number from the existing balance sheet.

Simplicity is the big benefit of the book-value method, but it comes with an extreme built-in disadvantage for the seller. It has no relationship to the shares' fair market value. For accounting purposes (and this is strictly an accounting measure), book value equals net assets, meaning assets minus liabilities. Assets are always recorded at their historical cost; what you paid for it is the number that hits the books. So if your corporation bought a building for $100,000 in year one, that number would never change even if the corporation could actually sell that building for $1,000,000 today.

Wait—it gets worse. Physical assets, like buildings, depreciate in value, at least for accounting purposes. ▸▸ **After years of depreciation, the net book value of that asset (the original building cost less any accumulated depreciation) could be just a fraction of its purchase price.** And here's one more negative. The books don't include the value of the company's goodwill, another accounting term that puts a price on the company's good name when it comes time to sell to outside buyers but doesn't get recorded on the corporation's books. Goodwill is often a small company's most valuable asset. It's that intangible quality that makes customers come to your company instead of any other, the reputation of your corporation. Nothing you can really put your finger on, but it brings in business and increases the value of your business—just not the book value.

Fair Market Value

Fair market value offers the seller a share price equal to its worth. In that regard, it is the most fair of the three methods, since the seller will walk away with the true approximate market value of his shares. On the downside, this method requires professional appraisal for all the assets on the books and a professional determination of the corporation's goodwill. That means a lot of money and time spent, unless your buy-sell provisions include some kind of clause that allows you and your co-owners to agree on an informal version of the fair market value. If you can't agree, you can always call in appraisers.

As an extra backup in the case of disagreements about valuation issues, your shareholders' agreement can direct the discussion to mediation or arbitration. This tack is generally less costly and time-consuming than the formal appraisal process.

Using a Formula Approach

Putting a value on shares of your corporation can be tricky. Book value is inherently unfair to the seller. Fair market value can be a tough nut to crack, and defining it can involve a lengthy, expensive process. To avoid those difficulties, many small-business owners turn to a formula approach instead. This method attempts to come close to fair market value simply by using a mathematical equation.

The most basic calculation starts with book value, then adds a specified percentage (typically in the 5 to 10 percent range) to that. The point of the added percentage is to bring the book value closer to fair market value and account for goodwill. For example, suppose you and your four fellow shareholders agreed on a 7 percent markup. The corporation's current book value is $100,000, and each of you owns 100 shares. The added percentage brings the total formula value to $107,000, or $214 per share. The selling shareholder would receive a total of $21,400 for all of his shares.

Another commonly used, but slightly more complex method, starts with average earnings over a set period (usually three to five years). Then those earnings are capitalized using a pre-set percentage, and that process is supposed to come close to refiguring the corporation's total assets at fair market value. The next step is to subtract the corporation's total liabilities to come up with its net fair market value. Divide that by the number of shares outstanding, and you've come up with your new formula price.

Putting numbers in makes it easier to see how this version works. Suppose the corporation's average annual earnings over the past three years came to $50,000, and your shareholders' agreement set the capitalization rate to 10 percent. That would put the formula asset value at $500,000 ($50,000 divided by 0.10). If the corporation had $275,000 of debt, that knocks the net fair market value down to $225,000. With 500 shares outstanding, the per share price would be $450; the selling shareholder would get $45,000 for 100 shares.

These formulas are the most commonly used, and you can use them as is or determine your own. Once the formula is in your shareholders' agreement, there is no wiggle room when it comes to application. The only way to make a change is to hold a shareholders' vote and formally amend the agreement. You can also use different formulas or different percentages for different situations; for example, you can set the capitalization rate at 10 percent when an owner sells due to disability, but 5 percent if he's selling due to personal bankruptcy.

In the Absence of an Agreement

When there is no shareholders' agreement in effect, state law dictates how issues will be decided. The default rules may not be in your best interests. In fact, some issues important to you may not be covered by statute at all, and in those cases it's every shareholder for himself. For example, many states impose no statutory restrictions on transfers of ownership interests, and that can pose a lot of problems for small-business owners (as you saw earlier in this chapter).

Should the solution to a dispute not be found within state statute, co-owners may be left with no choice but to pursue outside intervention. That can be both costly and divisive and may lead to the dissolution of your corporation. Court costs can add up rather quickly, and court proceedings can suck up a lot of time. Both of these conditions can spell death for your company, as its owners will be forced to spend their time, attention and resources in the legal system rather than on their corporation (where it's probably desperately needed). However, with a thorough shareholders' agreement in place, issues can be resolved before they ever come up. Plus, in instances where there is no preplanned resolution, the agreement can point you toward mediation or arbitration, both of which are less costly and less conflict-ridden than a full-fledged court battle.

Disagreements aren't the only items normally covered in a shareholders' agreement. A comprehensive document sets forth individual rights and responsibilities and details ongoing corporate maintenance tasks. Without an agreement to refer to, formalities may be overlooked, and that could lead to loss of limited liability protection.

 TEST DRIVE

Gather your thoughts about what should be included in your shareholders' agreement before you talk to your co-owners or to the corporate attorney. This way, you won't be distracted by other people's comments, and you'll make sure that issues that concern you are adequately addressed. Use these questions to help figure out which items matter to you most:

➲ Are any of the shareholders married, or likely to get married in the near future?

➲ Are all shareholders personally financially stable?

➲ Would you like to bring in additional equity investors (family members, employees)?

➲ Will all shareholders contribute roughly equally to the daily management of the corporation?

➲ Do you want to allow shareholder loans to and from the corporation?

Maintaining Your Corporation

PART 4

Regular Board Meetings

Every year, your corporation must hold its annual meeting of the board of directors. This meeting follows the schedule set in your corporate bylaws, which include the processes necessary to call and hold the meeting. Each director must get ample written notice of the date, time, and location of the annual meeting.

Depending on the setup of your corporation, these meetings may be quite casual, held right in your main office. Or, if you have board members outside the inner circle of owner-shareholders, the meeting may be formal, held at an off-site venue. When you are the sole director, you may hold the entire meeting in your head, including the recitation of motions and the vote-taking. Regardless of the form your corporation's annual board meeting takes, you must make certain that the meeting is actually held and the minutes are properly kept, especially when you are the sole director.

Unanimous Written Consent

Many small, closely held corporations have directors who are also shareholders, officers, and employees. Since they are involved intimately in the business, they know what's going on, what they want to see happen next, and how they plan to make that happen. Rather than holding full-blown meetings for every board decision, they may instead opt for a unanimous consent document.

Here's how it works. Whenever these directors make decisions that call for board approval, they can simply document them as having been made by unanimous consent rather than by holding a meeting. The corporate secretary writes up the consent document, and all directors must sign and date it. If you take this route, make sure to file the signed document in the corporate minutes, and your meeting requirement is fulfilled.

The first order of business at an annual board meeting is to call the roll and note the directors present. The second item on the agenda is to read and approve the minutes of the last meeting. After that, the board can begin to discuss the business of the corporation and review any motions before them. They may hear presentations made by the corporate officers. The board will also typically hear or review the most recent set of corporate financial statements, including any special financial reports that may be applicable to this particular business.

At minimum, each year the directors must elect the corporate officers for the upcoming year. Even if there is no change in the selection of officers, they must be appointed and accepted annually through a vote. Other common voting issues include whether or not to purchase major assets, enter into significant leases or contracts, change primary vendors or banks, expand the company into new product lines or geographic areas, and other material business decisions. Once all votes are counted and decisions documented, the last matter on the agenda is the meeting adjournment.

Annual Shareholders' Meetings

Much like the board of directors, the shareholders of a corporation must meet each year at an annual shareholders' meeting. The primary goals of these meetings are to elect directors to the board (directors' positions, much like those of officers, come with one-year terms) and hold votes on any items for which shareholder approval is required.

Shareholders meetings must be called and held following the protocols set out in the corporation's bylaws. Notice must be sent to each shareholder of the date, time, and place of the annual meeting. When your corporation has some uninvolved shareholders (purely investors), it helps to have a pre-set agenda to keep the meeting moving along. Such an agenda might include these standard items:

- ➲ Roll call (to make sure you have a quorum)
- ➲ Reading of the previous meeting's minutes
- ➲ Presentations by directors or officers
- ➲ Report on the current position of the corporation
- ➲ Election of directors to the board
- ➲ Address of any open business items
- ➲ Discussion of new business items
- ➲ Vote on any new business items that call for a shareholder vote

Once all agenda items have been completed, the meeting can be formally adjourned.

➤➤ **In closely held corporations, where all shareholders act as business owners and participate regularly in daily operations, you can use a consent document in lieu of an annual meeting.** Depending on specifications in your corporate bylaws, that document will require either majority or unanimous consent. To prepare this consent, simply document the items that would have been discussed at the meeting, along with any actions that have been approved by the majority of shareholders (or all, if required), and state that this agreement is in lieu of the annual meeting. Each consenting shareholder must sign and date the document, which is then filed in the permanent corporate records book.

Special Situations Call for Special Meetings

Annual meetings offer directors and shareholders a time to come together and discuss the state of the business. The agendas for each contain pretty standard fare: a little discussion of things past, a look toward the future, and a vote to appoint directors (at the annual shareholders meeting) or officers (at the annual board meeting). Sometimes, though, things come up that simply can't wait for the annual meeting to get approval, and these situations call for special meetings.

Your bylaws spell out exactly who can call special meetings. Once the appropriate party has made that request, the next step is notification. The procedures for this are similar to those of the annual meetings, with a little twist. Here, the notice has to specify the items that will be addressed at this special meeting, and no other items may be discussed. At the meeting, role will be called, a quorum ascertained, the matter at hand debated, and a vote taken. Once the matter that's at the center of the special meeting has been decided, the meeting can be adjourned.

Special Shareholders Meetings

Special meetings of the shareholders can be called by whomever you name in your bylaws. Typically, the named parties include directors, specific officers, and a majority of shareholders. Reasons to hold special shareholders meetings can include the following:

- ➲ The sudden loss of a board member who must be replaced
- ➲ Amendment of the articles of incorporation
- ➲ Amendment of the corporate bylaws
- ➲ Approval of changes in the stock class structure (such as a new non-voting common class)
- ➲ The opportunity to merge with another company
- ➲ Decisions on whether to sell off substantially all assets of the corporation
- ➲ Dissolution of the corporation

Should any discussion bring up another issue that the shareholders wish to vote on, they cannot do it at the particular special meeting they are in. Instead, they must vote to hold another special meeting, with that new issue on the agenda.

Special Meetings of the Board of Directors

Directors may have meetings throughout the year even when no vote will be taken. In large corporations, board members may meet to simply discuss the state of the business and to consider new objectives going forward. In smaller corporations, directors may get together to have a more formal meeting than they would in their other roles as officers and employees of the company. However, it's much more common for small, closely held corporations to have these meetings as part of the normal course of business, in their capacities as officers, in order to avoid the extra procedural requirements involved in calling a special board meeting.

There are plenty of times, though, when voting matters arise during the year, and at those times the purpose of the special meeting is to proffer votes. The most common reason is to declare dividends, and that's closely followed by proposing changes to either the articles or the bylaws.

Taking a Vote

Whether it's the shareholders who are voting or the directors, the procedures laid out in your corporate bylaws must be followed to the letter to ensure the outcome is valid. A full quorum must be present for the vote to take place, and the required number of favorable votes must be rendered in order for a motion to be approved. Virtually all major decisions affecting the corporation will be subject to a vote, from electing directors to selling off a major asset.

In most cases (unless you choose otherwise), each shareholder casts one vote for each share he owns, and each director gets a single vote. Power can be concentrated through proxies, where one shareholder signs over his voting rights to another, to be voted however the second shareholder wishes.

Setting the Quorum

One key factor in all corporate votes is the quorum. A quorum represents the minimum presence required before a valid vote can be held. State law sets out guidelines for quorum counting, but your bylaws can override that number, either way. For shareholder votes, the quorum is often expressed in terms of shares. For example, you can set a quorum of 500 shares, meaning that the shareholders who show up must among them own at least 500 shares to meet the quorum rules. For board votes, the quorum is expressed in the number of directors. In this case, your bylaws might order that three directors be present to achieve a quorum.

The best way to set your quorums, for both shareholder and director votes, is to use a percentage rather than a fixed number—if, that is, you choose not to default to state guidelines, which usually call for simple majorities. Using a fixed number can cause problems when the number of outstanding shares or the number of directors changes. Should either of those scenarios occur, you would have to amend your bylaws to encompass the change, and doing that calls for a vote (which could get messy if you can't achieve a quorum).

Suppose your corporation has authorized 2,000 shares, and 500 of those shares are currently outstanding, split evenly among five owners, and the board currently has five directors. If you set the corporate quorums at 400 shares and four directors, at least four of you have to be present in order to hold any kind of votes. Then suppose your corporation grows, and you end up issuing 1,000 more shares; your shareholder quorum would be less than a third of outstanding shares. An opposite scenario holds true, too. Suppose two of the owners want out of the business and sell their shares back to the corporation. Now there are only 300 shares outstanding and three current directors; neither of which constitutes a quorum.

If you and your co-owners are not comfortable with a simple majority quorum, consider setting percentages instead. This allows for much more flexibility should changes in numbers occur, as they almost inevitably do. For the shareholders' meetings, set the quorum as a percentage of outstanding—not authorized—shares. For the board meetings, use a percentage of active directors for your quorum count.

How Directors Vote

State law dictates that each director on the board gets one vote when it comes to making decisions at their meetings. Under most state law, a simple majority of directors satisfies the quorum requirement. That means that most of the directors must be present at the board meeting in order for a vote to take place. However, if a majority can't be easily reached or if you want more than simple majority of directors present, your corporate bylaws can specify the number that best suits your company.

Once you've got a directors' quorum, votes can be held. Again, most state law calls for a simple majority vote to make decisions. That means that the majority of directors must vote "yes" for a motion to pass. In your bylaws, though, you can set a different "yes" rate for motions to be approved.

Now, math gets involved once again. Suppose that your bylaws call for four directors on the board, a majority quorum, and a majority to pass votes. That means you need three directors present in order to hold a vote. Then, depending on whether three or four directors show up, a decision will be carried with either two or three votes, respectively.

Typical items voted on by directors, in addition to their annual officer-electing duties, include approving shareholder dividends, revising employee compensation guidelines, and making major decisions about the direction of the corporation.

How Shareholders Vote

The procedures for shareholder votes are set out in the corporate bylaws and may also be discussed in a provision of the shareholders' agreement. In order for a vote to be called, there must be a shareholders' meeting in progress, and a quorum must be present. Once that quorum is established, issues to be decided will be presented to the shareholders (though they will already know of these issues from their meeting notification). When it's time to cast votes, each shareholder votes his shares. Unless otherwise specified in the bylaws, majority rules.

With shareholder votes, though, it's the shares that have to be present, not necessarily the shareholders themselves. It's pretty uncommon to have full shareholder attendance at meetings (unless there are only one or two shareholders), so many corporate bylaws allow for vote by proxy. That means a shareholder hands over his voting power to someone else who will attend, and vote his shares, on his behalf.

Minority shareholders (those who hold relatively few shares) have voting rights, but they can feel like those votes do not count. One way to protect their rights when it comes to electing directors to act for them is through cumulative voting rights. Here, the votes of each shareholder are multiplied by the number of directors up for election. Then shareholders can use those votes however they want. For example, suppose a corporation has three directors on its board and three shareholders, two holding fifty shares and the other holding thirty-five. In straight votes, the majority shareholders could always outvote the minority shareholder, giving him no voice in director election. With a cumulative vote, though, the minority shareholder would have a total of 105 (thirty-five shares times three directors) votes to cast. The majority shareholders would have to use 106 votes to secure their choices, but they could only do that twice before running short. This guarantees that the minority shareholder can elect at least one board member of his choice.

Empowering Minority Shareholders
Can Attract Capital

Jane Michaels and Gerald Mann own Clean Up, Inc. They each own fifty shares of stock, giving them equal ownership status. When they needed to raise some capital, they agreed to sell thirty shares to an investor, someone who would not participate in the daily running of the business. They shopped their business plan around among some venture capitalists they'd heard about but were turned down every time. Then they asked an associate, Harold Levine, if he would like to invest in their company. They offered him thirty shares in exchange for his capital contribution of $6,000.

Harold read over their business plan, liked the prospects, and expressed interest in becoming a investor. He did, though, demand a couple of changes. The first was to change the number of directors on the board from two to three. The second was to grant cumulative voting rights for director elections. He explained to Jane and George that while he was happy to be a silent investor, he wanted to feel that his investment was protected. By having a seat on the board of directors, he could have a say in the business without being directly involved. With cumulative voting, he was assured that his choice would always make it to the board.

Once Jane and George amended their articles and bylaws to accommodate those changes, Harold felt more secure in his investment, and Jane and George got the funding they needed to expand their corporation. Plus, these changes would help Clean Up, Inc. attract additional minority investors when they needed their next cash infusion.

Keeping the Minutes

With corporations comes lots of documentation, not the least of which is keeping the minute book complete and up-to-date. From the very first board meeting to the final shareholders' meeting (and everything in between), everything that goes on at these meetings must be meticulously recorded and filed for posterity.

The actual task is much simpler than its importance implies. Really, keeping the minutes just means taking thorough notes during meetings, the primary job of the corporate secretary. In many cases, you can even use a standardized fill-in-the-blanks form to keep the record, rather than writing out all of the repetitive parts (and there are a lot of those). Whether you use those forms or write up the minutes yourself, there are some basic items that must be included for proper documentation.

First comes the page header, which identifies the document as minutes. That's followed by some general information, such as the type of meeting (annual board, special shareholders) and the name of the corporation. Third comes the information specific to this meeting: its time and location, the name of the chair (the leader of the meeting), and the acting secretary (usually the corporate secretary). Then you come to the meat of the minutes, where the meeting is described in step-by-step format, starting with the call to order. This section also includes the roll call, which usually includes officers and directors by name, and a shareholder count, to document that a quorum was present. Next, the minutes list the motions heard, the votes taken (for example, seven in favor and four against), the outcome of each vote, and a detailed description of any resolutions adopted during the meeting. The last action is the meeting adjournment.

Once the minutes are prepared, which may not be until a couple of days later, the secretary signs off on them with his signature and title. The completed document gets filed in the corporation's minute book along with the other permanent records.

Why Keep the Minutes?

The point of the minutes, from a legal perspective, is to provide a comprehensive record of the matters discussed and decided during each session. From your perspective as a corporate owner, keeping the minutes serve two very important purposes. First, it helps maintain and preserve your entity, and second, it serves as proof of the decisions made and agreed upon by you and your co-owners.

Filing Annual Reports

As part of the ongoing corporate maintenance formalities, most states require that every corporation submit an annual report every year. (In some states, the requirement is biannual instead.) Unlike the fancy annual reports of large, publicly held corporations (typically magazine-length, and similarly bound and glossy), your small corporation may only have to submit a simple one- or two-page form. In many states, the state business office will send you the completed form, full of last year's information. In other states, you may be able to download a blank form directly from the secretary of state's Web site.

The standard form contains basic identifying information, including this:

➲ Federal tax identification number
➲ State tax identification number (where different)
➲ Formal and DBA names of the corporation
➲ Address of the registered office
➲ Name of the registered agent
➲ Names and addresses of all directors
➲ Names and addresses of all corporate officers

If all of the information on the printed form is correct, sign it and mail it in to the appropriate state office along with a check for the full amount of the required annual fee. Some states allow you to make particular changes right on this form—for example, if you've appointed a new registered agent—saving you the additional fees that would be required with a separate change of information filing.

Make sure to complete this process by the due date, or your corporation may be assessed fines. If you don't submit the form on time, the state will send out at least one reminder notice. Should your corporation fail to comply, the state may dissolve it (though they will send notification before taking such action).

How to Avoid Penalties

Corporations mean big business for the states. Many of the formalities come with a fee attached, not to mention all the costs of incorporating in the first place. A primary way the government (federal, state, and local) makes money is through business fees and taxes, and those are considered ordinary and necessary costs of doing business. However, some fees are completely unnecessary, and these can be easily avoided by simply adhering to the rules and watching the calendar.

The vast majority of government-imposed penalties are about filing paperwork on time and paying the right amount due. Take taxes, for example. Just like with your personal income taxes, any time you pay corporate taxes late or in the wrong amount (underpaying, as there's generally no penalty for overpayment), a penalty will be assessed. Even if your corporation isn't subject to income taxes, it will probably still have to pay sales taxes, employment taxes, and possibly general business taxes. As long as you file on time, you'll save the corporation a late filing fee, and as long as you pay enough, you won't be subject to interest, underpayment penalties, or late payment (as opposed to late filing) fees. These are all excellent reasons to get the help of a good accountant.

Other official business documents come with due dates and payment requirements as well. Business permits have to be obtained and renewed periodically. Professional licenses must be maintained and kept current. Annual corporate reports have to be filed. As long as you keep on top of all the government paperwork, filing on time with properly drawn corporate checks, you can keep your corporation free from penalties.

Create your corporate records book. Supplies you'll need include a large three-ring binder, a three-hole punch, section dividers, and plastic prepunched document pockets to protect papers that shouldn't be marred. Make your section labels, which should include things like incorporation documentation, loan documentation, major asset titles, minutes (you can separate this further into directors and shareholders), and resolutions. Sort through your existing paperwork, and place each document in the appropriate binder section. Place the most recent documents on the top.

The Advantages of Limited Liability

When it comes to owning and operating a small business, limited liability protection can be your best friend. That protection keeps your personal assets out of the line of fire should the company ever be unable to fulfill its financial obligations. Without the shield of limited liability, you could be held personally financially responsible for unpaid business debts and unmet business obligations.

Every business has liabilities. From supplier invoices to payroll taxes to the monthly electric bill, no company can exist without owing something to someone at some time—and these are just the ordinary and usual debts. In addition to debt incurred in the normal course of business come more unusual liabilities, like lawsuit settlements and court-ordered reparations. When the company can meet all of its debts, personal liability typically doesn't come into play. However, when a company is struggling financially and not paying its bills, creditors turn to the owners for satisfaction, usually through protracted court proceedings. Where the business entity doesn't provide protection, those creditors will prevail.

That's where the corporate limited liability advantage comes in. As a corporate shareholder, your personal assets are shielded from business debts. While you can lose your full investment in the company (as creditors take priority over equity investors), you cannot lose more than that as long as the shield stands firm.

When Liability Protection Does Not Apply

Limited liability offers a great deal of protection, but the shield is not completely impermeable. First, you always stand to lose your investment in the business—that, in fact, is where the "limited" part of limited liability comes from. When a corporation struggles to meet its financial obligations, creditors come before investors when it's time to dole out whatever money is left. Second, limited liability does not apply to your own acts of negligence or malpractice. If you personally mess something up, you will be held personally liable for the damages. Third, you may be held liable for such acts committed by your employees. Because your employees are under your control, you can be sued for negligent hiring or supervision practices.

One instance where the shield has no bearing is improper document signing. When an owner-employee of the corporation signs documents on the company's behalf, she must also include the name of the corporation and her representative position. For example, should Claudia Owens, president of Owentech, Inc., sign a note borrowing $10,000 for the corporation, she must include "president, Owentech, Inc." as part of her signature right on the contract. If she signed only her name, then she has entered into the contract rather than the corporation, at least in strict legal terms. In that case, Ms. Owens could be held personally financially responsible for that contract.

Losing Your Protection

The beauty of the corporate form is that it creates a legally distinct entity, one that is completely responsible for its own obligations and that in legal terms is completely separate from its owners. Maintaining that separation is crucial to the corporation's survival. ▶▶ **It is your responsibility as a corporate owner to keep all business and personal dealings fully differentiated at all times.** In addition, it is your responsibility to comply with all the legal requirements necessary to keep your corporation "alive." Failure to meet even a single requirement, including that complete separation, can result in the loss of your limited liability protection and the loss of personal assets.

Loss of limited liability protection is absolute. Though the corporate veil typically gets pierced based on the rulings in a lawsuit brought on by a single creditor, once it's gone, it's gone completely. As soon as that personal financial liability is imposed for one creditor, it's out there for all of them.

Why Your Corporation Needs Insurance

Limited liability protects you from the debts of your corporation and protects your corporation from your personal debts. However, nothing shields the corporation from the responsibility of paying its own debts and obligations. Just as you can be held liable if someone is injured on your property, your corporation could be liable for any injuries or other forms of damage suffered in connection with the business.

Standard business insurance provides a strong line of defense for your corporation. There are two basic forms to consider: liability insurance and property insurance. Liability insurance takes care of claims by outside parties, when the corporation is responsible for damages to someone else or his property. Property insurance, on the other hand, covers your corporation for damages to its own property. Within these two big categories, there are dozens of more specific policy choices, including specialized provisions to cover particular incidents or properties.

Don't Rely on Your Homeowner's Policy

If you conduct any business out of your home, you may need to adjust your homeowner's insurance policy, or risk losing everything. Many policies specifically exclude business-related events. In some cases, operating a business out of your home—in any capacity at all—can invalidate your homeowner's policy completely.

Different insurance companies have different guidelines regarding business use of the home, mainly depending on the extent of business use. For a simple home office, the norm is to attach a specific rider to your standard policy. When the business use is more extensive, a separate policy may be called for; this could be the case if you see customers or clients in your home, store inventory on the premises, or have expensive equipment.

Know What You Have to Get

In some states, certain forms of insurance are mandatory. Motor vehicle insurance is required in many states, for example, and malpractice insurance is required for many professions. Though legally you may be able to get away with minimal coverage, it's a bad idea to confuse legal sufficiency for what your corporation really needs.

Every state has different rules concerning mandatory insurance coverage. Even within a state, requirements may vary by industry. For example, restaurants that serve liquor may need more or different coverage than beauty salons. Failure to obtain necessary coverage can result in the revocation of your business license or in steep fines. Make sure you know what policies are required, as well as minimum coverage requirements, and get on the phone with your insurance agent before you open the doors for business. Keep your agent apprised of any major changes (like adding delivery to your list of services) so he can add coverage as needed.

Consider an Umbrella Policy

Most insurance policies come with limits and deductibles. That means your corporation may be on the hook for payments even when your claim is covered. For times like these, an umbrella policy can keep your business solvent.

Umbrella policies offer liability insurance coverage for the excess, after your other policies poop out. For example, suppose your corporation is sued for $2,000,000 in damages, and your insurance company helps settle the claim for $1,500,000. The corporation has a $50,000 deductible, and the policy payout is limited to $1,000,000. That leaves your corporation liable for $450,000. If you have an umbrella policy in place, it will pick up some or all of that $450,000 and may even cover all or part of your original deductible.

Keeping Things Separate

Separation of personal and business transactions is critical when it comes to maintaining your corporation's unique identity. Mixing the two can lead to trouble down the road, both in minor ways (like having to sort business transactions from personal ones) and in more serious ones (like losing limited liability protection).

Your corporation must have its own bank accounts, completely separate from any of your and your co-owners' personal accounts. Checks written for the business must be out of the corporate account, and checks written for personal items must come from your personal account. Should the need arise for a personal payment to be made using a corporate check (or vice versa), write the corporate check to yourself and use your own check to make payment. An interchange of the two is the most common evidence used to eradicate the veil of limited liability.

This separation applies to credit cards as well. Many new and small-business owners use their personal credit cards to buy things for their companies, rather than going through the bother of applying for and waiting for corporate cards. Then, when the corporation does receive its own credit cards, those are often used to make personal purchases. This cross-use has the exact same impact as commingling cash and checks and can result in the same lack of separation issues.

Commingling assets does not only refer to cash and credit cards, though those are the most commonly floated back and forth. The separation issue applies to all assets of the corporation equally. These are the other assets that often make the trip back and forth:

- ➲ Laptops
- ➲ Motor vehicles
- ➲ Boats
- ➲ Rental equipment
- ➲ Recreational properties

Using assets interchangeably in both personal and business applications sets the stage for creditors to sue the corporation under the alter-ego theory (in the section beginning on page 204). When you have contributed such personal assets to the corporation in exchange for shares, make sure to sign title over to the corporation immediately, and stop using those assets for personal activities.

When an Existing Business Is Incorporated

Many small businesses start out without the formality of incorporation and often run for many years under other entity forms. If you make such a change, and your company becomes a corporation, make sure to switch absolutely everything over to the corporation and begin using the full corporate name immediately. Cancel all old bank accounts, even if you have hundreds of checks left; shred them, and throw them out. Cancel all old credit card accounts. Get rid of the old letterhead stationary, purchase orders, invoices, and any other preprinted paperwork that contains the

Separated Is Not the Same as Separate

Inside Track

When Jason Drake incorporated his business, a martial arts studio, he carefully followed all of the required corporate conventions. He was the sole shareholder, officer, and employee of Kick It, Inc., a statutory close corporation. He held solo shareholders' meetings, kept a corporate records book, had a corporate bank account and credit card, and carefully tracked business expenses. Jason believed he had followed the rules for keeping things separate, but he was wrong, as he learned when he had the first quarterly meeting with his accountant.

Jason did have a separate corporate checking account, in the same bank as his personal checking account. When one account was running low, he simply transferred in funds from the other. He took cash advances on the corporate credit card and deposited that money in his personal checking account. He kept careful records of all the transfers, entering every transaction into his corporate files. Jason also kept a detailed mileage log in his car to track business and personal mileage. At the end of every month, he made an entry to record the corporate mileage expense.

The accountant explained to Jason that keeping separate records, even having separate accounts, was not good enough to stand up as a legal defense. By moving money back and forth at will, by booking a corporate business expense for use of a personal vehicle, he was actually commingling some assets. To remedy the situation, Jason had to stop making random transfers among accounts. Instead, he had to make official interest-bearing loans to the corporation when he transferred cash in and declare official dividends when he transferred money out. As for the car, he was a corporate employee, using a personal vehicle for business purposes; that could be deducted on his personal income tax return as an employee expense.

old business name. This is particularly important if the old business name was your name. (Many sole proprietors use their own names as business names, for example.)

The moment your company is incorporated, open new bank accounts and apply for new credit cards, all in the corporate name. Retitle every single asset that has come over to the corporation. Get new business cards, new letterhead, and new preprinted invoice and purchase order forms. Every piece of paper that leaves your corporation should have the full corporate name on it, indicating the new entity.

Failure to take all of these steps could result in the loss of limited liability protection. If other entities (businesses or individuals) do not know they are dealing with a corporation, they have a reasonable expectation of payment from you, personally, should the corporation fail to pay. When your corporation uses checks from the old business checking account, for example, it is effectively using assets that it does not own, impairing its entity status. In addition, it gives the recipients the impression that your business has not undergone any changes.

How to Use Assets and Stay Separate

Consider this. You have a lake house up in the mountains, and you decide it would make a perfect corporate retreat. Or your corporation sells antique furniture, and it just acquired a piece you'd love for your house. Or the business is a landscaping company, and you need your lawn cut. Any of these situations could result in commingling of assets—unless, that is, you treat them like business transactions. In that case, you get to have your corporation and share assets with it, too.

All that's required to keep everything aboveboard is an arm's-length transaction. You need the lawn cut? Pay the corporation to do it, the same amount as any other customer would be charged. (If some customers or other employees get discounts, you can give yourself the discount, too). Have the corporation pay you fair-market rent for the use of your lake house. Check with your tax advisor: if the property is rented for fewer than fourteen days, the rental income you receive may be tax-free to you, while still deductible to the corporation.

When the Veil Is Pierced

Frustrated creditors can attempt to have the corporate veil pierced, allowing them to seek financial relief from owner-shareholders. Chapter 9 discusses why you absolutely should avoid allowing this to happen. Basically, should the corporate veil be pierced, creditors of the corporation can reach your personal assets, everything from your checking account to your mutual funds to your motorboat. Once it happens, every single debt of the corporation crosses over, not just those due to the creditor who initiated the lawsuit that resulted in the veil piercing.

Here's how the process unfolds. First, your corporation has trouble meeting its debts. After repeated collection attempts by the creditor in question, the company is still unable to pay up. The creditor then goes to court, suing the business owner personally, claiming that right under the state's prevailing "pierce the veil" doctrine. Then that creditor has to prove that the doctrine fully applies in this situation.

This Works Both Ways

Switch your focus for a moment. Put yourself in the place of the frustrated creditor, unable to collect monies owed to you by a particular corporate customer. Your company has been making collection attempts for over a year, and not a single payment has been received, despite your company's litigation threats and that corporation's promises. As you're looking back through the file, you notice that some older invoices were paid with personal checks. Now your company can take that corporation to court, attempt to pierce the corporate veil, and finally get paid if your company does prevail.

The creditor will prevail if he can prove either of the two following legal concepts: the "alter-ego" theory or the "undercapitalization" theory. The essence of the alter-ego theory is that the corporation really isn't a separate financial entity, that the corporation and its owner are one and the same. The undercapitalization theory holds that the company was purposely underfunded when it was created and nothing was done to remedy that situation; worse, the owners continually drain funds from the company to pay themselves at the expense of creditors.

Should either theory be proven, your limited liability shield will be dissolved. Creditors will be able to sue you and your co-owners personally for any unpaid debts owed by the corporation. Your personal assets would be at stake here: cash, cars, vacation homes, mutual funds. The courts will order you to pay the creditors, and the corporate debts—all of them—may become your personal debts.

The Alter-Ego Theory

The alter-ego theory comes into play when owners of a corporation do not make sure to keep all things corporate separate from all things personal. There are a couple of ways that this manifests, but the commingling of funds is by far the most common. This lack of separation between personal and business finances demonstrates the creditor's point for him: When the owner ignores that separation, the courts should as well.

Commingling funds doesn't just mean putting corporate money into personal bank accounts, or vice versa, though that does satisfy the definition. It includes using the corporate checkbook for personal expenses, something many small-business owners get into the habit of doing when they're running short on personal funds. It includes writing checks to yourself when dividends have not been formally declared. It even includes using your personal checkbook to pay corporate expenses. This lack of financial boundaries indicates to the courts that the corporation is not in fact a separate financial entity and that its owners should therefore be held responsible for outstanding corporate debts.

In addition to the commingling factor, failing to treat your corporation like a corporation can also allow the invocation of the alter-ego theory. For example, if you never hold board meetings or shareholders meetings, never keep a corporate records book, or fail to keep up with all other required corporate formalities, a court could decide that the corporation did not really exist.

Remember: Other Assets Must Be Separate, Too

Most of the time, proof of the alter-ego theory revolves around money, but this is not always the case. Treating any corporate assets as personal property can bring this theory into play. For example, the lawn mower of an incorporated landscaping company cannot be used to mow the company owner's lawn unless that owner is a paying customer of the corporation. The corporate boat can't be used for the owner's grandson's graduation party, unless he rents it from the company. When an owner wants to use an asset of the corporation, he must behave as though he is dealing with any other unrelated company or risk being called out for treating the corporation as an alter ego.

The Undercapitalization Theory

The name of this theory makes it sound easier to prove in court. After all, these lawsuits are about unpaid creditors. If the corporation were fully capitalized, the creditors wouldn't be unpaid. That's not exactly how this theory works, though. It's more about the owners' intent to defraud creditors by intentionally underfunding the company.

In order to prove this theory, a creditor must show that the owners set up a company for the purpose of stealing. They created a corporation in order to buy stuff or receive services that they didn't intend to pay for. When they incorporated this business, they did not put up enough funds to reasonably run a company, and they did it on purpose. Should those allegations be proven to a court's satisfaction, the limited liability shield will be terminated.

Accidental Loss of Limited Liability Protection

Even if you have kept meticulously separated records and fully funded your corporation, there are still some circumstances that could trigger the loss of your personal limited liability protection. These are generally circumstances that trigger an inadvertent dissolution of the corporation, and once the corporation is dissolved the limited liability shield no longer exists.

Since such dissolution is unintentional, it probably goes unnoticed by the owners. They typically continue conducting business, unaware that they are no longer operating as a corporation. This means they are operating instead as either a sole proprietorship or general partnership (depending on how many owners there are). In either case, though, all owners would become 100 percent personally liable for all existing debts of the business.

Though inadvertent dissolutions can happen by way of standard statutes, these actions can often be prevented (or at least controlled) by the company's articles of incorporation or its bylaws. The most common accidental dissolution event is usually a simple oversight: failing to renew corporate status properly and on time. The state in which your business was incorporated has specific annual procedures that must be followed to ensure continued existence as a corporation. Most, though, stick to a basic pattern, requiring corporations to file an annual report and pay a fee. Neglecting to do this puts your corporation into a "bad" standing in the state roster. Let it go long enough, and the state will automatically dissolve your corporation.

Along the same line, a defective incorporation can nullify any liability shield. This situation occurs when someone forms a corporation, either on his own or with capital from others, and does something incorrectly. Due to that error, the corporation was never properly formed and doesn't legally exist; however, the owners think they've incorporated, and they carry on as if that were the case. Everything goes along normally until the corporation can't meet its obligations. Then, depending on the severity of the defect, the courts will decide whether the shareholders acted in good faith and deserve personal limited liability protection. Cases here can go either way. The outcome is based on a number of factors, but courts mainly look at how well the owners kept up with corporate formalities and the fully separate corporate identity.

Charging Orders

With a corporation, limited liability protection flows both ways. The owners bear no personal responsibility for business debts, and the business bears no responsibility for the personal debts of its owners. That's how things operate under normal circumstances, but there are times when the corporation may suffer due to the unpaid obligations of its shareholders.

When a creditor sues a corporate shareholder for debts owed and not yet satisfied, that creditor can't dip into the corporate bank accounts to get paid—not directly, anyway. However, that creditor can get something called a charging order, which allows him to participate in corporate management in place of the shareholder.

Here's how that works. The creditor brings a lawsuit, the courts find in his favor, and they allow him to acquire corporate shares through attachment. That attachment allows the creditor the powers of the shareholder, including voting rights, but not direct ownership of any assets owned by the corporation. So while he cannot take possession of corporate equipment, he can vote to sell that equipment.

Once the creditor holds those voting rights, he may hold the power to liquidate the company or take other actions unfavorable to the original shareholder's interests. This scenario is most likely to take place with a small, closely held business, where power is concentrated in very few hands.

Surviving Lawsuits

Lawsuits can cripple small businesses and their owners. You can better protect your corporation (and yourself) by simply understanding the rules of the game. Even with the best liability protection planning and the best insurance, you could still find your corporation being hauled into court. Being prepared will help your defense substantially.

That said, the very best way to survive lawsuits is to try and keep them out of the court system. ▶▶ **Just because a legal action is brought against your corporation does not mean it must be settled inside a courtroom**—you do have other options. One way to accomplish that is for the involved parties to reach an agreement, called a settlement. Settlements can be reached in a few different ways:

- ➲ Through negotiation by both parties' lawyers
- ➲ Through mediation
- ➲ Through arbitration

All three of these methods are strictly consensual, meaning both parties must agree to enter into the proceedings. They can agree to that before the dispute gets formalized or afterward. In fact, as your corporation enters into new contracts, it can request the insertion of a mediation or arbitration clause, requiring these courses of action before starting an official legal action.

Keep this in mind: The longer a legal disagreement drags on, the more it costs all the parties involved (except the lawyers). Your corporation's best chance of survival here is to get through the process as quickly as possible. A $200,000 settlement today, hard as it may be to deal with, is better than a $175,000 settlement three years from now after three years of attorney's fees and court costs and lost time.

Choose Mediation and Arbitration

If your corporation has to choose between going to court or undergoing mediation or arbitration proceedings, choose one of the latter options. Your company will benefit substantially. ▸▸ **Either mediation or arbitration almost always costs less than taking a case to trial.** There's no jury, so you don't have to worry about who will be deciding your company's fate. There are no complicated rules of evidence, making it much easier for talks to go ahead. For these reasons, including mediation and arbitration clauses in all of your corporation's contracts makes good business sense. Why include both? Mediation is typically less expensive, making it a good first choice. However, mediation requires the agreement of the parties, which does not always happen. Arbitration is a more formal (and slightly more costly) proceeding, but the decision will be binding, ensuring that the matter does get settled out of court.

Mediation calls for a professional mediator, who listens to both parties and may try to get a dialogue going. He acts as a middleman, to smooth rough spots in the conversation and return discussions to the topic at hand (as these discussions can get emotional and easily off track). The mediator facilitates the meeting and may make recommendations to help the parties resolve their disagreement. However, unless both parties agree, there is no resolution.

Arbitration also involves a professional disagreement handler. This one, however, has the power to hand down a decision that is binding on both parties. That sounds like what happens in court, and it is, with a very critical distinction. This is a private hearing, with only the pertinent parties and the arbitrator involved. There is no judge, no jury, and no court system involved. It is still a hearing, though, with both sides presenting their arguments and evidence. After that hearing, the arbitrator renders a decision. When the arbitrator decides in favor of the plaintiff, an award will be entered (similar to the judgments entered as the result of courtroom trials).

The Personal and Financial Impacts of Lawsuits

Even when a lawsuit is a strictly business matter, it can take an extremely high personal toll. Defending a lawsuit successfully can still result in severe financial loss, as the costs of that defense may be quite high and in all likelihood not reimbursed. Most small-business owners dip into their personal funds to defend their companies and will never see that money again.

It can take a lot of money to defend against a lawsuit, and that money spent cannot guarantee a favorable outcome. The defense alone can use up vast amounts of corporate resources, not to mention the personal resources as well. Even when your side does prevail, and your corporation is not forced to pay out a settlement, the process itself could cause serious financial setbacks and severely impair corporate cash flow.

Many people believe that the losing side of a lawsuit will be forced to pay the court costs of the winning side. This is not always the case, so don't expect to be reimbursed for all the cash that you and your corporation have laid out.

While the financial impact can be awful, the personal psychological impact can be devastating. Professionals being sued for malpractice or incompetence may begin to doubt their abilities. When personal injury is involved, overwhelming feelings of guilt may ensue, even if you and your corporation aren't held legally responsible. Defendants may fear for their future reputations. And the constant fear of loss can be crippling: loss of future customers and income, loss of a home and a nest egg, loss of a lifelong profession.

Protect Yourself

From the very first day your corporation is created, treat it like a corporation. Maintain fully separate finances. Retitle every asset you contribute to the corporation. Follow and document all corporate formalities. Pay every fee, and file every form on time. Operate your business in a fair and ethical manner. This diligence creates a legal defense, a mountain of paperwork proving that your corporation is indeed a separate entity. It doesn't have to be perfect. A misstep here or there won't negate the facts shown by the overwhelming evidence in your favor.

Even if your corporation ends up on the losing side of a lawsuit, your personal wealth will remain protected. Your business may be forced to struggle to cope with the losses, and you may even lose the business entirely, but your personal assets will remain intact as long as you have taken the necessary steps to protect them.

▶▶ TEST DRIVE

Are you 100-percent sure that your personal assets are wholly distinct from your corporation's assets? If you can answer even one of these questions in the positive, you may have some commingling to untangle:

- ⮕ Do you pay corporate expenses with personal funds without filling out expense reimbursement reports?
- ⮕ Do you use your personal vehicle to make business deliveries?
- ⮕ Do you bring inventory home for personal use?
- ⮕ Does your corporation have its own credit card?

The Business of Business Is (Mostly) the Same

Corporations come with some extra bells and whistles, but when it comes to conducting business, they aren't really much different than other entities. They have the same types of daily transactions, the same cash flow patterns, the same irate customers, and the same impatient vendors. Unlike other entities, the corporation owners can also be employees. Expanded benefits options are available; the company itself enters into contracts; and some accounting rules are unique. Those differences don't typically impact everyday business issues, though, bringing things back around to the fact that the normal business conducted isn't so different after all.

To run a company successfully, aside from all of the corporate formality requirements, small-business owners must be well versed in lots of standard issues, such as these:

- A working knowledge of accounting
- Familiarity with employment regulations
- An ability to attract, motivate, and keep top-notch employees
- Some marketing know-how
- Basic salesmanship
- An understanding of business law
- Strong negotiating skills
- Computer and Internet proficiency

The best entrepreneurs—and the most successful—know what they know, and they hire out the rest. To join that elite group, figure out which areas are your strongest and get to know them inside and out. As for the rest, compensate for your weaker areas by surrounding yourself with knowledgeable others, whether they be co-owners, employees, directors, officers, or professional consultants.

Contracts

One of the areas of particular importance for corporations is contract law. You will likely negotiate many contracts on behalf of your corporation, and it's important to understand what you are signing. For more complicated deals, it's a good idea to have your corporate attorney review the documents before anyone signs them. For more common agreements, though, running to the lawyer's office each time would seriously impact your schedule and your corporation's cash flow.

Leases are among the most common business agreements. Whether for rental property or office equipment, your corporation will probably be a party to some kind of lease. Most of the time, terms (like rent payment, due date, length of agreement) are straightforward. Some business leases may include things like escalating rent clauses (which allow for rent increases under particular circumstances), assignment or subletting terms (which dictate whether you can rent all or part of your rental space or equipment to someone else), and improvement and alteration language (which speaks to tenants modifying the space or equipment to suit their needs).

Purchase orders and sales agreements also constitute contracts. Some of the terms commonly included in these contracts are glaringly obvious, like price and quantity. Others may not be quite as clear to novice entrepreneurs, like shipping or payment terms, which seem to operate with unique coding systems. Once you have the key, cracking the codes is very simple. As for shipping, the terms will typically be either FOB (free on board) shipping point or FOB destination. The big difference here is ownership: with FOB shipping point, the buyer owns the merchandise as soon as it hits the truck; with FOB destination, the seller owns the goods until they reach the buyer. As for payment terms, the most commonly used look like this: 2/10, n30. That letter and number combination simply means the buyer can get a 2 percent discount for paying within ten days, or pay the net (the "n") balance in thirty days.

Dealing with Employees

Employees come with a multitude of paperwork. From the ads you place to find them, to employment applications, to termination documentation, each employee that sticks around will end up with a very thick folder. In addition to myriad forms, there are also dozens of rules that govern hiring and firing practices, payroll, workplace safety, and (of course) taxes. These laws exist at every level, from federal down to local, and they primarily exist to protect the employees. As you begin hiring people to work for your corporation, familiarize yourself with the applicable statutes to avoid opening the company up to lawsuits.

As a corporation, your business has a unique leg up on employee motivation. Unlike any other business entity, you can offer employees stock or stock options as benefits or as rewards for continued good performance. When employees own a piece of the pie, they are more likely to work harder and smarter; after all, now they're working for themselves. You can learn more about these excellent incentives in Chapter 24.

Employees Add a New Liability Dimension

Every business has liabilities and potential liabilities, some more than others. A business with employees has inherently more liability issues than one without. Consider all the problems that can crop up with employees: injury on the job, sexual harassment claims, theft, poor performance—the list goes on.

In addition to all that, though, employee negligence can create liabilities that put corporate assets in jeopardy. For example, the guy you hired to drive your delivery van could hit another car, or a member of your landscaping team could inadvertently weed-whack someone's prize-winning roses. Incidents like this are hardly rare, so keep the liability factor in mind as you make the choice to hire employees.

Amending Your Articles of Incorporation

Once your original articles of incorporation have been filed, they're set in stone. Should you need to make a change, you will have to formally amend those articles and refile with the secretary of state. All this requires is a little paperwork, and a (usually) small fee.

Before any official paperwork is prepared, the amendment must first be accepted by the shareholders. The board of directors must present proposed changes at a specially-called shareholders meeting. The shareholders then vote to adopt or reject that amendment.

Though the procedures to get this done seem like a big hassle, they really only come into play for major issues. For example, if the corporation wants to authorize more shares, an amendment to the articles is a must. Other items that may call for amended articles include these:

➲ Adding a new class of shares
➲ Changing the required number of directors
➲ Changing the DBA name of the corporation
➲ Redefining cumulative voting rights
➲ Altering transfer restrictions

The more you put into your original articles of incorporation, the bigger the chances that something will need to be amended down the line. For that reason, many incorporators choose to include only the bare minimum information, as required by state law, in the articles of incorporation. Everything else is taken care of through the corporate bylaws and the shareholders' agreement. These documents also require shareholder votes for amendments, but nothing needs to be filed with the state.

Maintain a Strong Corps of Professional Advisors

It's not hard to maintain a corporation, but it does take attention. Unfortunately, slip-ups and oversights can result in the loss of your company's corporate status, so vigilance is of the utmost importance. To help you keep things flowing smoothly, consider professional help.

The five most important (and common) professional advisors, used by corporations in virtually any line of business, are the following:

1. CPA
2. Attorney
3. Insurance agent
4. Banker
5. Retirement plan manager

Your corporation is not required to hire these professionals, but they will make your corporate life a whole lot simpler. Yes, with the possible exception of the banker, they all tend to charge fees, typically on the high end of the scale. The best of the bunch will let you do what you can to keep costs down, getting involved only when a situation truly calls for a professional of that level. You'll find that plenty of those situations crop up, and you'll be glad to have a trusted ally already in your corner.

The CPA

When it comes to corporate tax returns—and there can be a lot of them—your CPA (which stands for certified public accountant) may be your best friend. From income tax to payroll tax to sales tax, with a lot more specialized taxes thrown in, the CPA is well-versed in the lingo and loopholes. She'll know what your corporation needs to file and when, how much the checks should be written out for, and where it's safe to get more aggressive with deductions.

That's how most small businesses use their CPAs, but they could be getting a whole lot more for their money. In addition to being experienced tax preparers, many CPAs also specialize in small businesses and all of their financial intricacies. Tax preparation often leads neatly into tax planning, a set of strategies designed to minimize the overall tax burden both now and in the future. That opens the door for other forms of financial planning, both for your corporation and your personal estate.

A qualified small-business CPA can help you put together a first-rate business plan. She can help you figure out how much money your corporation needs to raise and the best way to bring it in. She can help you optimize corporate cash flow, maximize profitability, and grow your business in a sustainable fashion.

▶▶ **Here's what you don't need a CPA for: regular bookkeeping tasks.** Even if you hire out this cumbersome job, you don't need to pay CPA rates. The CPA who takes care of the heavy lifting may have staff that can handle your more routine needs at a much lower cost. If not, look into hiring a part-time bookkeeper to handle the day-to-day accounting chores.

The Attorney

Every small business, regardless of its entity, should be well acquainted with an experienced attorney. From the initial idea phase through incorporation to that unexpected lawsuit, you want a qualified and familiar lawyer by your side. Tiny missteps early on can have monumental consequences later, and your corporate attorney can make sure that doesn't happen. Plus, developing this relationship during good times saves you the stress of trying to find someone while your corporation is in crisis mode.

That does not mean you need a lawyer to do absolutely everything for you, especially when you are trying to preserve your precious start-up cash. There are many formation steps you can do on your own when you are creating a bare bones small corporation and don't intend to issue any shares to the general public. For more sophisticated arrangements, ones that don't fall neatly into the preprinted forms you can download from the home state's Web site, talk with an attorney. State securities laws vary widely, and though they can get pretty tricky, full compliance with every requirement is a must. You don't necessarily need to hire someone to create your incorporation paperwork, but it pays to have a qualified small business attorney who is familiar with the particular state laws at least review the documents you have prepared.

When you do begin to look for a lawyer, talk to other members of your local small-business community. You'll get an idea of which lawyers are more willing to work with you than around you, and which have the most experience in this area. The best recommendations will come from the business arena. Great personal lawyers may not make great business lawyers.

Once you've chosen an attorney, talk explicitly about fees. Not only do you want to find out the rates, but you must also know how your corporation will be billed. Some attorneys bill by the job for particular tasks, some by the hour. Some attorneys who bill on a time-spent basis charge by different benchmarks: half-hour, fifteen-minute, or ten-minute segments are all commonly used.

The Insurance Agent

Like every other business out there, your corporation needs insurance. The types of policies and the levels of coverage it needs, though, are not the same as every other business. Insurance agents get a bad rap as boring salesmen who talk about death and actuarial tables, but the reality is much different. These are the guys who can save your business from bankruptcy, who can help you rebuild after a catastrophe, and who can make sure you're covered when you rush your wife to the emergency room to deliver your first baby.

Business insurance isn't just one single thing. It's a broad range of coverage, some of which you absolutely need and some of which you probably don't. Every business needs basic liability coverage and some kind of property damage coverage. ▶▶ **Companies with employees are required to have active workman's compensation policies.** In most states, any business that owns and operates motor vehicles must insure each of them. The optional column contains everything from health and life coverage for you and your employees to umbrella policies.

There are many variables to consider: policy type, coverage level, deductibles, named property clauses. A trusted insurance agent can walk you through it all, getting you the policies you really need at a price that fits your corporation's budget. As your corporation changes and grows, he'll be right there with you to adjust coverage as needed, before you actually need it.

The Banker

Every business can benefit from a solid working relationship between its owners and a local banker. Chances are, when you first formed your corporation, part of its funding came from a bank loan. That means your corporation already has a banking relationship in place, and you can build on that by meeting payment deadlines and using other bank services. Even if your initial financing did not include a bank loan, you can still begin to build a relationship with both a bank and a loan officer. By laying a solid foundation now, and earning a reputation as a favored customer, you may be able to score better loan terms when your corporation does require such financing in the future.

When you have a relationship with a banker, your loan application packet may make it more quickly to the top of the pile. A loan officer who is familiar with your company's business cycle, cash flow, and seasonality can help you out by incorporating special terms into your loan agreement. Those terms can help your company remain in compliance with any covenants required by the bank. For example, if your company takes in most of its cash toward the end of the month, you and your banker can schedule payment dates that take that into account.

The Retirement Plan Manager

Should you choose to offer an employee retirement plan, consider hiring a professional to take over all of the administrative duties. In addition to helping you choose the best plan for all parties involved (your employees, your corporation, and you), a retirement plan manager can take care of piles of paperwork and help ensure your plan remains in compliance with a complex body of tax law.

Whether or not you hire a plan manager, you will be considered a plan fiduciary, as someone who has authority and control over the plan and its assets. If you've participated in the selection of the plan provider or the investment options, you are a fiduciary. Along with that designation comes awesome responsibility, both ethical and legal. Fiduciary responsibilities include the following:

- ⮕ The duty to act in the best interests of all plan participants and beneficiaries
- ⮕ Knowledge of and full understanding of all expenses paid by the plan
- ⮕ Prudent decision-making concerning the plan, from the choice of a service provider to the investment options
- ⮕ The monitoring of plan investments
- ⮕ Constant action in accordance with all plan documents

Not knowing about or fully understanding fiduciary responsibilities does not exempt you from performing them. When fiduciary responsibilities are not met, there can be legal and financial repercussions (including jail time!).

Keeping up with the laws, filing all the required forms, and managing the plan can be a full-time job in itself. The rules governing retirement plans are hard to understand, and they change fairly frequently. While plan sponsors (meaning the financial institution in which you house that retirement plan) can help guide you through some of the finer points, a plan manager will actually take care of them for you.

Determining Optimal Salaries

Every corporate shareholder who works for the company has to draw a salary. The trick is to come up with just the right number to keep income taxes as low as possible without annoying the IRS.

The basic rule of thumb depends on what type of corporation you have. In a C corporation, you want your salary to be as high as possible. With an S corporation, though, you want your salary to be as low as possible. In case that raised your eyebrows, remember that there is more than one way to get money out of your corporation, so you don't have to rely on salary alone to bring home cash.

The logic behind the high/low salary puzzle is all about taxes. With a C corporation, you want to avoid the double taxation that comes with dividend distributions, and your paycheck only gets hit with income taxes once. With an S corporation, dividend distributions are not separately taxable, but your salary comes with an employment tax hit (Social Security and Medicare) on top of straight income taxes.

While your goal is to minimize taxes, the goal of the IRS is to collect as much in taxes as possible. With that in mind, they put some guidelines in place that basically say S-corporation owner-employees must take a reasonable salary, and that C-corporation owner-employees cannot take too high a salary. You do have a lot of wiggle room with these guidelines, as long as you can show that the salary figure you chose is reasonable compensation for the work you do as a corporate employee.

For S-Corporation Shareholders

The owners of corporations are also often their officers. Corporate officers are expected to draw a salary, as are other shareholder employees. There is one glaring difference, though. The salaries of corporate officers are listed separately on the corporate tax return, while other salaries are just lumped in with employee payroll. Sure, every employee's salary is reported individually to the IRS with the annual payroll tax returns, but those are completely separate from the company's income tax return. On that return, IRS agents look to see that corporate officers are being compensated "fairly."

The Definition of Reasonable

Brenda Jones was the sole shareholder and officer of her S corporation, a stationery store. The company had been in business for three years and was just starting to turn profits. In addition to Brenda, two sales clerks and one store manager worked for the corporation. The clerks each earned $16,000 per year, and the store manager earned $28,000 per year. Brenda paid herself $25,000 per year in salary, and took 80 percent of the year-three profits as dividends. She did that against the advice of her accountant (Joanna Richards), who told her to pay herself at least as much as she paid the store manager.

As the corporation entered its fourth year, Brenda received a notice from the IRS, which she brought to her accountant. Joanna read the notice, and told Brenda that her salary was being questioned. Joanna explained that they'd have to justify her salary to the IRS. If they couldn't do that to the agent's satisfaction, part of her dividends could be reclassified as salary, subject to back taxes, interest, and penalties.

Brenda said that she kept her salary lower than the manager's because she also spent some time as a sales clerk. She had settled on an in-between salary, on the higher end because she spent more time as a manager. Joanna explained that she could try to sell that to the IRS, but there was a good chance it wouldn't fly.

A few weeks later, the IRS officials sent their response to Joanna's explanation. They disagreed with the reasonableness of Brenda's salary and reset it to $35,000 for year three. Their logic? She should earn more than a mere manager's salary because she also filled the roles of corporate president and secretary. Brenda and the corporation had to pay some back taxes, along with a few penalties and a little interest. For year four, she set her salary to $40,000, just to be on the safe side.

The temptation in an S corporation is to pay virtually no shareholder salaries and pay more profits out as dividends. That lowers the overall tax burden by minimizing employment taxes. It's fine to keep your salary minimal, as long as you can prove it's reasonable. First, it can't be zero; no one works for free. Even if your salary turns a tiny corporate profit into a loss, you still have to pay it. Second, it should work out to be at least the minimum wage, or you could find your corporation in violation of state or federal statutes. Third, it should sound reasonable to you for the type of work you're doing and the number of hours you're putting in. If it makes sense to you, you can sell it to the IRS.

For C-Corporation Shareholders

For C-corporation shareholder-employees, the goal is often to maximize salary and minimize dividends. This strategy has a double purpose. First, salary payments are deductible expenses to the corporation, and dividend payments are not. Second, dividends get taxed twice, and salaries only once. Again, the IRS looks to see that shareholder-employees get reasonable compensation, but here reasonable means not too much. If they determine your corporation is paying you an unreasonably high salary for the work you do, they can recharacterize some of that salary as a constructive dividend. (See Chapter 21 for more details.) That reduces the tax deduction for the corporation and increases its taxable income, just like a regular dividend would have done. Plus, IRS recharacterizations may result in the assessment of penalties, which are never considered deductible expenses.

The Corporate Home-Office Advantage

Many small-business owners operate at least a portion of their companies from their homes. Sometimes it's just a quiet spot to do some end-of-the-day paperwork. Sometimes it's a full office, where employees and clients may come. In some cases, sheds, garages or basements are used as inventory storage or manufacturing (assembly-type tasks) facilities. Regardless of the reason, if your corporation is using work space in your home, one of you (either you or the company) may be entitled to tax deductions for the associated expenses.

The biggest issue to decide here is which entity will take the expense deduction. When you take the deduction personally, you will have to take it as an employee expense. That means your deduction may be subject to a 2 percent floor. In other words, the total deductible expenses must be greater than 2 percent of your personal adjusted gross income, and only the excess will be deductible. On top of that, the IRS rules are pretty strict about whether your home office qualifies. You have to be using space at home "for the convenience of your employer." So if the corporation provides an office for you somewhere else, your home office won't qualify for the home office deduction, but that doesn't mean you can't still deduct expenses that are strictly business related. For example, if you had to purchase additional insurance to cover your home business activities, that expense could be traced directly to business purposes.

There is a way the corporation can get a deduction, but it means a little more paperwork for you. It's one of the benefits of having a separate entity, one unique to corporations. ▶▶ **Your company can rent space from you.** It has to pay you rent, and it gets a rent expense deduction. You have to report the rental income but can deduct all of the rental expenses from that. Those may include things like these:

- ➲ Utilities
- ➲ Cleaning services
- ➲ Security
- ➲ Pest control
- ➲ Repairs and maintenance

This treatment will result in an extra schedule in your personal tax return, Schedule E. That form acts like a statement of profit and loss for your rental property. The resulting profit or loss flows onto the first page of your Form 1040.

Getting Additional Financing

Sometimes your corporation may need more money when you and your fellow shareholders have none left to give. At those times, you will need to turn to outside sources to deliver the cash infusion. Corporations are often in a better position to do this than any other entity because they can sell off equity shares without giving away any control. At the same time, corporations can opt for debt financing; small corporations can take advantage of federal programs specially designed to help such businesses.

At different times in your corporation's life, different options will make more sense. If your corporation is already shouldering a lot of debt, an equity transaction will be less taxing on the cash flow. When debt is minimal and you want to keep the number of shareholders small (like for an S or close corporation), consider taking out a business loan. Either way you go, there will be a price to pay. Investors want to see a return on their investment, often in the form of steady dividend payments. Lenders want to get their money back, on time, with interest.

On the other side of the deal is the impact on your corporation's income taxes and cash flow. Equity financing typically has a tax-neutral effect, meaning it won't impact your bottom line one way or the other. Their will be an ongoing cash flow impact, though.

At first, their will be a large inflow of cash, the infusion you were looking for. Part of the payback may be in the form of dividends, which drain cash from the company without a concurrent tax deduction. Loans also come with a big chunk of cash up front, but they affect both taxes and cash flow. Loans call for steady repayments, a constant cash outflow. The interest portion of each payment is tax-deductible, so you can recoup some of that cash outflow through a smaller income-tax payment (due to lower taxable income).

It's Time to Update Your Business Plan

Now that you're looking for some outside funding for your corporation, it's time to dust off your business plan and give the numbers an extreme makeover. Your company has a track record, hopefully a successful one, and that can help attract investors and lenders. The corporation now has an experienced staff in place, a reliable customer base, and strong relationships with vendors, all things that should help you obtain external financing. Here's the catch: You have to put that all in writing, making sure it sounds good and looks polished.

Even when you have a solid relationship with your banker, and even when you and your potential investors go way back, they will all want to see a current business plan. That plan must reflect what your corporation has been doing lately, where it's going, what it needs the money for, and how it plans to pay that money back.

Applying for a Bank Loan

Bank loans can be hard to come by for new small businesses. After all, most new businesses fail. That makes the possibility of repayment pretty risky business for the bank, and banks are well known for their conservatism. That said, a small business with some success under its belt is much less risky than an unknown entity. Armed with your corporation's success story, however short or limited that story is, you have a good chance of getting a "yes" from your banker.

It's your job to make it easy for him to approve your loan. Supply all the paperwork he asks for, in the exact format requested. Adapt your business plan to include the elements he needs to see. Complete all the forms he asks, on time. Be prepared to answer questions on the spot. That doesn't mean you need to memorize every number, but you should know what your business plan says and why this loan practically comes with a guarantee of prompt repayment.

Visit the SBA

If you are considering taking out a business loan, check out the U.S. Small Business Administration (SBA). This federal agency was formed primarily to make sure small companies could get reasonably priced business loans. Since new and small businesses pose bigger payback risks to the bank than larger, more established companies, lenders tend to charge them more for the same loans. Other terms may be much more strict as well, making it nearly impossible for the standard small company to qualify. So the SBA comes to the rescue by guaranteeing small business loans and policing loan terms to make sure they're fair. The actual loans are made by regular lending institutions, like banks.

Though the SBA has many different loan programs, the three most commonly used are the basic 7(a) loan guaranty program, the certified development company/504 loan program, and the micro-loan 7(m) program. The 7(a) program and the micro-loan program can each be used by start-up company or existing businesses for virtually any business purpose; the 504 loan program is strictly for "brick and mortar" financing, meaning that physical asset purchases must be involved. For more information on SBA loan programs, visit their Web site at *www.sba.gov.*

Taking on More Business Partners

When your corporation needs more cash because it's growing quickly, taking on another co-owner or two may help your company as much as the cash they bring in. Even though these owners are called shareholders, they are truly business partners. These guys will roll up their sleeves and join you in the trenches. In return, they will get comparable equity stake in the company, as well as the rights and responsibilities of other shareholder-partners.

If your corporation already has multiple owners, there is probably a shareholders' agreement in place (if not, have your attorney draft one right away). However, if you've been running a one-man show until now, you will need to draw up a comprehensive shareholders' agreement before your corporation has additional owners. The agreement will serve to protect all of you, provide guidelines for settling disputes, and spell out the steps to take should this new arrangement not work out as expected.

Attracting Equity Investors

When you want to raise equity capital but don't want to dilute your power base, you can look for investors. Sometimes these are big-money guys, known as venture capitalists, looking for bigger growth and returns than they'd get on the stock market. They don't want to be involved in the day-to-day chores of running a company. That doesn't mean they will necessarily relinquish all control; very often this type of investor (particularly when smaller, unproven companies are involved) will want a voice in major decision-making.

If your corporation has employees, you may have another market to tap into, a sort of captive audience. If it makes sense for your corporation, you could initiate an ESOP. That's a form of retirement plan that invests mainly in the stock of your corporation. Your employees get to participate in a retirement plan, and they get to own a little piece of the company they're already committed to. At the same time, your corporation gets tax deductions for its contributions and expenses plus a cash infusion from its stock sales. These plans can be complicated to set up and administer (as described in Chapter 24), so make sure you get some professional help.

▶▶ TEST DRIVE

Hiring the right professionals takes time and patience. These relationships will be long-term, so make sure that you factor personal feelings into your choice. Consider the following questions as you choose the professionals who will help you build and shape your corporation:

1. Did he listen to what I was saying before responding?

2. Did he try to make my plans work, or did he fit my corporation into an existing set of plans?

3. Would I feel comfortable disagreeing with him?

4. Would I feel comfortable questioning advice that made me uncomfortable?

5. Do I really want to be involved with this guy for the next ten years?

PART **4**

Maintaining Your Corporation

What Kinds of Records Should You Keep?

Accounting for a business is a significant undertaking, and it won't be any easier for your corporation. Depending upon your company's transactions volume, daily bookkeeping could be voluminous or minute. Regardless of transaction volume or type, though, each and every single one has to be accounted for in your bookkeeping records.

Typical transactions that most businesses record repeatedly include these:

- Sales (cash or credit)
- Accounts-receivable activities
- Cash receipts
- Cash expenditures
- Inventory movement (purchases and sales)
- Accounts-payable activities

A Few Sets of Books

Does your company have more than one location or multiple product lines? If so, you may want to track each separately, and that calls for multiple sets of books. Recording transactions this way can be very useful for you, letting you know which product lines are succeeding or which locations are bringing in fewer sales.

Keeping more than one set of books can be time-consuming, and it will add another level of complexity to your accounting system, but it's worth the trouble when it comes time to make business decisions. Should you decide to do this, keep these two things in mind: You'll still need to know how the business is doing overall, and there may be expenses (like your salary) that must be allocated among the units.

To support those bookkeeping records, your corporation will need to maintain source documents for its transactions. That includes things like cash register tapes, bank statements, cancelled checks, credit card statements, expense receipts, customer invoices, and vendor invoices. It's a lot of paper, and it takes up a lot of room. When the IRS calls for it, though, you may be required to supply transaction proof for up to three years after the date of the applicable tax return. That means you should hold on to such records for four years. Essentially, your corporation may be called upon to prove that the transaction actually occurred, for the amount in question.

Introduction to Basic Bookkeeping

Keeping accurate records of business transactions is required of every company, regardless of the entity. Every time your business buys or sells anything, orders or promises anything, it has conducted a transaction, regardless of whether money exchanges hands at the time. Recording those transactions is the first job of bookkeeping.

Most of your company's transactions are probably recorded at the time they occur. When you write a check, you're recording a transaction. The same goes for billing a customer, adding customer receipts to your checkbook balance, or writing up an order. Others may get temporarily bypassed and will need to be accounted for later. For example, most cash transactions (from buying stamps to paying cab drivers) result in receipts that get tossed in a box somewhere.

After a while, you will start to notice patterns among your transactions that allow you to start grouping them. You might have ten receipts for postage, or a pile of paid phone bills. Every logical grouping can be treated as a single account for accounting purposes. Those ten receipts will go into an account called postage expense, the phone bills into telephone expense. On the flip side, those transactions all impact your cash and will get recorded there as well. Every single transaction will affect at least two accounts, sometimes more.

Meet the Basic Account Groups

As you set up your books, you'll become intimately involved with the five basic account groups:

1. Assets
2. Liabilities
3. Equity
4. Expenses
5. Revenues

The first three groups are made up of permanent accounts, meaning they carry balances from one period to the next. Assets represent everything of value your business has. This group includes things like money, inventory, office furniture, vehicles, and equipment. Liabilities are the debts of your business, and are considered claims against the assets. Equity, simply, is ownership. To paint a better picture, consider that your house is your asset, the outstanding mortgage your liability, and the portion you own outright is the equity.

Expenses and revenue are measured for specific periods of time and get folded into equity at the end of each accounting period; for this reason, these groups are considered temporary accounts. Revenues are everything earned by the corporation. Expenses represent all of the money spent in order to earn that revenue. Expenses are often broken out into product costs (for companies that sell physical products) and operating expenses (which are incurred regardless of sales). When revenues exceed expenses for a given period, the corporation has turned a profit; when expenses are greater than revenues, the company has sustained a loss.

Debits and Credits

One of the most basic premises of accounting, and one of the hardest to grasp, is that of debits and credits. As soon as you read those terms, words like plus, minus, add, and subtract may come to mind—if they do, put them out. Yes, debits and credits may cause additions and subtractions to account balances, but that is not what the terms actually refer to. In the world of accounting, debit means "left side" and credit means "right side."

When all bookkeeping was done manually, accountants used forms called T accounts (because they looked like Ts). All debits to an account were written down on the left side of the T; all credits were recorded on the right side of the T. Though debits always go on the left and credits always go on the right, they don't always impact accounts in the same way. Some accounts are increased by debits and decreased by credits: assets and expenses. Some accounts are decreased by debits and increased by credits: liabilities, equity, and revenues. The proper balance of the account (meaning debit or credit) depends on which type of entry increases the account. For example, assets are increased by debits and therefore normally have debit account balances.

Use Accounting Software

Bookkeeping is labor-intensive and time-consuming. The easiest way to keep on top of this task (other than hiring a bookkeeper for $15 to $50 per hour) is to buy some basic accounting software. There are several good programs out there, and they all have the same general capabilities; buy whichever one is the most comfortable for you to use. Most offer trial versions of the program, either free or for a nominal fee that gets deducted if you purchase the product.

Using accounting software for basic bookkeeping functions—paying bills, recording deposits, tracking inventory—can cut your work time in half. If you are unfamiliar with both the software and bookkeeping in general, have a professional set up your accounts, and walk you through the basic transactions.

Every transaction must contain equal debits and credits. How those debits and credits affect the particular accounts involved doesn't really matter, as long as the total debits equal the total credits. Along the same lines, the overall accounts must balance—the total debit account balances must equal the total credit account balances.

Maintaining Accounts

Although a lot of small business bookkeeping gets done haphazardly (and in the checkbook), every transaction does need to be formally recorded in both the accounting journal and ledger. Journal entries keep track of transactions in chronological order, while the ledgers hold all of the collected information by account. In the old days, when most bookkeeping was done manually, people would record transactions as they happened (or at least fairly frequently), then post them to the ledger every once in a while. Today, though, automated accounting software takes care of both jobs simultaneously, substantially cutting down on the amount of time it takes to keep the books up to date.

Unique Corporate Transactions

While most transactions that run through your company are the same as they would be if you were using any other entity, there are some transactions that only corporations record. As you might expect, these transactions are all directly connected to equity, which is structured uniquely for corporations. For example, only corporations issue and sell stock, and only corporations declare and pay dividends. In addition, only C corporations pay taxes on their own income, a burden no other entity bears.

Issuing Stock

No matter when the corporation issues stock, the transaction will always be the same. Something of value, usually (but not necessarily) cash, is contributed to the corporation in exchange for shares of ownership. Those shares of ownership come in the form of corporate stock.

In this transaction, both corporate assets and equity are increased. This transaction is recorded in the company's general journal, then posted to the appropriate general ledger accounts. The accounting will include a debit (increase) to the asset account, and credits (also signifying increases) to any equity accounts involved. The specific accounts depend on what was contributed to the corporation and whether the value of those assets exceeds the par value of the shares received in exchange.

Dividend Transactions

Whenever the board of directors decides to pay out dividends, the transaction takes place in two parts. First, the dividends are declared, meaning the board officially states that the dividend will be paid, specifying when and how much. Second, the dividends are paid.

The first transaction, the declaration, is a promise to shareholders that dividends will be paid. That explicit promise creates a liability for the corporation, and that liability must be recognized on the books. That transaction results in a decrease to the retained earnings account (where dividends come from) and an increase to the dividends payable account (to recognize the liability).

Transaction number two occurs when those dividends actually get paid to the shareholders. In this case, the dividends payable account is decreased, as the obligation is fulfilled. At the same time, the cash account is also decreased.

Income Tax Transactions

Corporations have to pay income taxes on their profits. They don't, however, have paychecks from which income taxes get withheld. Instead, corporations have to make quarterly estimated tax payments to make sure that the majority of their tax burden for the year is paid throughout the period. It sounds tricky, and it is. At least initially, have your tax accountant help you figure out the estimated income tax payments.

Once your accountant gives you the payment amount, you can record a transaction. The accounts involved will be income tax expense and income tax payable; this acknowledges the estimated tax liability. When you write out and send the check, usually on the due date, record another transaction to decrease both the tax liability and the cash account.

At the end of the year, when the corporation's profit for the year is a known quantity, you will learn the true amount of the income tax due. If your estimated payments have exceeded the balance due, no additional payment will be necessary. When the corporation is owed a refund, the standard operating procedure is to let the remainder ride as a partial estimated tax payment for the upcoming year. If your payments have underestimated the total tax bill, you'll write a check for the remaining balance due. In that case, record an additional journal entry to increase the expense to its true balance, and decrease the cash by the amount of the check paid.

A Special Equity Section

Compared to every other business entity, the equity section of the corporate balance sheet has the most elements. That is because the total equity is comprised of several pieces, and some of those pieces can be broken out even further. The main headings are as follows:

1. Stock
2. Additional paid-in capital
3. Treasury stock (only where applicable)
4. Retained earnings

The big distinction for balance-sheet readers outside the day-to-day company management, such as investors and bankers, is contributed capital versus earned capital. That distinction can have important implications for you. All states allow dividends to be paid out of earnings, but not all allow dividends to be paid from paid-in capital.

Capital Stock

Stock shows up on the balance sheet by class; for each class of stock, there will be a separate line item. The classes get listed in order of their equity preference, which really just means who would collect first should the company be liquidated. For example, if your corporation has both preferred and common stock, and the preferred shareholders would get the first shot at payouts when the company is folded, preferred stock would be listed before common on the balance sheet. (This "first dibs" information should be spelled out explicitly in your company bylaws.)

▸▸ **Unlike other items on the balance sheet, you can't just list the name of the stock class and be done with it.** For each class of stock, include the par value of the stock, the number of shares authorized, and the number of shares issued and outstanding. This level of detail is required when you present statements to readers outside your corporation, but it may be optional for purely internal statements. Here's an example:

Common stock ($10 par value, 10,000 shares authorized, 4,000 shares issued and outstanding)

As for the dollar balance that goes along with this rather lengthy account description, simply multiply the number of shares issued and outstanding by the par value. Using the numbers from the example above, the balance of the common stock account would be $40,000.

Additional Paid-in Capital

Whenever stock is issued and sold for more than its par value, the excess over par is called additional paid-in capital. This happens rather often, as par value is an arbitrary amount, often set as low as allowed under state law to minimize the corporation's tax bill. Since par value rarely bears any resemblance to real market value, the shares get sold at a price higher than par.

Look back at the example in the previous section. Suppose the shareholder actually paid $50,000 for that stock. The balance of the common stock account would not change; that's set in stone, courtesy of the par value. The excess over par, or $10,000, would be charged to the additional paid-in capital account.

The separation of these components of price is more than just an accounting issue, though. It can also impact just how much your corporation will be allowed to pay out in dividends. The rules on this vary by state (no surprise there). Corporations are allowed in every state to make distributions of current or previously accumulated earnings (collectively referred to under the law as earned surplus). After that, the rules may part ways, and some become much stricter. Some states allow distributions to be made from contributed capital surplus, accounted for as additional paid-in capital in excess of (and wholly separate from) the minimum stated capital. However, many states do not allow this type of distribution, allowing only those based on earnings. The distinction is critical as making disallowed distributions may constitute fraud.

Treasury Stock

Though treasury stock may sound like it has something to do with the federal government, it doesn't. Treasury stock is simply outstanding shares that the corporation itself has bought back. Those shares are still issued but no longer outstanding. As such, they decrease the overall outstanding equity balance.

Large corporations may buy up shares of their own stock to push up the current market price; fewer circulating shares can drive up prices. Treasury stock rarely pops up on small corporation financial statements, but there are some circumstances where it may. For example, if one owner wants to sell off his entire interest but can't find a suitable buyer, the corporation may buy the shares.

Whatever the reason, treasury stock does remain in the equity section of the corporate balance sheet. When the corporation buys back some of its own stock, the transaction is recorded at the amount of the purchase, with a debit to treasury stock and a credit to cash (or whatever asset was used to pay for the purchase). Once that is done, your corporation has two choices. It can resell those shares or simply retire them (sort of like un-issuing them). Should the shares be sold, the transaction involves a debit to cash for the full amount of the sale, a credit to treasury stock for the original cost of those shares, and a resulting debit or credit to paid-in capital from treasury stock to absorb the difference. When the shares are retired, they are deducted from outstanding stock. To accomplish this on the books, debit common stock and credit treasury stock, with any dollar differences hitting the appropriate paid-in capital account.

Retained Earnings

The retained earnings account holds a running total of the cumulative profits and losses of the corporation (from inception) that have been left in the corporate coffers. Any portion of earnings paid out as dividends, regardless of the form those dividends take, reduces the retained earnings account.

In the early years of a new corporation, it's quite common for the retained earnings balance to be negative. That happens when the company sustains a loss, as new businesses often do for the first few periods. As things begin to turn around, and the corporation begins to earn profits, that retained earnings balance will swing to positive. Once that happens, you'll be able to start paying shareholder dividends.

Some companies do hold on to their retained earnings as a sort of internal corporate savings account. That accumulated profit can be used to finance growth without taking on debt or further diluting equity ownership. It can be used to pay off large chunks of debt ahead of schedule, improving the company's future profitability and cash flow. It can be spent on major asset purchases or renovations. In fact, in order to preserve this sort of savings account status, some corporations actually create more than one retained earnings account: one restricted and one unrestricted. The restricted (or pledged, or reserved) account is used solely for its named purpose, while the unrestricted account is used for dividend payouts.

Beware the Accumulated Earnings Tax

Most small C-corporation owners try to keep their dividend payouts to a bare minimum. They jack up salaries and benefits (giving them plenty of take-home cash that's deductible to the company) and leave any leftover earnings inside the business. However, leaving earnings intact simply to avoid the double taxation that comes with paying dividends can result in a form of penalty taxation.

That penalty is called the accumulated earnings tax, which exists to sew up this very loophole. To avoid it, all you have to do is pay out a reasonable amount of dividends when your retained earnings balance is squarely in the black. The exception is when you have funds earmarked for a special project. That's considered an acceptable reason to let earnings accumulate.

Financial Statements Track Success

When you want to see in black and white just how your corporation is doing, it's time to put together some financial statements. The big three include a balance sheet, a statement of profit and loss (a.k.a., an income statement), and a statement of cash flows. While you can look at these statements individually—and many business owners do focus primarily on the statement of profit and loss—they work best as a package deal. The information you'll glean from reading the statements as a set can help keep your corporation on a successful track or get it back on the right track when it veers off.

In addition to internal uses, there are times when financial statements are necessary to satisfy the demands of outsiders. Information from both your corporation's balance sheet and statement of profit and loss will be needed to prepare your corporate tax return. To secure financing, your company will have to develop at least one full set of financial statements, sometimes two; the second set will use future projections, numbers that express what you expect will happen in the upcoming accounting periods. When your corporation has outstanding business loans, it may be required to maintain particular account balances to remain in compliance with loan covenants. The proof of compliance is in the financial statements, and the lender is likely to request them periodically.

The Balance Sheet

A balance sheet serves as a snapshot of your company's financial position on a particular day. It includes an accounting of all of the corporation's assets, liabilities, and capital and lists the balance of each account on that specific day. In addition, the total of the accounts must balance: total assets must equal the sum of the liabilities and equity accounts.

To make that information even more useful, assets and liabilities are typically split up into categories. On the asset side, you are likely to see three distinct classifications, and occasionally a fourth: current, fixed, intangible, and other. Current assets include those that are expected to be converted to cash within a year, including things like accounts receivable, inventory, and cash itself. Fixed assets are also known as "property, plant and equipment." These are physical assets expected to serve the corporation for more than one year. Intangible assets are also long-term assets, but these lack physical form. Common examples include patents, copyrights, and trademarks. Other assets include anything that really doesn't fit squarely into any of the other categories.

As for the liabilities, you will find only a two-way split there: current and long term. Current liabilities include those that will come due within one year of the balance sheet date. Accounts payable and taxes payable are accounts frequently found in this category. Long-term liabilities refer to those that have due dates later than one year from now. This classification normally includes things like business loans and mortgages. Long-term liabilities can cross over into current territory when a portion or all of the balance will come due within the next twelve months.

The Statement of Profit and Loss

When it comes to financial statements, this is the one most entrepreneurs flock to, the statement of profit and loss. This report gives you the score, showing exactly how well (or not well) your company has done for the accounting period. In form, it's a straightforward math equation: **revenues minus cost and expenses equals profit or loss.** When revenues exceed costs and expenses, there's a profit; when costs and expenses are greater than revenues, there's a loss.

Most eyes go straight to that bottom line, that one profit-or-loss number, but there's a wealth of information contained in this statement aside from the final outcome. It starts with the revenue section, where you see how gross sales are reduced by discounts, returns, and allowances (which are kind of like discounts that you give to major customers when they accept something other than what their order specifies). The resulting number after all of those subtractions is called net sales. If your company has lots of gross sales, but that great-looking number is diminished by excessive returns, you may have a problem on your hands. That knowledge can help you turn things around, and keep the majority of your sales intact.

Next up is the cost of goods sold section, pertinent only to corporations that deal in goods (as opposed to services). Every product your corporation sells cost it something. Either it bought the items shelf-ready or created them and paid for the component parts (or ingredients). The difference between the amount your corporation pays to purchase its products and the price it charges customers is called the gross profit (or gross margin). This key number tells you whether or not your corporation is charging enough for its products.

The next section covers standard operating expenses, those unrelated to product costs. These may be broken out into two groups of expenses, sales and administrative, if that makes sense for your corporation. Sales expenses are not incurred without corresponding sales. They include things like sales commissions, delivery charges, and shopping bags. Administrative expenses, also known as fixed costs, are incurred regardless of whether your corporation makes a single sale. This category includes things like rent, utilities, office salaries, and insurance.

Finally, you're at the bottom line. For product-based companies, the net profit (or loss) is calculated by subtracting the total operating expenses from the gross profit. With service companies, the cost-of-goods-sold step is unnecessary, so you get to the bottom line by deducting total operating expenses from net sales. When expenses are greater than revenues, your corporation sustains a loss. You can determine which items are contributing to that loss—prices set too low, too many product returns, excessive administrative expenses—by looking more deeply into your statement of profit and loss.

Don't Worry If You've Lost Some Receipts

You must have backup for every expense deduction that will show up on your corporate tax return. Usually that backup is a piece of paper: receipt, cancelled check, or bank statement, for example. However, it is very common for some of these documents to get lost in the shuffle. Don't worry if that happens, as the IRS provides an easy way to deal with it.

When an expense is obviously standard for your corporation, a lost backup document doesn't really matter (like missing September's phone bill). The IRS will look at your other documentation for the same type of expenditure, come up with a reasonable estimate (usually the amount you've already recorded), and let you deduct it.

The Statement of Cash Flows

Businesses, especially small businesses, live and die by cash flow. No matter how profitable a company is, no matter how many assets it owns, if a company doesn't have sufficient cash to cover its operating costs, it will fail. To understand how cash moves into and out of your business, you first must understand its three basic sources and uses: operating, investing, or financing activities.

Operating activities simply refer to normal everyday business transactions. On the source side, this mainly includes sales. On the use side, it includes all of the expenditures needed to keep your business up and running, like utilities, inventory, and advertising. Investing activities refer to sources and uses that involve assets. Sources would include things like interest and dividends received and cash received for the sale of an asset. Uses would include things like asset purchases and loans made by the corporation to other entities (like an employee or a shareholder). Financing activities impact the other side of the balance sheet, involving liability and equity accounts. Sources would include cash received in exchange for corporate stock, as well as loan proceeds (when the loan is to the corporation). Uses would include things like interest and dividends paid out by the corporation, loan repayments, and stock buy-backs.

All three of these activities come together on the statement of cash flows. On that key financial report, you will see the path that your corporation's cash has traveled over the previous period. That gives you solid insight into the path it will take in the upcoming period, with enough time left to make some changes when necessary. No company can survive for long when cash flow is consistently negative, meaning more flows out than in. Even with a positive cash account balance, a company with negative cash flow is in trouble.

Perform a Ratio Analysis

In addition to evaluating the numbers that appear on your financial statements, analyzing their relationships can provide helpful insights. This analysis is performed using standard business ratios, each falling into one of four basic categories:

- ➲ Liquidity
- ➲ Efficiency
- ➲ Profitability
- ➲ Solvency

Before you get started calculating these ratios for your corporation, it's good to have a frame of reference to work with. "Good" results vary by industry and by business size. What's considered standard for one company could spell disaster for another. You can check with your trade association for some comparative figures, or you can simply ask your accountant for a list of targets to hit.

Liquidity Ratios

Liquidity keeps your business afloat. It's all about corporate cash—your corporation's ability to bring in quick cash and its ability to pay bills as they come due. Millions of new and small companies face liquidity problems, and that can spell their doom. Keeping on top of your corporation's liquidity can help keep your corporation in business for the long haul. You can learn more about just how liquid your corporation is by doing a little bit of math.

Liquidity ratios pull numbers from your balance sheet and combine them to let you see just how well your business can generate cash. These statistics are a favorite of lenders, from vendors to bankers, as they indicate just how likely it is that they will be paid on time. ▶▶ **The two most widely used liquidity ratios are the current ratio and the quick ratio.** Determining which best represents your corporation's true situation depends mainly on whether the company primarily sells products or services.

The current ratio compares current assets to current liabilities to measure your corporation's capacity to meet immediate financial obligations. Industry standards vary, but the general rule for success is to have at least $2 in current assets for every $1 of current liabilities, for a current ratio of 2:1. That indicates that your corporation can easily pay its immediate obligations with a comfortable cushion. A ratio of less than 1:1 indicates that your company cannot meet all of its current obligations.

The quick ratio is used for companies with inventory, a current asset that may not be converted quickly into cash. As your company cannot really control when inventory will be sold, this account balance gets deducted from the total current assets figure before the ratio is calculated. Here, a ratio of 1:1 is generally considered good. It indicates that your corporation can meet its current liabilities even if the inventory proves hard to sell.

Efficiency Ratios

Efficiency ratios let you know just how well your corporation is using its assets to bring in cash and profits. These statistics speak mainly to productivity—after all, the purpose of assets is productivity. However, these ratios don't track the assets that may spring to mind when you hear the word "productive," like factory equipment and manufacturing machinery.

Rather, they look chiefly at accounts receivable and inventory, two of the most important assets to track.

First, take a look at accounts receivable. This asset represents sales for which your corporation has not yet been paid. As such, it's the number one reason a corporation might show profits while running out of cash. The only way to turn accounts receivable into cash is to make collections, and while your corporation doesn't have complete control over that, it can exercise quite a bit through stricter payment terms, balance caps, and credit checks run before extending customer credit. One great way to measure accounts receivable efficiency is the average collection period. Good results mean your corporation is doing a great job managing its accounts receivable, lesser results indicate the need for a customer collection crackdown.

Calculate the average collection period by dividing the accounts receivable balance on your balance sheet by average daily sales (total sales for a period divided by the number of days in that period). The result tells you just how many days your sales are tied up in uncollected accounts receivable. Whether that result is good or bad depends on your credit terms (though a smaller result is always better). If you set your credit terms allowing customers thirty days to pay and your average collection period is twenty-five days, that's good. On the other hand, with the same credit terms and an average collection period of sixty-eight days, your corporation needs to take some action to improve collections.

Next, put your inventory under the statistical microscope. What's most important here is turnover, just how fast that merchandise is moving out the door. If your company sells products, that's an important number to know. It tells you just how long the lapse is between the time the inventory comes in and the time it gets sold. Calculate this ratio by dividing the cost of goods sold for a set period by the average inventory for the same period. You can get the average inventory by adding the account balance from two consecutive balance sheets and dividing that sum by two.

The result here varies widely by industry. For example, milk inventory will turn over more frequently than minivan inventory. To find out what's average for your industry and companies about the same size as yours, you can check with your trade association. With inventory turnover, a bigger number is better, as that indicates your merchandise is moving more quickly. That said, the number you get should be in the same general ballpark for the industry average.

Profitability Ratios

When someone wants to know how the corporation is doing, they are usually referring to profits. You can measure your corporation's profitability every step of the way by calculating some basic profitability ratios, moving right down the most current statement of profit and loss.

First comes the gross-profit margin ratio, for which you divide the gross profit (sales minus cost of goods sold) by sales. That lets you know just what portion of each sales dollar is available to cover your corporation's operating expenses. Second, you can figure out your corporation's return on sales (another sort of profit margin) to let you know how much your corporation is earning before income taxes get deducted. This is accomplished by dividing the profit before taxes by sales. Finally, you can compute your net profit margin to learn just how much bottom-line profit is being generated by each dollar of sales. This is calculated by dividing the net profit by sales.

Solvency Ratios

Solvency ratios (a.k.a. risk factors) speak to your corporation's long-term financial health. They highlight just how much of your business is actually owned by you and your fellow shareholders and how much is owed to lenders. They measure corporate leverage, meaning how much the company has borrowed in order to finance its assets. Plus, they look at how easily your earnings are covering interest expense, sometimes the biggest expense of highly leveraged companies.

First up is the debt-to-equity ratio, calculated by dividing total liabilities by total equity. A result higher than 2:1 is a pretty clear indicator that your corporation will have trouble attracting additional debt, as higher numbers mean bigger risks for lenders. Many small businesses do have high ratios here, but the ideal ratio to shoot for is close to 1:1.

The Per Share Information

While the overall performance of your corporation is important, what that means for each shareholder may be even more important to them. For that reason, your financial statements may contain per-share information. If you've sold shares to the general public, you must provide that information to your shareholders. The figure most stockholders will want to see is the earnings per share, which simply means how much of the total corporate earnings (as shown on the statement of profit and loss) are allocable to a single share of stock. You can calculate that figure by simply dividing your bottom-line profit by the number of shares currently issued and outstanding.

Next comes the debt-to-asset ratio (a close relative of the previous calculation). For this statistic, divide total debt by total assets. When this result is greater than 0.50, it means that more than half of your assets are financed with debt. This is a very common occurrence for new and small product-based companies, which put a lot into inventory without knowing how quickly that inventory will turn over.

Finally, calculate the times-interest-earned ratio (a.k.a. interest coverage). To calculate this ratio, divide operating income (that's before deductions for interest and corporate income taxes) by interest expense. The result shows you how many times your operating profits can pay those interest charges. Here, a higher result is better, as it indicates your corporation can keep up with interest payments.

 **TEST DRIVE**

Does your corporation need a dedicated bookkeeper? You may think that the cost of a freelance or in-house bookkeeper outweighs the benefits. Consider these issues to help you measure the real cost-benefit profile:

1. How many transactions does your business have in one day?
2. How much time do you spend daily on other facets of running the company?
3. Do you have other employees?
4. Can you honestly keep up with the bookkeeping on at least a monthly basis?
5. What's the going rate for a part-time bookkeeper in your area?
6. Does your accountant's firm offer bookkeeping services at a discounted rate?

PART **4**

Maintaining Your Corporation

Deciding When It's Time to Leave

You've put so much of yourself into building a successful company that you may not remember what it's like to live without it. You may feel like your corporation is part of you, something you've created with your own two hands and molded into a thriving moneymaker. Your corporation may be such a big success, now providing almost effortlessly for you and your family, that you hate to see it go. Or it may have been less successful, and you may be looking forward to getting rid of it. Perhaps you started the business with the intent of selling it as soon as it showed signs of profitability and have no personal feeling about it either way.

Why You Need an Exit Plan Now

Even if you think you're years away from leaving your corporation, it's a good idea to consider what could happen to your family (and possibly your business partners) if you were to face unexpected circumstances, like sudden death or extreme disability. No one likes to think about these things, even less to plan for them. Without a plan, though, your family could lose everything.

Think about creating a business exit plan. This plan can cover things like succession, when your intent is to keep the business in the family. It can lay out the steps your family will need to take in order to sell off the business, or your shares of the business, for a just price.

Regardless of your personal situation, the decision to sell may be one of the biggest decisions you will ever make, and it may involve more money in a single transaction than anything you've ever done before. Unlike switching suppliers, redesigning product packages, or hiring employees, all which you may have done dozens of times throughout the life of your corporation, this is a one-shot deal. As soon as you sign the contracts, you're out for good. Before you take that final step, make sure this is what you really want to do, and carefully consider every term of the sale. That advice stands whether you are selling to outsiders or to fellow shareholders.

While selling the business to outsiders can be a complicated process, so can keeping it in the family. This scenario is based on the assumption that you have family members willing and able to take over and that you are comfortable handing your business over to them. Family transactions often don't involve lump-sum cash exchanges and may involve your maintaining an active (if much reduced) role in the company.

A third scenario involves a business that simply didn't succeed. That can lead to bankruptcy for you, your corporation, or even both. When an individual or business entity is overburdened with debt and sees no possibility of settling that debt, bankruptcy court offers a form of financial relief. Under this circumstance, the company may be treated like a yard sale, with the proceeds going to the creditors with the strongest claims first.

Look Back at Your Shareholders' Agreement

If you are not the sole owner of your corporation, there may be restrictions placed on share transfers. When the time has come for you to sell your shares of the corporation, first pull out your shareholders' agreement. (See Chapter 14 for more on this topic.) Most of the time, these agreements contain explicit buy-sell provisions that dictate the protocols you must follow when selling your shares.

The standard course of action involves first offering your shares either to the corporation itself or to the remaining shareholders. Many agreements also spell out exactly how a fair purchase price will be determined, and how that payment may be structured to help the corporation avoid a massive cash hemorrhage.

In the event that neither the company nor the other shareholders want to or can buy your shares, you may still face certain buyer restrictions. This type of provision is especially important for S corporations and statutory close corporations, where violation of shareholder restrictions can invalidate the corporate form. To protect selling shareholders, your agreement may specify that the corporation must buy back the shares if an appropriate buyer cannot be found through reasonable means (a very common occurrence with small, closely held businesses).

Keeping It in the Family

It's the American dream: building up a successful business, and passing it down to your heirs who eagerly take over the reins. The reality can be wonderful, frustrating, and rewarding, as well as a wonderful source of family wealth. The biggest challenge can be in creating an orderly succession among multiple family members; second to that can be the generational financial- and tax-planning issues. For the second, you can turn to qualified professionals to lead you down the most profitable path. For that first challenge, dealing with family members, you'll be cutting the path.

No matter how well you get along with your kids (or nephews or cousins), this business transfer isn't going to proceed like a dream. You won't be able to decide on Monday night that you want to retire, then sail off into the sunset on Tuesday while Junior starts running the company without a hitch. This is a long-term prospect, and doing it properly can ensure a long and prosperous life for your corporation. You must account for several factors, including the business itself, your family (both as individuals and as a whole), the family estate, and (of course) the potential tax consequences.

This is a daunting mix of ingredients, and getting it just right is so tricky that most families don't. In fact, less than one-third of family businesses last through the second generation, and the third-generation success stories are even more rare. By planning meticulously ahead of time, you can create a legacy rather than react to a crisis situation.

Successful successions involve two distinct plans, one for transferring power and one for transferring assets. Power will generally be more concentrated, put primarily into the hands of a just a few. Assets may be spread more thinly in order to include more people in the family business without making it impossible to actually manage the business.

Turning Over the Management Reins

When choosing someone to follow in your footsteps, start with the person most capable of handling the job. Preferably, this will be someone who has actually worked for your corporation in some capacity. This might be someone who has worked his way up through the ranks and who would jump at the chance to begin running the company. That must be balanced against a variety of other business and personal factors, including things like the amount of time a family member could commit to the corporation and that person's special skills areas.

In order to initiate a smooth transition, you must name your successor early on in the process. Training may take some time, and the learning curve for running the business is much steeper than it is for merely working there. ▸▸ **The corporate president must have a comprehensive understanding of everything about the company, as well as a vision for its future.** That doesn't come overnight and may take months (even years) to develop. The best strategy involves having your successor firmly in place before you make your exit.

Remember, also, that the next generation may have very different goals than you did, and they may implement strategies you never would have considered. That can be hard to swallow, as your way has proven successful, and theirs may not work so well. Separating yourself, and giving them the freedom to succeed on their own terms, may be the hardest parts of handing down the business.

Slicing Up the Company Pie

Not everyone in your family will want to work for the corporation. However, when you hand over shares and management responsibilities to one or more of your relatives, you can bet the others will feel slighted. That can often be remedied by handing over equity shares to nonparticipating family members. They can be connected with the business, even profit from it, without diluting the new concentration of power.

The trouble with handing out pieces of your business is the potential tax consequences for everyone involved. Here's where your tax attorney—as opposed to a tax preparer or a business attorney—should play a starring role. The pitfalls of improper structuring include big tax bills, while a carefully implemented game plan can minimize, even avoid, a current tax consequence. Keep this in mind, though: It's more important to start with the plan that works best for your family, then figure out how to make the tax part work, than to come up with a recommended tax scenario and squeeze your family's interests into that.

The Foster Family Business Changes Hands

Steve Foster had spent most of his life building up a business to pass on to his children. His company, Foster's Hardware Supplies, Inc., had been modestly successful for over thirty years. All three of his children had worked in the shop every summer and after school since they were ten years old. As they each turned sixteen, he gave them 100 shares of stock in the family business.

The oldest son, Frank, was enrolled in a Ph.D. program, and was heading back to graduate school in the fall. The youngest son, Evan, would be starting college in the fall. Brandon, the middle son, had just graduated from college and wasn't quite sure what he was going to do next. Steve had big plans for Brandon, though. He was about to surprise his son by turning over the business to him. As Brandon had always been the most enthusiastic about working in the shop and didn't have set plans of his own, Steve was sure that Brandon would be happy when he heard the big news. He wasn't.

Steve called a family meeting to find out if any of his sons was interested in taking over the hardware store. None of them was. They'd all liked the ease of working there, never having to hunt for jobs when they wanted some extra cash. None of the three wanted to own the shop, though, leaving Steve with a lot of thinking to do.

Steve had been counting on one of the boys taking the reins. Now he felt trapped, like he'd have to run the shop forever. Until he talked to his accountant, that is, who reminded him that he could just sell the business, which is what he did.

Some Potential Tax-Planning Issues

The United States has something called the unified transfer tax in place. This section of the tax code covers gifts made during your lifetime and at the time of death. Both are taxed at the same very high rates (up to 50 percent!), and both offer some solid planning opportunities through exclusions and exemptions.

First, take a look at the annual gift-tax exclusion. Every year, every tax payer can give away up to $12,000 to anyone, completely tax-free for both parties. Even better, a husband and wife team can give double that to a single giftee; that's considered a split gift under the tax rules, even if only one of you technically owned the gift property. For gifts bigger than that, federal gift taxes could kick in, but usually not until you hit the unified credit amount of $2,000,000. However, that first $12,000 (or $24,000) doesn't count toward that lifetime credit at all; it's a total freebie. Using a strategy of planned gifting, you can turn over corporate shares to family members without the worry of transfer taxes.

Now, take a look at the federal estate tax, which hits estates before any proceeds are distributed. The tax liability imposed comes under the umbrella of that unified transfer tax. This tax is calculated according to the value of the property included in your estate at death plus all the taxable gifts you handed out during your lifetime. If those taxable gifts surpassed the $2,000,000 limit (for 2006 to 2008), they get added to the total estate value. Though it seems like a huge number, it's not as far away as you might think. Add the value of your home, your retirement plan assets, investments, and your business—you're probably already in that ballpark. By making a practice of handing out tax-free gifts, you can substantially reduce potential estate taxes.

Selling Your Business

Whether you are selling a whole business or your ownership shares, the process may be long and complicated. One of the hardest parts is finding a qualified buyer. Then there are questions of valuation, deal structure, and financing options. The actual sales process contains several steps, and the deal could fall apart almost anywhere along the line—a sale of this magnitude takes a lot more than even selling a house. Common steps in this sales process include the following:

- ➲ Determining a fair asking price
- ➲ Attracting appropriate buyers
- ➲ Negotiating terms of the sale (including financing arrangements)
- ➲ Receiving a letter of intent (an informal agreement, stressing confidentiality)
- ➲ Completing due diligence (buyer's investigation of the corporation)
- ➲ Preparing a formal purchase agreement
- ➲ Fulfilling all state law requirements
- ➲ Closing the deal

To help you through this process, consider enlisting professional help. Small-business brokers specialize in these kinds of deals, the same way that realtors match up families with homes. Like realtors, business brokers charge steep fees to help you sell your company. Some charge a percentage of the total sale proceeds, while others take a flat fee off the top. What's equally important is to find someone that you trust and click with. You will be spending a lot of time with this person during a very unsettled time and personality clashes will make things much more difficult.

When There Are Multiple Owners

When you are subject to the terms of a shareholders' agreement, you must follow them to the letter. Those often involve giving either the corporation itself or fellow shareholders the first shot at buying your shares, typically for a preset price. If you find no takers inside the corporation, you may begin looking outside, though restrictions still may apply to potential buyers. For example, your shareholders' agreement may forbid you to sell to someone who can invalidate the corporation, like selling S corporation shares to a nonresident alien, or prohibit you from making a public sale announcement, as with a close corporation.

It can be very tough to sell shares of a closely held company. In addition to common business issues like profitability, cash flow, and market share, potential buyers will also have to contend with an established power base. Any of them will be coming in as the odd man out, and even a welcome addition may have personality and management style issues to contend with.

When You Are the Sole Shareholder

The mechanics work somewhat differently when you are the corporation's only shareholder and are looking to sell an entire business, rather than a portion of its shares. You have two basic options here: selling the business as a going concern, or selling off individual assets.

In most cases, the first option will net C-corporation owners a higher selling price and better tax treatment, as detailed in Chapter 21. Using this method, you'll be subject to capital gains tax based on your tax basis in your shares; in a C corporation, this is usually just whatever you initially paid the corporation for the shares. You sell shares, you pay some taxes, you're done. If you sell off individual assets, on the other hand, taxes will be imposed twice. The first time, if the sales price is greater than the assets' book value, the corporation will get hit with a capital gains tax for the asset sales. The second time, you'll pay taxes as the corporation is liquidated. Here, the taxable amount equals those sale proceeds minus your stock basis. That double bite can be avoided by just selling corporate shares.

Don't Overlook Your Employees

As you begin to search for buyers for your corporation, consider your employees. When you already have an employee stock ownership plan (ESOP) in place (more about that in Chapter 24), the equity transfer has already begun. ESOPs are excellent vehicles by which to transfer shares of your business to people who are already in place and already love the company.

The whole point of an ESOP is to allow employees to invest a portion of their salaries in your corporation. This gives them partial ownership, and the corporation gets some extra cash. The corporation may sell or give additional shares to the ESOP at any time, making it a convenient buyer when you're ready to sell your business.

All corporation owners (C and S) will find an extra benefit to selling shares rather than assets, though this one has nothing to do with taxes. When you sell a whole corporation, any currently unknown liabilities of the company stay with the company, becoming the buyer's problem. However, when you sell the assets instead, those potential future liabilities stick with you. A good lawyer and a carefully crafted sales contract can transfer those potential obligations to the buyer. Any glitch, though, and the default rules will apply.

Valuing Your Business

Now that you know what you're selling, you need to put a price tag on it. Potential buyers may use various valuation methods, some of which approximate your price and some that are miles out of the ballpark. To attract the right kind of buyer—the kind who can afford to pay you a big chunk upfront and won't squabble for months over minor details—you need to set a realistic and fair price. Consider also getting a professional appraisal done, either to confirm your hoped-for price or to change it before you float it in front of buyers.

Different valuation methods work best for different types of businesses; there is no one approach that is universally appropriate for every business. Here are some commonly used valuation methods, and the kinds of companies for which they work best:

Earnings multiple: This method works best for established companies with steady profits that can be maintained even without the current ownership in place.

Book value: This method works well for companies with a heavy investment in fixed assets, like manufacturing enterprises.

Service company approach: This method is used to value service companies (as the name indicates) based on annual billings and expected staff retention.

Each method comes with a wide range of factors to consider, based on the particular business and its industry. For example, with the earnings multiple method, the multiplier varies greatly depending on the current market position of the corporation and its recent profitability. The service company approach factors in the type of services offered, the number of high-level employees that will remain in place, and recent billings.

Dissolving the Corporation

Even the end of your corporation involves a lot of formality and paperwork. Unlike some other entities, like sole proprietorships, **you cannot just walk away from your business and consider it closed.** You have to take specific legal steps, some of which may vary according to your corporation's home state law, to officially dissolve your corporation.

The first set of steps is completely internal, starting with a resolution. Once the internal part is done, articles of dissolution must be filed. Next will come all of the final tax returns. In addition, every creditor of the corporation must receive official notice of its dissolution, and all outstanding claims must be settled. The last step is to distribute the remaining assets of the business to all of the corporate shareholders.

Once all of these steps are completed, your corporation will be legally and actually dissolved. That means you can no longer enter into agreements in the name of the corporation, use the corporate checking account, or conduct business as a corporate representative. It doesn't mean, though, that you are forever free from all liability that might arise from earlier corporate business. There may still be some contingent liabilities on the horizon, such as ongoing product liability issues. If these contingencies pose a substantial exposure risk, consider protecting your personal assets with an insurance policy to cover such events.

The Internal Steps

In order to dissolve your corporation properly, you must take the following steps to get the ball rolling. Though most dissolutions follow the same basic format, look to your bylaws and shareholders' agreement for specifics.

The first item on the list will be a resolution that the board of directors draft, vote on, and then approve. Once the directors have given approval, the resolution is turned over to the shareholders for their approval. Even if all the directors are also shareholders, both votes must be taken. After both groups have approved the resolution, document those actions for your corporate records book.

Articles of Dissolution

Now that the board and the shareholders have agreed it's time to end the corporation, it's time to let the state know of your intentions. The exact process varies a bit by state, so check out the rules of every state in which your corporation transacts business. That includes the home state and every state in which the business is registered as a foreign corporation; each will require separate official dissolution procedures to be performed.

In some states, you must file official dissolution documents before starting the creditor-notification process. In other states, you cannot file that paperwork until all creditors have been notified and claims settled.

Some states also require special tax clearance for a corporation before they'll allow a certificate of dissolution to be filed. To get that clearance, all outstanding taxes due must be paid in full. Finally, some states may require you to file a notice of intent to dissolve, then settle up all outstanding obligations, and then file final articles of dissolution.

Whichever order is required for these steps, at some point in the process you'll be filing articles of dissolution, along with the appropriate fee. Again, specific items may vary according to state law, but here are the basics you'll likely need to include:

1. Name of the corporation
2. Date of incorporation
3. Date the dissolution was authorized
4. Brief acknowledgment of shareholders' approval of dissolution
5. Brief statement about creditor notification and settlement

As with most corporate forms, you may be able to find a fill-in-the-blank version on the state Web site. Absent that, most states post instructions on how to dissolve a corporation in accordance with state statutes.

Dealing with Creditors

Before you begin procedures to pay off the regular creditors of your corporation, prepare the final tax returns. The government (at all levels) counts as a creditor, and all taxes must be paid before dissolving the corporation. On the federal level, you can go to the IRS Web site (at *www.irs.gov*) and print out their "closing a business" checklist, which includes not only the forms you'll need to fill out for them but also the links directing you to more information about state and local rules. Remember, you are not dealing only with income taxes now. The corporation has to settle up payroll, sales, excise, and any other outstanding taxes as well. Also, at all government levels, you will have to file a special final return, clearly marked as such. If you don't, your corporation's tax file could remain open, exposing you to future nonfiling penalties and the like.

As for the regular creditors of your corporation, you must give them written notice of the dissolution. That must include a specific statement saying the dissolution (or intent to dissolve) has been filed. In addition, you must include an address where outstanding claims can be mailed, along with the information they must include in their claim in order for it to be processed and paid promptly. You will include a deadline for submitting claims, usually 120 days from the date of the notice, and a statement specifying that after that deadlines, no claims will be accepted.

Some states also allow for claims of unknown creditors, meaning the corporation is not aware of the creditor or the claim. In these states, you may be required to publish a public notice in the local newspaper as a notification of the dissolution. This can be a tricky area, so consider talking with your attorney if any state your corporation was registered in allows this provision.

As claims begin to trickle (or flood) in, you can either accept or reject them. Those that are accepted must be paid, or other settlement arrangements must be agreed upon with the creditor. For example, a creditor that submits a claim for $5,000 might agree to accept $4,000 instead in order to be paid now. When claims are rejected, that has to be in writing. This is another tricky area that may be subject to specific state statutes, so involve your attorney in these rejected claims as well.

Sharing the Spoils

Once all taxes are paid and all creditors satisfied, it's time for you and your fellow shareholders to split up the remaining assets of the corporation. These assets have to be distributed in proportion to ownership percentages. If you own 40 percent of the shares, you must receive 40 percent of the remaining corporate assets.

Your corporate bylaws will spell out how to distribute the assets. Where there are multiple classes of shares (preferred and common, for example), distributions may have to be made in a specific order. **When the assets are all in the form of cash, your bylaws may dictate that they must first be sold before final distributions can be made.**

However the distributions are made, all of them must be reported to the IRS. Your tax advisor can help you through this process, as there are circumstances in which a corporate dissolution will trigger a personal income-tax liability.

When Dissolution Is Involuntary

Sometimes, corporate dissolution happens without your intent. This can happen when the business is unsuccessful or through technical legal means. Many small corporations fold for very personal reasons, the top three being death, disability, and divorce. Regardless of the reason for the dissolution, many of procedures outlined in the previous sections must still be completed. Even though it may be effectively dissolved, if the corporation is not officially dissolved, it still may be required to file periodic reports with state and federal government authorities or to continue to pay business fees and taxes. Failing to meet these requirements can result in fines and penalties.

The Bankruptcy Option

Not every business succeeds. In fact, most new businesses don't make it for the long haul. When your business is struggling to get by and simply can't get out from under an overwhelming debt burden, you may turn to the bankruptcy courts for help. Should this be the case, talk with your corporate attorney before you file anything. He can help you determine which type of bankruptcy filing will work best for your unique situation.

If your corporation files for bankruptcy, the courts will set up an order in which creditors will get paid with the existing assets. All corporate assets may be taken and sold, usually not for top dollar. Those proceeds will be used to pay as many creditors as possible, as fairly as possible. Secured creditors will be paid first, followed by unsecured ones. The courts will discharge most of the corporation's remaining debt.

Many debts can be eliminated through bankruptcy proceedings. However, some debts will not be discharged by the courts and will remain outstanding until satisfied. One example is secured debt. If there is an outstanding debt with collateral attached to it, those creditors must either get paid (installments are fine here), or the debtor will have to turn over the collateral. In addition, the law specifically exempts particular debts from discharge, like payroll taxes. Finally, there's no relief from debts that are first incurred after the bankruptcy filing.

Automatic Dissolution

There are some circumstances under which your corporation will be automatically dissolved by state statute. When this happens, your business does not dissolve. It simply reverts to an unincorporated form of business, and that means the loss of your limited liability protection.

One of the most common causes of this undesirable situation is the failure to renew your corporate status. Every year corporations must file annual reports, along with any requisite fees, to their home states. Failure to do either task can put your corporation into a bad status with the state business office. After a period of noncompliance, and usually some notices, the state will simply dissolve your corporation.

In some states, your corporation also may be dissolved if you fail to register it as a foreign entity in a state (other than its home state) where it conducts business. While this won't set off dissolution procedures in all states, it will in some.

The bottom line is that you have to keep up with the paperwork or risk losing your corporation.

▶▶ TEST DRIVE

It can be hard to know when it's really the right time to leave your corporation, especially if it has been successful and you truly enjoy the business. To find out if you're really ready to make a change, and exactly what kind of change you want, ask yourself these questions:

- ➲ Do I want to keep working steadily?
- ➲ Do I want to keep my hand in as an occasional consultant?
- ➲ How will I feel if I'm completely uninvolved with the company going forward?
- ➲ Do I need a big chunk of money right now?
- ➲ Would a steady stream of payments over the next ten years be better for my cash flow?
- ➲ Do I want to start another business?

Taxes, Taxes, Taxes

PART **5**

Keep Abreast of Frequent Changes

Tax law changes quite often, and it can be challenging to keep up with the changes as they happen. Some of these changes will be implemented by the government with barely a dent in your operations; others can cause serious complications and require major changes to keep your company in compliance. Many come with catchy names or acronyms, making them sound more user-friendly than they actually are. Some are immediate, some phased in, some permanent, some to be phased out. No one expects you to keep all of this information in your head, or even on hand; that's your tax accountant's job. However, since many tax laws will impact your company, you need to be aware of the basics and keep up with changes that may affect your corporation.

Some of the most recent tax changes, the two that may affect your business right now are the Job and Growth Tax Relief Reconciliation Act (JGTRRA) and the American Jobs Creation Act (AJCA). Both of these acts contain provisions that you may be able to use to your corporation's advantage, once you know the score.

JGTRRA Basics

The JGTRRA began to kick in back in 2003, and by now all of its provisions have been activated. Some will have already gone away, others will last until 2010—that is, unless Congress changes things again (which is a virtual certainty). Certain provisions benefit all American businesses, no matter the entity, while others apply only to corporations. Here, you'll see a simple sketch of this comprehensive act. Let your CPA help you determine which tax strategies can be implemented to best serve your corporation over the long haul.

Some of the biggest changes will impact your income-splitting strategy, a particular perk unique to corporations detailed on pages 275–76. Under JGTRRA, individual income tax rates were lowered, while corporate tax rates were not. When individual tax rates are lower, it may benefit your overall tax picture to take more money out of the corporation in salary and bonus. The act also lowers the tax rate on shareholders who receive corporate dividends, whether or not they own the company. Double taxation still exists, but now it comes with a spoonful of sugar in the form of a

15 percent dividend tax cap. For some shareholders, that tax rate may be as low as 5 percent. This rule, however, is due to disappear in 2008.

On the other hand, the act also makes it more attractive to keep retained earnings inside the corporation. Now you can keep more cash inside without drawing big tax penalties, and the new tax penalties (when they do apply) are lower than they used to be. (More on this in Chapter 23.)

Finally, the JGTRRA makes the tax bite easier on owners of small corporations who sell their qualified small business stock. Part of the gain (up to 50 percent) on such a sale may be excluded from tax altogether; the rest may be subject to a special capital gains tax rate of 28 percent. Plus, if you sell at a loss, or your shares become worthless, you may be able to deduct up to $100,000 of losses against your other income (called ordinary income, as opposed to capital gains) rather than the standard $3,000 maximum offset.

The AJCA (In a Nutshell)

The AJCA was passed in 2004, with some provisions taking effect as early as January 1, 2005. Some of its provisions apply directly to small corporations. Talk with your accountant to discover which may benefit your business.

One major section provides special tax deductions for manufacturing companies, though the definition of what qualifies here is a bit gray. The act allows corporations to deduct 3 percent of income pertaining to U.S. manufacturing operations from total taxable income. That percentage is slated to increase to a whopping 9 percent by 2010. There is a cap, though. This deduction cannot be more than 50 percent of the total gross wages paid to employees, including shareholder-employees, for the year. Here's how it works. If your corporation has $50,000 of taxable income, $20,000 of which is derived from manufacturing, you can deduct an additional $600 ($20,000 times 3 percent). That knocks your corporation's taxable income down to $49,400, decreasing the income tax liability as well.

S corporations also get special attention under the AJCA. This act both simplified and eased some of the restrictions placed on S corporations. Now, S corporations can have up to 100 shareholders (the prior limit was seventy-five). Even better, all members of a single family count as a single shareholder, no matter how many of them actually hold shares. Previously, family members were counted individually, and that rule saw shareholder counts add up to the limit very quickly.

Employee Compensation

When your business is formed as a corporation, it automatically has at least one employee: you. Since you and your corporation are wholly separate legal and financial entities, you have to be an employee and get a paycheck from the company for the work you do. In addition to you and your fellow shareholders, you may have regular employees. Regardless, as soon as a business has a single employee—and yours does—it enters the wonderful world of employee compensation and taxation. (Chapter 23 tells the full story about payroll taxes.)

One of the biggest areas of confusion for novice corporation owners is how much to pay employees, including themselves. The parameters for figuring out your own salary are much different than coming up with employee wages. You want to get as much money out of your corporation as possible, while minimizing the overall tax burden (as described in the discussion of income splitting on pages 275–76). You want to pay your employees as little as possible, at least during the early days when cash is tight, while still attracting the cream of the crop. Luckily, there's more than one way to pay an employee (no, not cash under the table).

As part of your employees' total compensation package, you can include these things:

- Base salary (or wages)
- Bonuses
- Health insurance
- Retirement plans
- Fringe benefits
- Employee stock options

Of course, these components can be used to increase the total salary packages of you and your fellow employee-shareholders as well.

Initially, many of your employee compensation decisions will be based on just how much your corporation can actually afford. All of the items listed above, with the sole exception of employee stock options, are deductible expenses to the corporation. Employee stock options are not, but they come with a special benefit for the company—they don't call for an outlay of precious cash.

Setting Employee Compensation Levels

Setting appropriate salary and wage ranges for employees is actually easier than it seems. While it may appear that you have lots of flexibility, that's not really the case. First, there are legal minimums governing how little you can pay employees. Second, there are the going market rates for particular positions. You can deviate from these somewhat, but they do set the "reasonable" guideline. Employees generally won't work for less money than they can get elsewhere unless you make it worth their while in other ways.

Your first constraint is the minimum wage set by the state. The local state, where employees are actually working, rules; the corporation's home state minimum wage rules impact only employees working in that state. ▶▶ **A state's minimum wage cannot be set lower than the federal level, but it can be higher.** Check with the state employment office in every state where your corporation has employees to learn what appropriate minimum wage is.

Next, check out what your competitors are paying their employees. You will find a range here among different companies and even within companies, but that range will likely be fairly narrow for equivalent positions. Remember to take the whole salary package into account. For example, one company may pay a little less but offer health benefits, and another may pay top dollar for wages and offer no benefits at all. Once you've got the general range, you can set your wage and salary guidelines, again remembering to factor in any other bonuses and benefits your corporation may offer.

Offering a Little More

Everyone likes to be appreciated, and your employees are no different. They all like getting holiday bonuses (either cash or gifts). They like going to the annual picnic, and they like it when the company picks up the dinner tab when they've had to work especially late. All of these gestures can go along way toward boosting employee morale, retention, and productivity. They will cost the corporation some money, but the resulting goodwill can be well worth that.

Here are a few other extra-special benefits that can help your corporation attract the best of the best:

- ⮑ On-site day care (doesn't have to be fancy)
- ⮑ Discounted health club memberships or an employee gym
- ⮑ Occasional pizza-and-beer parties
- ⮑ Employee discounts for company products and services
- ⮑ Birthdays off with pay
- ⮑ Bagels and donuts at the monthly morning meeting

Remember, every perk you offer to employees is available to you and your fellow owners as well. If there's something you want (like an on-site masseuse), ask your accountant if it can be turned into a deductible expense for the corporation if other employees have access to it as well.

Employee Stock Option Plans

One of the best things about forming your company as a corporation is your ability to motivate employees by giving them a piece of the pie. As part owners of your corporation, the people who work for you have a personal stake in the outcome of operations—the corporate profits are their profits, too. This unique benefit, available only with corporations, allows you to give small portions of equity to large numbers of people while simultaneously scoring significant tax benefits for your business. While these are not the same as traditional retirement plans, they do share some similar traits.

In addition to the obvious benefits (increased employee motivation and tax advantages), giving your employees equity shares also helps stabilize your corporate cash flow. That's especially important during the start-up phase, when every dollar is precious but you want to attract and keep the best employees. Handing out equity conserves cash, but it makes your job offers much more attractive on a long-term basis. After all, no one knows what those shares could be worth some day, or what giant corporation may want to buy up your company's shares for a hefty premium.

When it comes to employee stock option plans, you have several choices available. Some of them are rather obscure, and won't be introduced here. The more common (which also happen to be simpler) varieties will be discussed, along with how you can use them in your corporation. As you're reading, don't be scared off by what seems like a lot of technicalities; you can hire an experienced professional to deal with the fine points, as long as you have a firm grasp of the big picture.

About Stock Options

Before you can understand the incentive stock option (ISO) plan, you need to know how stock options work. Basically, a stock option is the right to buy shares for a specified price—called the strike price—at some time in the future. For example, a stock option could let an employee buy 100 shares for $10 each. If the share price goes higher than that, the option holder can buy at her low price, and sell for the higher market price, turning a tidy instant profit.

With small corporations, though, there may not be a big market for shares. In those cases, employees may buy the stock at the strike price, and hold on to it until a bigger market develops.

Qualified Incentive Stock Options

Qualified incentive stock options (ISOs) get special tax treatment for corporate employees, and that can include you. Unlike standard retirement plans, this one allows you to give the benefit to only the employees you choose. In fact, each year, your corporation's board of directors gets to decide who gets the stock options, a plan that allows a lot of discretion in keeping and motivating key employees.

Here's where the tax bonus kicks in. With an ISO, taxes aren't levied until the shares are eventually sold, and then they're levied at the lower capital gains rates. As with most IRS rules, there are tons of conditions attached; however, some of them are much more likely to impact your corporation. For example, the options can only be given to employees. Independent contractors and board members who aren't employees won't qualify. Any shares bought by exercising an ISO have to be held on to for at least a year—and that purchase date has to be at least two years since the option was granted. Plus, when an employee owns more than 10 percent of the total outstanding voting stock (very common in small corporations), the strike price can't be less than 110 percent of the fair market value of a share on the grant date. There are more rules, and they get more complicated as you go, so make sure to talk to an experienced professional before you initiate an ISO. If any rule isn't followed to the letter, the options convert to nonqualified, with less favorable tax benefits.

The tax benefits of an ISO are pretty substantial, and they're worth protecting. Again, the full rules are intricate and best left to the accountants, but the basic benefit is easy to understand. There are no regular income taxes due at all until shares are eventually sold. Normally, as soon as an employee gets compensation (like a stock option), he pays tax on it, but that's not the case with an option given under an ISO. Figuring out the taxes when they're due is complicated (and, again, let a tax expert figure this out), but the taxes are based on capital gains rates, which are typically lower than income tax rates.

Nonqualified Stock Options

Any time your corporation offers ISOs that don't pass all the IRS tests, the benefit transforms into a nonqualified stock option (NSO) plan. NSOs do not offer the same advantages as their rule-bound cousins, but your corporation can still benefit by using them.

Without the restrictions of ISOs, you can give NSOs to people who aren't employees: board members, independent contractors, even your accountant or your favorite supplier. That flexibility does come with a tax trade-off. NSOs don't get preferred capital gains tax treatment. However, they do retain some key tax advantages, like deferred taxation—there's no tax due when the options are handed out.

Deductible Benefits

Deductible benefits come in many shapes and sizes, from minimal fringe benefits to formal employee benefit programs. ▶▶ **Essentially, anything you give an employee (other than salary and bonus) in exchange for their work counts as a fringe benefit.** The employee gets a freebie (most of these don't count as taxable income), and your corporation gets an expense deduction. Even better, as a corporate employee, you share in these benefits, a perk not available to unincorporated business owners.

From the accounting perspective, your corporation categorizes the benefit in whatever expense category it naturally falls into. For example, providing employee meals would be deductible to the corporation as a meal expense; letting an employee drive a company car falls under corporate automobile expense; club memberships can be categorized as dues and subscriptions expense. That may seem irrelevant, but it's not. Allowing these benefits to be classified as regular expenses rather than as payroll saves your corporation a lot of money in employment taxes.

More formal employee benefit programs cover things like employer-sponsored health insurance, retirement plans (more on these in Chapter 24), educational assistance (like tuition reimbursement plans), and group-term life insurance coverage. The IRS imposes some restrictions on some of these items pertaining to their full deductibility. Mainly, though, payments made by employers on behalf of employees in these types of plans will be counted as business expenses. For example, group-term life insurance premiums are not deductible to the corporation when it is the policy beneficiary.

Income Splitting

One of the most valuable benefits of incorporating your business is income splitting, an advantage unavailable with any other entity. All corporations share this advantage, though it is somewhat more limited for

S corporations and their owners. The most beneficial income splits are unique to each circumstance. They may vary from year to year and are largely dependent on current tax law, which changes all the time. To come up with the best deal for your situation each year, talk to a qualified tax professional.

One big advantage of C corporations is that owners get paid salaries, which are fully deductible to the corporation and taxed only to the employees at individual income tax rates. That gives you the flexibility to decide which entity will pay income tax (you or the corporation) on how much money. When individual income tax rates are lower, you can pay yourself a higher salary; when corporate income tax rates are lower, you can pay yourself a smaller salary and let the corporation pick up more income. Of course, there's a lot of math involved, partly because both individual and corporate income tax rates are graduated (and not on the same scale, either).

Dividends are a mixed bag for C-corporation shareholders. In C corporations, dividends are subject to the dreaded double taxation. That means taxes are paid on the same income twice. First, the corporation pays income tax on its earnings, and then shareholders pay income tax on the earnings distributions (a.k.a. dividends) they receive. That can double the total tax hit on those earnings. On the plus side, dividends are now taxed to individuals at no more than 15 percent (some very low-income taxpayers may be charged only 5 percent on their dividend income); that's compared to the highest regular personal income tax rate of 35 percent. The dividend rate makes the double-taxation issue less taxing financially.

S corporation owners, on the other hand, pay all of the income tax on the corporation's earnings whether they get dividends or not; that's just how pass-through taxation works. For these shareholders, getting more in dividends and less in salary is almost always beneficial. That's because dividends are not subject to employment taxes (Social Security and Medicare) and salaries are. Though that tax gets split between the two parties (shareholder and corporation), it still adds up to an extra 15.3 percent of your money going to the government.

Keep It In or Pay It Out?

One of the toughest decisions to be made in a small corporation is whether to pay out dividends or hold on to retained earnings. Tax matters aside, this decision speaks volumes about the company's growth potential. No company can expand without financing, and at least part of that funding will be expected to come from the company itself. At the same time, owners want to grow their personal nest eggs, and paying themselves handsome dividends is a great way to jumpstart personal wealth.

The JGTRRA makes it much easier for small corporations to build up large retained earnings balances. Your corporation can hold on to up to $250,000 with no questions asked. More than that, and you need a valid business purpose for the accumulation, or your corporation may be charged with an accumulated earnings penalty tax. Though that tax used to be set at close to 40 percent, it's now tied to the highest rate people pay on dividends. Basically, the same tax will be paid on these excess earnings whether they get distributed as dividends or held by the corporation.

Of course, if your corporation needs the money and is using its retained earnings as an internal savings account, keep the money in the business. Valid business reasons include things like retiring debt (bank loans or bonds, for example), expanding the business, and gathering a reserve for future expected expenses (like defending a lawsuit). In addition, if your company has accumulated earnings but no cash, it may not be able to distribute earnings to shareholders.

From a personal perspective, keeping earnings inside rather than distributing them currently may be part of your long-range personal financial or estate plan. For example, when you sell the corporation, you'll get those retained earnings back. However, they'll now be in the form of capital gains, rather than dividends or salary, and capital gains tax rates are usually among the lowest. It's even better for qualified small business corporation owners, who may now be able to exclude up to 50 percent of the gains from the sale of their corporations under JGTRRA. (Talk to your tax advisor to see if your corporation qualifies.)

Retained Earnings Score a Bank Loan

When the owners of The CD Side of Town, Inc., went to their local bank for an expansion loan, they were turned down flat. When Josh and David, the corporation's two shareholders, asked the loan officer why, he told them that their company didn't meet the bank's criteria for a loan. Most importantly, he told them, the relatively new and small corporation wasn't putting up much of its own money.

David and Josh's music store had hit the ground running, earning profits even in its first year in business. The guys had taken most of those profits out in salary and dividends, leaving just enough cash in the company to cover the bills. After leaving the bank, they had a meeting in which they decided to leave this year's profits in the company and try to fund their own expansion next year.

By the end of the next year, the corporation had enough funds in retained earnings to cover about one-third of the expansion costs, not nearly enough to get the job done. So Josh and David headed back over to the bank, with their updated business plan and current financial statements. This time, the loan officer asked for some time to look over their plans; he would get back to them within two weeks.

Ten days later, the bank called the guys back in for a second meeting, one in which they were told that the bank would lend them the money. Even better, since the corporation was putting up such a substantial chunk of its own money, it qualified for one of the lower interest-rate programs.

The Corporate Tax Year

Every business, including every type of corporation, has to figure out its taxable income and file all required income tax returns. The time span for this activity is an annual accounting period called the tax year. Your corporation's tax year may match the standard calendar year, but it does not have to. Any twelve-month period will do, as long as that period remains consistent from year to year. For accounting and tax purposes, any twelve-month period that differs from the calendar year is called a fiscal year.

As far as the IRS is concerned, your corporation makes its tax-year choice when it files its first income tax return. Unless your company falls under guidelines that force it to use a required tax year (in which case you have to comply), anything goes. When a fiscal year is the tax period of choice, your corporation's books and accounting records must be kept using the same time period. If the tax year runs from April 1 to March 30, the bookkeeping and financial statements must also cover that period.

Changing the Tax Year

Even if your corporation has been filing tax returns for a decade, it still may be allowed to alter its tax year. This change requires IRS notification and approval. Most of the time, automatic approval is granted. Occasionally, though, the request requires a special ruling from the IRS. In those circumstances, you have to pay a fee along with your application.

To get the process rolling, the corporation has to file IRS Form 1128, Application to Adopt, Change, or Retain a Tax Year. The form is short and to the point, and it's quite easy to complete. You can download this form from the IRS Web site, at *www.irs.gov*.

When a Fiscal Year Makes More Sense

For many small businesses, it's just plain easier to use a calendar year for a tax year. There are some circumstances and some industries for which a different fiscal year makes more sense. Consider this: Even if you have a dedicated bookkeeper and a CPA on retainer, you will still have a lot of extra work to do come tax time. Think about the extra tasks that come at the end of your corporation's fiscal year:

- Conducting employee performance reviews
- Calculating bonuses
- Taking physical inventory
- Reconciling all bank accounts
- Preparing and finalizing financial statements
- Analyzing financial performance and budget deviations
- Getting together documentation for tax deductions
- Making dividend determinations

That's a lot of work, and doing it at your company's busiest time can be an overwhelming burden. If the year-end holiday season or the spring is your corporation's busy season, that's no time to tack on dozens of administrative tasks. For companies with that time flow, moving the fiscal year end to a slow time of year, like the middle of summer, can make life a lot easier. Plus, you'll get more attention from your accountant if you're working with her outside the standard tax season, from February to May, when she's busiest.

When a Calendar Year Makes More Sense

Companies that have level business cycles, meaning similar transaction volume all year round, may not benefit from using a fiscal year. Service-oriented companies don't have that extra burden of taking physical inventory at the end of the year. Since all corporations must have employees (talking about you here, as a shareholder-employee), they have to prepare calendar year-end paperwork for payroll anyway. For companies that fall into these categories (especially more than one), fixing the fiscal year to the calendar year may be easier.

For S corporations, calendar years are almost always the annual accounting periods of choice. That's because they have pass-through taxation, meaning the income taxes pass through the corporation on to the personal tax returns of its shareholders. Individual taxpayers virtually always use a calendar-based tax year. For the S corporation, using a tax year that is different from that than the primary shareholders adds unnecessary complications (and will almost certainly ratchet up your tax-return preparation fees).

TEST DRIVE

New companies tend to have limited resources and unlimited needs, one of which is often manpower. Employees do expect to be paid, but you can get creative when you put together a compensation package. Consider the following factors as you figure out your corporation's optimal employee compensation package profile:

- What type of employees do you have: seasonal or year-round? Full-time or part-time? Long-term or project-based?
- What is the corporation's projected cash flow for the next year? (You can use the pro forma from your business plan or your current corporate budget.)
- What is your personal need for employee benefits like health insurance, life insurance, and a retirement plan?
- What is the availability of authorized but not issued corporate shares?
- What classes of shares are set forth in the articles of incorporation?
- What are the terms of your shareholders' agreement?
- Would employee discounts on corporate products be well received?

How C Corporations Are Taxed

At the federal level, and often at the state level, corporations must pay taxes on their own income. To figure out the tax bill for the year, you first have to figure out the corporation's taxable income. Once that number is squared away, the income tax due will be calculated according to the current corporate income tax table, published and easily available on the IRS Web site (*www.irs.gov*).

That sounds simple, but coming up with the taxable-income figure can be a little complicated. That's because the net income (or net profit) that appears in your financial statements may not be the same as the corporation's taxable income. ▶▶ **The basics are the same: corporate gross income minus cost of goods sold and operating expenses.** On top of those, though, special tax credits, deductions, and exclusions may come into play.

Getting to Taxable Income

Calculating your corporation's taxable income is pretty much like calculating its actual income, with a few small differences. (Your accountant will handle this as part of the income tax return preparation.) Start with revenues, deduct expenses, and you've got your net income.

There are many corporate tax preference items, special deductions, and deductibility rules, but most of these will have no bearing on the tax return of an average small corporation. Items that may make your corporation's taxable income look a little different than its book income include these:

Meal expenses: On the books, your meal expenses will match the receipts, but for tax purposes only a portion of them will be deductible.

Dividends received deduction: On the books, all of the dividends your corporation receives from its investments count toward net income; for tax purposes, you may be able to exclude 70 percent of those dividends from taxable income.

Net operating losses: On the books, income and losses stay in the year they happened; on the corporate tax return, losses can be carried forward for several years and used to offset that future income.

The Corporate Income Tax Forms

Each year, C corporations are required to file IRS Form 1120 (or 1120A, a simpler form some small corporations may use). In addition to that, any corporations that expect to owe at least $500 in income tax at the end of the year must make quarterly estimated tax deposits (along with IRS Form 8109). The annual tax return must be filed by the fifteenth day of the third month after the end of its tax year. For example, if your corporation's tax year ends on December 31, the return would need to be filed by March 15 of the following year. Estimated tax payments are due four times a year, in months four, six, nine, and twelve of the corporation's tax year, each time on the fifteenth day. For a calendar tax year, that turns out to be April 15, June 15, September 15, and December 15.

Form 1120 looks like an income statement and a balance sheet. The numbers from your financial statements will roll over on to your tax forms, though maybe not in the exact same way. Many times, several financial-statement line items will be combined into a single line item for income tax reporting purposes. The first couple of pages follow a modified income-statement format, starting with gross revenues, moving down through cost of goods sold and operating expenses, and ending with net taxable income. The next couple of pages (which your corporation may not be required to complete, depending on revenue levels), mimic a balance sheet. One section holds assets, the other holds liabilities and equities, and the two sections must total to the same figure.

Other information is included on this form as well. Page one asks for a lot of identifying corporate information: name, tax identification number, mailing address, and date of incorporation, for example. Questions also appear throughout the return, asking for things like the accounting method and inventory valuation method. Finally, the return must be signed by an authorized corporate officer and by whomever you paid to prepare the return.

Don't Try This at Home

There is a preponderance of DIY tax software out there. This software is generally less expensive than having your corporate income taxes prepared by a qualified tax professional, at least on the surface. While hundreds of complex tax rules, calculations, and forms are programmed into these software packages, they are no substitute for a human tax expert, and paying too much in taxes won't save you money in the long run.

A tax professional will talk with you and likely uncover deductions you didn't know you had. She can help you minimize overall taxation and develop a tax-saving strategy for the upcoming year. She can help you understand why your corporation didn't earn as much as expected. Most important, she can deal with the IRS if something goes awry.

Understanding Corporate Tax Rates

Very similar to personal income-tax rates, corporations are taxed using a graded rate schedule. The effective rate your corporation ends up paying depends completely on its taxable income.

Federal Corporate Income-Tax Rate Schedule

$0 to $50,000	15% of total taxable income
$50,001 to $75,000	$7,500 plus 25% of taxable income over $50,000
$75,001 to $100,000	$13,750 plus 34% of taxable income over $75,000
$100,001 to $335,000	$22,250 plus 39% of taxable income over $100,000
$335,001 to $10,000,000	$113,900 plus 34% of taxable income over $335,000
$10,000,001 to $15,000,000	$3,400,000 plus 35% of taxable income over $10,000,000
$15,000,001 to $18,333,333	$5,150,000 plus 38% of taxable income over $15,000,000
More than $18,333,333	35% of total taxable income

Check out this example, in which your corporation has earned $225,000 of taxable income. The total income tax due for the year would be $71,000 ($22,250 plus $48,750, which is 39 percent of $125,000). Of course, the corporation wouldn't be expected to pay that in one lump sum; in fact, there would be a penalty applied in that case. Rather, the corporation should have been making estimated tax payments throughout the year, which divides that eye-popping number into four payments instead of one.

A Multitude of Tax Advantages

In addition to the legal benefits like limited liability protection, C corporations come with certain tax advantages that are simply unavailable with any other entity. In fact, many other business entities offer their owners limited liability protection (such as S corporations, LLCs, LLPs), but only regular corporations offer such extensive tax planning and minimization capabilities. These opportunities include the following:

- ➲ Expanded income-shifting methods
- ➲ Tax rate control
- ➲ Tax-free fringe benefits for all shareholder-employees
- ➲ Dividends-received exclusion

To get the greatest advantage, and pay the least possible taxes, consult with your tax professional. Strategies that work well for one company may increase the tax liability of another, and methods that save taxes one year could have the reverse effect in the next. Part of that inconsistency is due to changes in the makeup of both corporate and personal income from year to year, and part is due to ever-changing tax laws.

Income Shifting and Tax Rate Control

Unlike any other business entity, when you own a corporation, you have two different tax tables to work with. The rates change at different income points, giving you expanded opportunities to funnel income toward the entity that enjoys the lower rate. When the corporation will pay less taxes on income, you can leave more profits inside the business, in the form of retained earnings. No other entity has this capability; in those, all earnings are taxed to owners whether or not they are distributed, while C corporation owners only pay taxes on income they actually receive. When the opposite is true, and the corporation's tax rates are higher, you can increase payments to yourself through tax-deductible (for the corporation) means, like higher salary or lease payments. (See Chapter 20 for a more detailed discussion of income shifting.)

Tax-Free Fringe Benefits

Employee benefits is an area where C corporations shine. This is the only entity where the benefits that are normally tax-free to employees are also tax-free to shareholder-employees. The corporation gets a full tax deduction on its payments for all portions of the benefits plan, and the shareholder-employees receive the full benefit, no taxes due. With S corporations, shareholder-employees may get the benefits, but their value is included in each shareholders taxable income. Such benefits are detailed in IRS Publication 15-B, Employer's Tax Guide to Fringe Benefits, available free on their Web site at *www.irs.gov.*

Tax-advantaged employee fringe benefits that you (as an owner-employee) may also enjoy include things like these:

- ➲ Premiums paid for group term life insurance coverage up to $50,000
- ➲ Company cars
- ➲ Public transportation passes (up to $105 per month)
- ➲ Parking passes (up to $205 per month)
- ➲ Educational assistance (up to $5,250)

There are a lot more benefits defined under the IRS code, but these are just some of the highlights. The key to swinging tax-free benefits for yourself is employees. Your corporation has to have other employees, and they have to be able to benefit from these benefits as well.

The Dividends-Received Exclusion

Once your corporation starts turning profits and bringing in positive cash flow, you could end up with a pile of retained earnings. Rather than have those earnings sit in a checking or savings account and earn a pittance, you and your fellow shareholders may decide to invest all or some of those funds. When you invest in the stock of other unrelated corporations, your corporation gets a tax break—a very big tax break. Under the current corporate tax rules, your corporation may exclude 70 percent of those dividends from taxable income. So if the corporation invested in a bunch of blue-chip stocks and earned $1,000 in dividends during the year, it would owe taxes on only $300.

If instead the corporation paid out dividends to you, and you invested that money in the same blue chip stocks and earned the same $1,000, you would end up paying a lot of taxes. First, you'd pay tax on the dividends you received from the company. Then, you'd pay taxes on the full $1,000 of outside dividends earned.

Some Distinct Tax Disadvantages

When you put the words "C corporation" and "tax disadvantage" together in a sentence, the next logical phrase is "double taxation." That's the most commonly touted tax drawback for regular corporations, but it is not the only one or even the worst. In fact, thanks to the JGTRRA, double taxation is taking a smaller bite out of everyone's pockets than ever before. That said, being taxed twice on the exact same income at the exact same time is still disadvantageous. Plus, **there are times when the IRS can decide that another kind of transaction between the shareholder and the corporation should count as a dividend, rather than as a deductible business expense.**

Also on the downside list are extra corporate taxes that may or not be imposed depending on the particular circumstances. These include the following:

- ➲ Accumulated earnings tax (see Chapter 23)
- ➲ Corporate alternative minimum tax
- ➲ Personal holding-company penalty (see Chapter 23)

For many new and small corporations, the only real tax disadvantage is dividend-related. It's nearly impossible to avoid all double taxation once your corporation starts turning a profit. Plus, should your corporation sustain losses, those remain trapped inside the entity until such a time as it has income against which to deduct those losses, delaying their tax impact.

Constructive Dividends

As long as corporations have been around, shareholders have been looking for ways to take out money without paying more taxes. Virtually every kind of distribution comes with a tax bite: salary, dividend, loan payments (the interest portion), or lease payments. All of those count as taxable income to the shareholder. So people try to sneak money out in other ways, like having the corporation pay personal expenses, while taking a business expense deduction. If the IRS gets wise to this, they will deny that corporate expense deduction and charge the shareholder with taxable dividends. No official dividend was declared by the corporation, but the character of the transaction suggests otherwise. That's called a constructive dividend, and it's 100 percent taxable to the shareholder, with possible tax consequences for the corporation as well.

Other transactions that may result in constructive dividends include these:

⮞ Charging the corporation much higher than market rent
⮞ Buying property from the corporation for substantially less than its market value
⮞ Borrowing money from the corporation with no intention to pay that money back
⮞ Receiving excessive salary as a shareholder-employee

If the IRS does find constructive dividends in one tax year, you can be pretty certain that they'll pore over your records for other years as well.

Corporate Alternative Minimum Tax

Just like people, corporations may be subject to an alternative minimum tax (AMT). This extra tax kicks in if the corporation has too many (according to IRS guidelines) tax preference items, which reduce the corporate

The Payments that Turned into Dividends

Elizabeth Jackson had a thriving designer dress shop, formed as a corporation of which she was the sole shareholder. The corporation was earning lots of profits (a great problem to have) and getting hit with a pretty steep tax bill. This year in particular, the corporate profits were sky-high, and Elizabeth wanted to minimize the tax bill. Since her personal tax rate for the same income level was lower than the applicable corporate rates, she paid herself an enormous bonus at the end of the year, one that made her annual salary almost triple what it had been the year before.

Even with that huge salary payout, the corporation still had lots of profits. Elizabeth wanted to enjoy those profits, but she really didn't want to pay additional taxes. Instead of bumping up her salary even more or paying herself a fat dividend, she decided to borrow the money from the corporation. Since she was the only shareholder and had no one else to answer to, she didn't bother with loan paperwork. Instead, she made a quick bookkeeping entry that would suffice as documentation that the transfer was a loan.

A couple of years down the road, Elizabeth and her corporation were audited by the IRS. After weeks of document requests and meetings with the accountant, the agency reclassified half of that triple salary as dividends, along with 100 percent of the "loan." They explained that since there was no note, nothing in the corporate records book, and no evidence that a single loan payment had been made, the transaction did not qualify as a loan under IRS guidelines. In addition, they considered her suddenly huge salary unreasonable, as her role in the business had not changed.

income tax bill. Luckily, there is a small corporation exemption, just to protect small businesses from this extra tax. Corporations just starting out may not have to worry about this tax, as it won't kick in until the company's average gross receipts (a.k.a. revenues) are greater than $7.5 million. Plus, all corporations are exempt during their first year of existence.

Should your corporation lose its small corporation status—not such a bad thing, as it means your business is successful—and turn out to be subject to this tax, the AMT rate is 20 percent. Once the corporation loses small corporation status, it's a permanent loss; subsequent revenue dips won't restore it.

Qualified Small Business Stock

In many ways, small corporations are treated just like their gargantuan, multinational cousins. They share many of the same legal formalities, the same tax reporting requirements, and the same complex accounting treatment. Occasionally, though, the government gives the little guys a break, and one pretty substantial break comes in the form of qualified small-business stock treatment. That benefit gives the original shareholders a chance to keep more of their hard-earned profits when they do eventually sell their shares. When this rule applies, shareholders can keep half of those gains tax-free, paying tax on just 50 percent of the profits from the sale. Before you start spending that windfall, there's something you should keep in mind. The taxable portion of the sale will be hit with the full 28 percent rate (higher than the typical long-term capital gains tax rate). So you still get a good deal, just not as good as it seems at first glance.

Of course, to qualify for this huge tax break, there are a lot of hoops to jump through:

- ➲ You must have held the stock for at least five years.
- ➲ You have to have purchased the stock directly from the corporation.
- ➲ The stock cannot have been paid for with other stock.
- ➲ The company has to be set up as a regular C corporation.
- ➲ The corporation's total capitalization at the time your shares were issued can't have been more than $50 million.
- ➲ At least 80 percent of the revenue earned has to come from active trade (not passive investments).
- ➲ The corporation's business cannot include the performance of personal services.

Even once you've made it through all of those hoops, it's possible that a portion of your profits will still be excluded from this special treatment. There's a cap on just how much can be excluded. The advantaged portion of your gain can't be greater than ten times the current adjusted basis of the stock you sold; that's even further limited by a cap ($10 million for married couples; $5 million if you're single or married but filing separate income tax returns).

Figuring out the best allocation of corporate profits involves some basic math. Follow these steps to get an idea of which money-dividing method makes the most sense: more for you, or more for the corporation:

1. Print out the most current corporate income tax table (from the IRS Web site).

2. Print out the most current individual income tax table that applies to your situation—married filing jointly, married filing separate, head of household, or single (also available on the IRS Web site).

3. Prepare a year-to-date statement of profit and loss for the corporation.

4. Multiply your salary by the appropriate individual tax rate.

5. Multiply the corporate profit by the corresponding tax rate.

6. Add 60 percent of the corporate profits to your salary, and deduct that same amount from the original corporate profit.

7. Recalculate steps four and five.

Special Issues for S-Corporation Shareholders

S-corporation shareholders face different tax issues than owners of regular corporations. Most of the differences stem from the fact that S corporations are invisible entities for federal (and some state) income tax purposes. The corporations don't pay tax on their business income, but the shareholders do. On the flip side, shareholders also report business losses on their personal tax returns, and that little gem sets off an entirely different path of issues.

Some issues unique to S corporations and their shareholders include these:

- ➲ Pass-through taxation
- ➲ Special tax forms
- ➲ Higher dividend tax rates
- ➲ Different income-shifting parameters
- ➲ Trickier accounting records
- ➲ Taxable fringe benefits
- ➲ Different federal and state entity recognition
- ➲ Less calendar flexibility

Some of these items benefit S-corporation shareholders, but others can be disadvantageous. Many tax-related issues are particularly complex and require the insights of an experienced professional for tax-planning and tax-return preparation purposes.

Individual Tax Rates Matter More

All of the income earned by an S corporation is taxable to its shareholders. The company's income is split up among the shareholders in direct proportion to their ownership shares. Then, each owner's portion of income shows up on his personal income tax return.

Even though all of that income counts as personal income, there's still some wiggle room when it comes to managing the total tax bill. That's because there are two main ways to get cash out of your corporation: salary and dividends. Salary is subject to employment taxes, and dividends are not. By carefully splitting the money you take into these two piles, you can minimize your income tax bill without setting off any alarms at the IRS.

Keep in mind, though, that S corporation dividends do not enjoy the same very low tax rates as regular corporation dividends. That 15-percent rate cap applies only to dividends that have already been taxed as corporate earnings, which is not the case with S-corporation dividends. Here, corporate earnings will be taxed to shareholders at their personal income tax rates, regardless of whether those earnings are distributed as dividends. You won't have to pay additional taxes when you do take dividends, though.

Pass-Through Taxation

Pass-through taxation is really just what it sounds like. The corporation's income passes through the company directly to the shareholders, and they pay the tax on that income. On the tax return, it's as if the shareholders earned that income directly. For example, if the S corporation earns interest income, the shareholders report interest income. If the corporation has capital gains, the shareholders report capital gains. It's as if, for tax purposes, the corporation is invisible.

That doesn't mean S corporations aren't required to file annual income tax returns; they are. However, the federal tax returns of S corporations are for informational purposes only, and no corporate income tax is calculated. In addition, each shareholder's individual income tax information must be reported to him (and to the IRS) on a form called Schedule K-1. The data included on the K-1 flows through to the shareholders personal income tax return, in addition to any salary received from the corporation (reported on Form W-2). ▸▸ **The tax calculations can be tough, and filling in the forms correctly can be daunting.** (If you've ever received a Schedule K-1 before, you know just how daunting this is.) Have a professional tax preparer take care of all the year-end income tax requirements, from the corporation's informational return down to your own Form 1040.

The Corporate Income Tax Form

When the tax year is complete, it's time to gather up the records necessary to prepare your S corporation's income tax returns. The federal form number is 1120S, and it looks quite similar to a regular corporation's income tax return (Form 1120) with a few key differences. (State forms and form numbers vary widely; check out the home state's business tax Web page for forms and instructions.) This form is purely for informational purposes—there will be no tax due.

The Form 1120S is due March 15 in almost all circumstances, as S corporations are required to use a calendar year for their tax year unless they have a very good reason to switch it. If that is the case, and your S corporation's tax year end falls on a date other than December 31, the return will be due on the fifteenth day of the third month following the end of the tax year. ►► **The reason for the March 15 deadline is that shareholders need the information from the Form 1120S in order to complete their personal income tax returns, due April 15.** When the corporation requests an extension (which it can using Form 7004, an automatic six-month reprieve), the shareholders must do so as well.

Form 1120S asks for basic identifying data, like the corporate name and EIN, home state, and mailing address. When that's all completed, the next step is to fill in the financial information for the year, basically just a statement of profit and loss and a balance sheet. Though the numbers may show up in a different order or in different combinations here than they do on your financial statements, the overall information is the same.

That's where the similarity to a standard Form 1120 ends. In addition to information about the corporation, information about each shareholder is also required on the 1120S. Every shareholder must be listed by name, and the form also requires their addresses and social security numbers. The other major difference is that the Schedule K-1 must be sent along with the corporation's tax return, one for each shareholder.

Schedule K-1

As part of the whole Form 1120S package, the tax preparer will also create a Schedule K-1 for each shareholder. These schedules are used to detail each shareholder's proportional share of the corporation's net profit or loss; this share is not reported as one lump sum, but instead as a laundry list of income elements. In addition, the Schedule K-1 typically summarizes stock basis activity for the year.

Elements of income and expense are listed separately when they require different treatment on the shareholder's personal tax return. Most standard revenue and expense items are lumped together in a modified net income (or loss) that flows through as a dividend. However, other individual items will pass through more directly. For example, interest income of the corporation is reported as interest income on the shareholder's return. Here are some other items that are separately stated:

- Capital gains and losses (divided into short-term and long-term categories)
- Section 1231 gains and losses (sale of business property)
- Charitable contributions
- Tax-exempt interest
- Investment income and expenses
- Rental income and expenses
- Section 179 deductions (a special form of accelerated depreciation)
- Nondeductible expenses (such as tax penalties, or 50 percent of entertainment expenses)

There are also other less common separated items, like taxes paid to foreign countries, but those don't typically come into play for small businesses. As for the other, more common items, those appear on your tax return on the appropriate schedule (often specifically listed on the K-1). However, some elements are more complicated than others and may require the advice of an experienced tax accountant.

Your Personal Tax Return

If you've never filed more than a standard 1040 before, get ready to attach a lot of schedules. Some may be familiar, like Schedule A (itemized deductions), Schedule B (interest and dividend income), even Schedule D (capital gains and losses). Now, you'll become intimately acquainted with Schedule E as well.

As you go through Schedule K-1, you'll report each listed item separately in the appropriate spot within your tax return. Though some reporting requirements may be different for particular shareholders, the majority of items can be reported as follows:

➲ In most cases, the ordinary net profit (or loss) from the corporation will be reported on a single line on Schedule E.

➲ Interest and dividends earned are reported on Schedule B. Unlike the rest of your interest and dividends, which are itemized by payer, these will flow through as single figures, with the S corporation as the source.

➲ Schedule D will be used to report regular capital gains and losses, as well as Section 1231 gains and losses.

Most home tax-preparation software comes with a Schedule K-1 entry screen, where you can type in the items as they appear on your document. Then, the program takes care of which number goes on which form. However, these programs are not as sophisticated as an experienced professional, who may know a more beneficial presentation for a particular line item.

Understanding Basis

Basis is one of the most complicated concepts concerning S corporations. It's also one of the most critical, as it controls not only the current tax value of your shares but whether corporate losses may be deducted on your personal tax return. Basis is similar to the book value of an asset. It starts with your original investment in the corporation and then changes based on various additions and deductions over time. Unlike basis in other kinds of shares, though, an individual shareholder's total basis here may include the value of corporate liabilities and shareholder loans.

Each shareholder's equity basis is tracked in his individual capital account. Entries to this account include investments, withdrawals, and the proportional share of annual corporate revenue and expense items. Shareholders may also have loan basis, which can absorb corporate losses that pass through to the personal income tax return. Loan basis starts out with the amount the shareholder lends the corporation. It can be increased by additional loans and unpaid interest, or decreased by loan payments, debt forgiveness, or corporate losses in excess of equity basis. (The impact of shareholder loans is described in greater detail in the section beginning on page 305.)

When you have a good understanding of basis, you can take advantage of fluctuations to maximize your personal tax situation. For example, your corporation is more likely to sustain losses when it's just starting up than when it's running at full steam. If you want to take full advantage of those losses to keep your income taxes minimal, you can increase your basis before year end. Keep an eye on the income statement throughout the year, with special attention to the numbers as tax time approaches. ▸▸ **When your share of the expected losses exceeds your basis, dump some cash into the company.** Later on, when the company starts turning profits, you can pull that cash back out with absolutely no tax consequence; it's simply an equity transaction.

Negative Basis

Technically speaking, there's no such thing as negative basis, as a shareholder's basis cannot go below zero. Real-life situations, though, often result in negative basis. In those cases, shareholders may not deduct any losses until basis is restored (meaning brought back to a positive value). Typically, these situations occur only in the company's early years, when losses are common and shareholders can use the tax break. Once the company starts earning profits, though, situations in which basis goes negative are rare.

On the books, neither equity basis nor loan basis may be reduced below zero. When that actually happens, though, the real negative basis gets treated as nondeductible losses. That means you cannot deduct even $1 of current S-corporation losses on your personal income tax return—instead, the losses are temporarily suspended. You don't lose the losses, so to speak, but rather save them (indefinitely) for use in the future. As soon as your basis is restored to a usable balance, you can use those losses against other income, no matter how many years later it is.

An Example with Numbers

Barbara Johnson is one of three shareholders of Every Day, Inc., an S corporation. She purchased her shares for $12,000 in cash, $2,500 in computer equipment, and $500 in office furniture. On day one, her capital account had a balance of $15,000. Throughout year one, Barbara didn't invest or withdraw any funds or make any loans to the corporation. At the end of the year, her pro rata share of corporate losses came to $7,000. She used that loss on her personal income tax return to offset $7,000 of other income, reducing her basis to $8,000.

During year two, the corporation was still struggling. Now and then, Barbara made purchases for the company using her personal credit card, then submitted expense reports for reimbursement totaling $2,500. The company didn't have sufficient cash to pay her back during that year. In fact, the corporation sustained another year of losses; Barbara's share of those losses for year two came to $9,000. Barbara was able to deduct the full $9,000 of those losses against other personal income in year two; she used up her total equity basis of $8,000 plus $1,000 of her loan basis. Now her equity basis had a zero balance, and her loan basis was reduced to $1,500. That did not mean the loan balance had been reduced, just her basis for tax purposes.

In year three, the corporation started turning a profit. Every Day, Inc., paid Barbara back the full $2,500 it owed, causing a negative loan basis of $1,000. Barbara loaned the corporation an additional $1,000 to bring her loan basis back to zero. At year end, Barbara's share of profits was $3,200. That boosted her equity basis up to $3,200.

You don't have to wait for the corporation to turn things around to rebuild your basis, though. You can accomplish the same thing by investing more in the business (to build equity basis) or loaning the business more money (to restore loan basis).

The Benefits and Drawbacks

In addition to the legal protections common to all corporate forms, S corporations have some unique advantages and disadvantages. On the plus side, you've got pass-through taxation, no double taxation on dividends, the ability to deduct corporate losses against personal income, and the avoidance of the penalty taxes many regular corporations may be subject to (like the accumulated earnings tax or the personal holding company tax). On the downside, your corporation can't have more than 100 shareholders without losing S status. It can have only one class of stock, and there are more income tax forms to deal with as well as more accounting issues. Finally, fringe benefits aren't usually tax-free to shareholder-employees who own more than 2 percent of the business.

This combination of benefits and drawbacks works best for new small corporations that start out with relatively few shareholders. The early years of a business are when most losses occur. Only the S corporation allows you to apply those losses against your other personal income in the current year. C corporation losses are stuck inside the entity forever (though they may be applied against corporate income going forward). When the corporation starts turning profits, there's no double taxation to deal with (like with C corporations) since only shareholders pay taxes. When earnings start getting seriously large, as in the multiple millions range, and the corporation is ripe for expansion, you can change it to a C corporation and bring in as many new shareholders as you want.

The Financial Benefits

With careful tax planning, your S corporation can help you hold on to more of your company's profits than any other business form. First, income is taxable only once, not twice. Yes, it's taxable at personal income tax rates, but right now those are (mostly) better than corporate rates. When you pay yourself dividends, there is no income tax involved.

You're also able to reduce the overall tax burden with income shifting. Both salary and earnings income are taxable to you at your personal income tax rates. However, only salary is also subject to employment taxes; those add up to more than 15 percent between you and the corporation. By keeping your salary minimal and maximizing your dividends, you pay less taxes. As long as your salary is reasonable (and by reasonable, the IRS means not ridiculous), you won't draw attention from the IRS. When your corporation is sustaining losses, a very low salary is reasonable. When your corporation is earning profits, your salary should increase to a reasonable proportion (certainly no less than 10 percent). To figure out the optimal salary-dividend balance, one that won't invite IRS scrutiny, have your accountant run some numbers and see what makes the most sense.

Accounting and Tax Drawbacks

The drawbacks that most impact shareholders involve accounting costs, which decrease corporate income and increase cash outflow, and employee benefits, which may not be tax-free for shareholders who own more than 2 percent of the business. Though the regular business accounting is the same for all types of corporations, S corporations face the added burden of tracking shareholders' basis. The capital account of each and every shareholder must be accounted for individually, all the time. Since all distributions and allocations are based solely and wholly on ownership proportions, those capital account balances matter enormously. An S corporation owner who holds 17.6 percent of the corporation's capital must be allocated 17.6 percent of profits or losses, separately stated income and deduction items, and dividend distributions. Plus, insufficient capital investment (a.k.a. low or no basis) can bring "at-risk" rules into play, making losses nondeductible.

S-corporation owners also have to deal with passive-activity losses. This is another set of rules that impact the current deductibility of pass-through losses. Basically, if you don't actively participate in the corporation, or if the corporation earns its money through passive activities, loss deductions against other personal income will probably be severely limited (if allowed at all). In many cases, passive-activity losses are only deductible against passive-activity income; the rest is suspended for a period of time. The passive-activity rules cover income from investment-type sources, like rental properties and mutual funds. These rules are pretty complex, so talk to your accountant if you think they might apply to your situation.

Employee Benefit Deductibility

One disadvantage of S corporations as compared to C corporations is that some normally tax-free employee benefits are not tax-free to shareholder-employees. Any shareholder who holds more than 2 percent of the corporate stock can't get tax-free employee benefits. In fact, in this case, an S-corporation owner is treated just like a sole proprietor, in that any employee benefit he receives are counted as part of his taxable income. The only tax-advantaged benefits that S corporation shareholders may be able to enjoy are health insurance and retirement plans.

The At-Risk Rules

The moment you become a corporate shareholder or lend money to your corporation, you have put some of your assets at risk, meaning you stand to lose those assets. Your total amount at risk equals your adjusted stock basis plus your adjusted loan basis. That at-risk total will vary over time.

You can deduct your share of S-corporation losses up to the amount you have at risk. Any losses exceeding that total must be suspended. That means you can't deduct them against your other income right now, but you may be able to in the future when you have assets at risk again. However, those losses still get figured into your basis, even when you don't deduct them for tax purposes.

Here's how these benefits work. The shareholder himself, on his personal income tax return, may deduct the health-insurance premiums from taxable income. That has the same effect as the tax-free version of the benefit available to C-corporation shareholders, with a little more paperwork involved. As for retirement savings, the S-corporation shareholder may establish a retirement plan. Contributions may be deducted on his personal tax return, also reducing taxable income.

The Impact of Shareholder Loans

Small-business owners frequently pour more and more money into their companies, especially during the early lean years. S-corporation shareholders do just the same thing, but here, the way they put that money in can make a very big difference at tax time. While the immediate economic effect to the shareholder and the corporation doesn't vary, the income tax treatment at the end of the year may, depending on whether the money was considered a capital investment or a loan to the corporation.

As you learned earlier in this chapter, S-corporation shareholders have two distinct types of basis: equity and loan. When they lend additional funds to the corporation, thereby increasing their loan basis, they can use that extra basis to deduct additional pass-through losses against their other personal income, even when their equity basis is zero. That results in a current decrease in taxable personal income and the resultant income tax due. In turn, that tax deduction decreases the shareholder's loan basis. It doesn't impact the actual loan. That liability remains fixed; the transaction impacts only the shareholder's basis in the loan. That is where a potential tax snafu enters the picture, where loan repayment can instigate a taxable event.

When a shareholder uses his debt basis to absorb pass-through losses in excess of his equity basis, loan repayments may trigger additional income taxes. Those taxes may be at the favored taxable gains rate, or they may be calculated using the usually higher standard income-tax rates. Which rates apply depends on the characterization of the loan (as described below). Fortunately, this entire tax trap can be avoided with some careful tax planning.

The Basic Loan-Basis Math

Debt basis starts with the full amount of the loan the shareholder has made to the corporation. From there, it gets increased by any additional loans and unpaid but accrued interest. It gets decreased by loan payments and pass-through losses deducted against personal income. When debt basis is less than the actual amount of debt (due to loss deductions), it can be restored with corporate income.

Consider the following example. Joe Smith is a one-half owner of ABC, Inc., an S corporation. Right now, the company is sustaining some losses and facing cash flow problems. Joe lends the company $10,000, at 4 percent annual interest. Previous losses have reduced Joe's equity basis to zero. This year's total corporate loss came to $6,000, and Joe's share of that is $3,000. Since the company does not have enough money to make loan payments, this year's interest ($400) gets added on to the loan basis, bringing it to $10,400. Joe deducts the full $3,000 of corporate losses from his other income. That reduces his loan basis by the $3,000, for a new year-end basis of $7,400.

The next year, the corporation starts showing a profit, but it still has some cash flow troubles. Joe's share of the profits comes to $2,100, increasing his loan basis to $9,500. Another $400 of unpaid interest accrues, bringing the basis up to $9,900. To restore his loan basis and supply the company with a little extra cash, Joe lends ABC, Inc., an additional $900. Now his loan basis equals the loan balance, $10,800.

The Tax Trap

Cash and a lack of profits often go hand-in-hand for new businesses. In those lean times, shareholders lend their own cash to the corporation and deduct pass-through losses on their income tax returns. That's fine, until things turn around and the corporation is finally able to begin repaying the loan. When payments are made in excess of the shareholders basis, they are considered income and may be taxable.

To figure out the taxable portion, you have to do a little math. The IRS sets up the equation like this: divide the reduction in basis by the face value of the loan, and multiply that result by the payment amount. Suppose that you loaned your S corporation $10,000, and you now have loan basis of just $4,000. The corporation makes a loan payment of $1,000. The taxable portion of the loan would come to $600. Here's how you get to that number:

$$\frac{\text{loan value} - \text{loan basis}}{\text{loan value}} \quad \text{X} \quad \text{payment} \quad = \quad \text{taxable portion}$$

$$\frac{\$10{,}000 - \$4{,}000}{\$10{,}000} \quad \text{X} \quad \$1{,}000 \quad = \quad \$600$$

That's part one of the tax trap. Part two involves the kind of tax (and rate) you'll have to pay on that $600 income. The choices are capital gains tax or regular income tax. Most of the time, capital gains tax rates are lower and therefore preferred. To qualify for the capital gains tax rate, there must be a formal note documenting the loan. Without an official note, the loan is classified as an "open account," and ordinary income tax rates apply.

How to Avoid the Tax Trap

The simplest way to avoid this tax trap is to not lend money to your corporation. Rather, when your corporation needs a cash infusion, make a capital contribution. This simple fix works well for corporations with a single shareholder, but it needs some extra attention in a businesses with multiple owners to make sure equity proportions don't get out of whack. Also, in the case of existing shareholder loans, the problem must be remedied before the new strategy can be started.

These shareholder loans and their basis issues usually come into the picture when the corporation is struggling. When business picks up, the corporation begins realizing profits which go first toward restoring loan basis (as long as they aren't paid out as dividends). As profitability improves, those partially taxable payments become feasible, but not mandatory. One way to avoid the tax trap now is to simply hold off on loan repayments until corporate income restores loan basis. Any cash you need to get out of the corporation can be taken as a dividend distribution or as a salary increase, rather than as a loan payment. That works because regulations give you another little break here. Concurrent earnings and earnings distributions (a.k.a. dividends) allow for the distribution to be tax-free, though the earnings are taxable as always.

For corporations with more than one shareholder, extra capital contributions can be made that don't upset the balance of power. There are two ways to accomplish this. You can all make equal contributions in exchange for additional shares (an equal number of shares, of course). Or you can make contributions without issuing any new shares, funneling proceeds right into the additional paid-in-capital account. That can increase one shareholder's equity basis without increasing his voting power.

TEST DRIVE

Can you and your corporation benefit from choosing S-corporation status? If you can answer yes to any of these questions, consider electing S status for your corporation.

1. Do you expect the corporation to incur significant losses during its first few years of operation?
2. Do you have a good deal of other income against which those losses could be offset?
3. Is your personal income tax rate lower than the corporate income tax rate?
4. Do you have plans to offer shares to the general public?
5. Do you have another source of employee benefits, meaning you don't need them from your own corporation?
6. Does your company earn the lion's share of its income from non-passive sources?

PART **5**

Taxes, Taxes, Taxes

Flat Tax for Personal-Service Corporations

Tax rules are often complicated, but that's not the case when it comes to personal-service or professional corporations. These specialized entities are subject to a simple flat tax rate on all of their corporate taxable income. That rate is currently 35 percent (and has been for quite awhile), and no other tax brackets apply.

This one-size-fits-all rate impacts only corporations whose primary business activities are the performance of specific personal services and in which virtually all of the stock is held by the corporate employees who perform these services. The following professionals typically belong under this umbrella:

- Attorneys
- Architects
- Accountants
- Engineers
- Actuaries
- Physicians
- Other health professionals
- Consultants

The main reason these personal-service companies incorporate is to protect their owners from personal liability claims. Those claims may be related to the normal business dealings of the corporation, or they may arise from malpractice committed by co-owners. (In most cases, no business entity will protect a professional from liability arising from his own malpractice.) Under state law, these corporations may need to purchase malpractice insurance in prescribed amounts and maintain those policies for the life of the corporation or risk dissolving the entity.

In addition to pricey malpractice policies, owners of these corporations typically pay themselves hefty salaries and take full advantage of all the fringe benefits corporations have to offer. After all of those payouts, there isn't usually much income leftover in most personal-service corporations to be taxed at that 35 percent flat rate.

Federal Corporate Tax Penalties

The IRS charges penalties to all kinds of businesses for all kinds of things. Your corporation is subject to those penalties and more. Corporations have their own special penalties section of the Internal Revenue Code. When you're aware of the penalties and how they're imposed, you can work with your accountant to make sure your corporation avoids being charged.

Some of these penalty taxes revolve around excess (at least according to the IRS) retained earnings. The point of the penalties is to make it very unattractive for corporations to hold on to their accumulated earnings and much more attractive to distribute dividends to shareholders. The IRS also leans harder on corporations that earn income passively, like through investments, rather than productively. Even when your corporation will earn a lot of passive income, and even when you want to leave as much profit inside the company as possible, your tax advisor can help you structure things to avoid being hit with these tax penalties.

The Accumulated Earnings Tax

When regular corporations hold excessive retained earnings, rather than distributing those earnings as dividends to shareholders, they may be subject to the federal accumulated earnings tax. This rule is in place to limit the avoidance of double taxation by corporation owners, essentially forcing them to distribute earnings or pay the piper anyway.

Your corporation is allowed to retain what the IRS deems a "reasonable" amount of earnings inside the business for bona fide business purposes. They allow professional-service businesses to hold a $150,000 retained-earnings cushion. Most other corporations can hold up to $250,000, no questions asked. When the cushion grows bigger than that, your corporation may be asked to justify the excess accumulated earnings. Proof usually entails a specific, detailed plan for the use of those retained earnings; common reasons include expansion plans, property purchase plans, and debt retirement plans. Basically, you have to show that you didn't have the corporation hold on to the earnings just to avoid paying extra personal-income taxes.

The accumulated earnings tax used to be pretty high, approaching 40 percent. Now, thanks to the JGTRRA, it's been knocked down to 15 percent. It's no coincidence that 15 percent is the new maximum tax rate on dividends (also a provision of JGTRRA). The total tax bill will be the same whether you keep the retained earnings in or pay the dividends out.

The Personal Holding Company Penalty

Under IRS guidelines, some small corporations may be reclassified as personal holding companies, making them subject to a 15 percent extra tax on their income. Corporations that fit into this category have five or fewer shareholders, who together own at least half of all the outstanding stock. In addition, the corporation earns at least 60 percent of its gross income from passive sources (like investments) and personal-service contracts. The complete set of rules can get pretty intricate, so if you think they may apply to your corporation, get your professional tax advisor involved.

The definition of personal-service contracts is specific. They are generally defined as contracts for the performance of personal services by a named person. Your corporate tax advisor can help you draw up contracts in such a way as to avoid having them classified as personal-service contracts under the federal definition.

➤➤ **If your corporation does get classified as a personal holding company by the IRS, it can still avoid the tax hit by paying out dividends to the shareholders.** Of course, that just switches the tax burden to the shareholders instead of the corporation. In some cases, though, shareholders may pay a rate lower than 15 percent (the new normal dividend tax rate) on their dividend income, making this transfer a better deal.

The S-Corporation Penalty Tax

S corporations don't pay any income taxes on their income. That's the general rule, but there is a gaping exception (of course). The exception applies to S corporations that earn more than 25 percent of their gross revenues from net passive-investment income and have accumulated earnings inside the corporation at the end of the tax year.

Passive-investment income includes things like these:

- ➲ Dividends
- ➲ Interest
- ➲ Royalties
- ➲ Rents
- ➲ Gains on securities sales
- ➲ Proceeds from annuities

To get to net passive-investment income, deduct all the expenses incurred to earn that income. Such expenses might include trading fees, account management fees, and broker commissions.

If your S corporation falls into this category, it will be subject to tax on that excess net passive-investment income (the part that's in excess of 25 percent of the gross receipts). The tax rate charged is the highest corporate tax rate, which is 39 percent right now. That tax is paid by the corporation and does not pass through to the shareholders.

Be careful with this. If this tax applies for three years in a row, your S-corporation election will be automatically terminated. If you think this possibility is likely, consult your business advisor about changing the business entity before it gets changed for you.

Tax Effects When Converting to a Corporation

Many small businesses follow a common order of progression. They start out as either sole proprietorships or partnerships (depending on the number of owners) and incorporate once their companies seem secure. That transformation comes with its own set of tax issues.

The mechanics of incorporating an existing business go something like this. The old company transfers all of its assets and liabilities into the newly formed corporation in exchange for shares of stock. Those shares are divided up among the owners of the old company in their original ownership proportions. For example, if the old company had four equal owners, each would receive one-fourth (25 percent) of the new corporation's stock.

Under the normal federal income tax rules, transferring assets in exchange for something of value (corporate shares, in this case) triggers a taxable event. When you sell an asset at a gain, you pay taxes on that gain. That gain, or profit, equals the excess of what you sold the asset for over your tax basis in the asset. (Tax basis equals the original purchase price, minus any depreciation, plus whatever you paid for improvements to the asset.)

If you'd rather avoid paying those taxes now—and most business owners would—you can elect Section 351 treatment instead. Under this IRC provision, the taxes that would have been due on the gain can be deferred until you actually sell off the shares you received. It's not that you'll never have to pay taxes on this transaction; instead, you get to postpone them until a later date.

The basic rules for Section 351 are discussed here, but the intricacies are complex. Every situation is different, and not all companies qualify for this treatment. In addition, there are circumstances under which tax deferral under Section 351 are not desirable. Sit down with your tax advisor before you incorporate your existing business, and the two of you can come up with the best strategy for your unique financial situation.

How to Qualify for Section 351 Treatment

In order to reap the benefits of this handy tax provision, certain requirements must be met. First, property must be transferred to the corporation, and the definition of property here is pretty broad. The transferred property can include cash, personal property, real estate, and intangible assets (like copyrights). Plus, the property doesn't have to come only from the business that you've incorporated. New shareholders—that is, people who were not involved in the original business—can contribute property as well and still qualify. What will not qualify is issuing shares in exchange for services to be performed on behalf of the corporation, and neither will debt forgiveness (such as if the old company owed you $10,000 but you accept shares as payment).

Second, the original business owners have to hold at least 80 percent of the voting stock after the transfer is complete. That means you and your business partners have to own a combined 80 percent of all the voting power when the deal is done.

The third rule is similar but much less common. The transferers have to own at least 80 percent of all other classes of stock issued. You don't have to turn away new investors to enjoy this tax deferral; you just have to limit their ownership to 20 percent or less of the business.

Qualification Snafus

Throughout the U.S. tax code, there are millions of tiny technical details, hard to decipher and easy to overlook. Section 351 is no different. With all the possibilities and all the situations that can crop up as you incorporate an existing business, it can be a little hard to tell at first whether your transfer qualifies. This section covers the two most common situations small-business owners face. Again, this portion of tax law is particularly complicated, so talk with a qualified tax professional.

Some exchanges come with a mixed bag of compensation, like a combination of property and services. Services as payment for shares usually prohibits Section 351 treatment. However, when you exchange those services in conjunction with property, you can still take advantage of the tax deferral benefit. There is one major caveat, though. The value of the property can't be nominal compared to the value of the services. In other words, you can't get around the exclusion by contributing $100 cash and $30,000 of services.

Another common snag crops up when the corporation gets stuck with more liabilities than the value of the transferred assets. It is irrelevant whether those liabilities are merely regular outstanding business debts or come attached to a piece of property, like a mortgage. Depending on the circumstances, the transfer may not be fully eligible for Section 351 tax treatment. Generally, the excess of liabilities over assets will be taxable, even though the balance may receive tax-deferred treatment.

State Tax Issues

With fifty states in the union, there are fifty different sets of tax laws. Every state's rates and rules and forms are different. To learn the specifics of the regulations impacting your corporation, check with the state taxing authorities for every state in which your corporation operates. Even with all of the differences, though, there is a lot of common ground.

Most states (Nevada and South Dakota are two exceptions) charge corporate income taxes on C corporations, and some even charge tax on S corporations, too. Most states also impose sales tax, and most states have personal income-tax laws on the books (which affects your corporation's payroll). In one way or another, your corporation will very likely have to make some sort of regular remittance to every state in which it conducts business.

States that do impose corporate income or franchise taxes base the tax due on income earned in that state. Those taxes are on top of any federal income taxes due, and they are usually deductible on the corporation's federal income-tax return. Speaking of which, most states follow the same general rules for determining taxable income as the federal government; they just apply different tax rates.

State payroll tax issues usually cover two separate areas: state withholding tax and state unemployment tax. The withholding tax is similar in nature to federal withholding tax, where the corporation deducts state income tax from each employee's paycheck and then remits that tax to the state on his behalf. State unemployment tax, on the other hand, is strictly an employer expense. This tax ranges widely and is generally based on a company's unemployment claims experience. If your corporation has a lot of ex-employees who have made unemployment claims, its state unemployment tax rate will be higher than a company that has few or no claims against it.

Sales tax regulations also vary widely among the states. ▶▶ **Most states do charge sales tax on goods sold to consumers.** Your customers pay the tax as part of the total price of whatever they're buying. Your corporation simply collects that tax and periodically remits it to the state. It's not an additional expense for your corporation, though there may be expenses involved in the reporting process.

Employee-Based Taxes

As soon as your corporation has one employee, even if it's only you, it enters the wonderful world of payroll taxes. Payroll taxes take two basic forms: those the company withholds from paychecks on behalf of its employees, and those the company pays for its employees. The corporation is responsible for filing all payroll tax returns (which can get into the double digits in a single year) and remitting all tax payments.

The basic payroll taxes include the following:

1. Federal income tax
2. State income tax
3. Local income tax
4. Federal unemployment tax
5. State unemployment tax
6. State disability insurance
7. Social security
8. Medicare

The first three are strictly withholding taxes. The corporation holds back a portion of the employee's paycheck as a courtesy and remits the taxes to the appropriate government authority on his behalf. Numbers four and five are paid by the employer as an added payroll expense. Number six, state disability insurance, is charged only in some states. Of those, some require employee withholding, and for others it's just another employer expense. Social Security and Medicare (together known as FICA) hit both sides of the fence. Both are withheld from employee paychecks, with a dollar-for-dollar employer match charged as well.

The Forms

For federal payroll tax purposes, there are several forms you'll become very familiar with. (State forms vary greatly; check with your state tax authority to learn what's required there.) The very first you'll come in contact with is the W-4, which all employees must complete, you included. This form dictates how much federal income tax will be withheld from an employee's paycheck, meaning you can't properly prepare payroll without this information.

Once withholding has begun, your corporation has to make periodic tax deposits and file payroll tax returns. Federal withholding tax and FICA get reported on the same return, IRS Form 941. On this return, you'll report total gross payroll for the specified period, along with total taxes withheld from employee paychecks and the matching portion of FICA. Typically, payroll tax deposits are made monthly and returns filed quarterly, so there may be no payment needed with the return.

Federal unemployment tax (FUT) gets its own return, IRS Form 940. This form is filed annually, though tax deposits are usually made quarterly. If your corporation is required to pay state unemployment taxes as well, that amount can be used as a credit against your FUT responsibility, reducing that federal payment.

At the end of the year, in addition to the payroll tax returns, your corporation must also send out a Form W-2 to each employee. (If you've ever been an employee, you've gotten a W-2 at the end of the year.) These forms let the employee know how much he earned during the year and how much he's paid in payroll taxes. The IRS gets a copy of each W-2 sent out, along with a Form W-3, which is a summary of all the W-2s.

Hire Someone to Do Payroll

Most accounting software packages include basic payroll modules, though you may have to pay a little extra for them. They claim to make payroll a snap. In a way, that's true. The software can make tracking employee hours, sick days, and the like much easier. As for actually doing the payroll yourself, even with this software, don't.

Payroll tax rates and tables change a lot, requiring frequent updates. If you forget to do an update, your payroll taxes may be calculated incorrectly, and that can lead to penalties. In addition, there are lots of different forms and lots of different due dates. It's hard to keep track of everything, especially at the same time you're trying to run your business. Skip a payment, file late, and you're looking at more penalties.

Hire a payroll firm. There are hundreds of them, many of which specialize in small businesses, and most of which charge very reasonable prices for the services they provide. All you have to do is call in the hours

Don't Mess Around with Payroll Taxes

John Knox and Cory Franks owned a sports gear shop. The two pals worked around the clock to make their corporation a success. John was the numbers guy, taking on administrative tasks; Cory was the salesman, schmoozing customers and closing sales. For years, it was just the two of them, and then the business began to take off. They hired two employees to work in the shop and began to increase inventory levels.

John was handling the payroll, from writing paychecks (including his and Cory's) to making tax payments—or so Cory believed. The inventory expansion, coupled with new employees, had put the corporation in a cash crunch. John paid the employees first, to keep them coming in to work. Suppliers came next, or they'd stop bringing merchandise. He and Cory had to be paid, because they had bills of their own. After the other regular bills got paid, there wasn't anything left over; so John let the payroll taxes slide.

After a couple of months, the corporation started getting a lot of mail from the IRS. There were penalties for failure to file the returns, for failure to pay the employment taxes, for withholding but failing to deposit the employees' payroll taxes. That last penalty can be huge, up to 100 percent of the tax originally due. When John didn't act upon these notices (since there wasn't enough cash), he and Cory began getting notices at home. What John hadn't known was that small-business owners who work in any management capacity may be held personally liable for unpaid payroll taxes and the penalties that go along with them, regardless of the business entity.

The corporation ended up filing for bankruptcy. John and Cory paid the balance to the IRS out of their own pockets, dissolving the corporation and their friendship.

(for hourly employees) at the end of the pay period—a task that takes about fifteen minutes of your time, compared to the hours it takes to prepare the payroll. These firms prepare the paychecks, the tax deposits, and the payroll tax returns, and they deal with all the extra year-end paperwork. Nothing gets overlooked, and nothing gets filed late—if it does, the firm often pays that penalty. The benefits your corporation will receive from farming out the payroll will be well worth the fully deductible cost.

Sales Taxes

If you've ever bought a product or eaten in a restaurant, you have probably paid sales taxes. Corporations are in the same boat. When they buy items that are subject to sales taxes, whether products or services, they pay the sales tax. However, corporations are businesses, existing to sell something to someone, and in that role, corporations may have to collect and remit sales taxes as well.

Sales taxes are strictly a state gig (so far . . . stay tuned). The system is supposed to work by having companies collect sales tax on behalf of the state, then periodically (usually quarterly) remitting everything they've collected. In instances in which sales tax is not collected, as when the seller ships something out of state (to a state in which he has no operations), the onus may fall on the buyer to report and pay the buyer's side of sales tax. This is called use tax (something that doesn't actually happen very often).

Who Doesn't Have to Collect Sales Tax?

Sales taxes are meant to be collected from the end-user of a product or service, also known as the consumer. If your corporation sells directly to those end-users, whether they're individuals or businesses, it has to collect and remit sales tax. However, if your corporation sells to middlemen or is the middleman, it probably won't have to deal with sales-tax collection at all. When your corporation sells its goods to a reseller, like a manufacturer to a wholesaler, it's out of the sales tax loop.

In addition, many states have exclusions, even for sales to end-users. For example, many states do not impose sales taxes on things like personal services or groceries.

As far as your corporation's responsibilities go, the first thing to do is to contact the state office that regulates sales tax. They'll help you figure out whether or not your corporation needs to collect sales tax. If it does, they'll direct you to fill out an application for a sales tax certificate and give you an ID number. They'll also tell you how much sales tax your corporation needs to collect and when to make remittance payments. At those times, a sales tax return will be submitted—the form numbers and design vary by state—along with a check for the sales tax due. These forms are pretty easy to follow. First, there's the basic identifying information (corporation name, address, sales tax ID number). Next, you report the total taxable sales for the period, multiply that by the sales tax percentage, and come up with the amount for the check. Sign the bottom, stuff it all in the pre-printed envelope, and get it postmarked by the due date.

The internal mechanics work like this. Your Corporation sells a kite to Buyer A, for $10 plus 5-percent sales tax, for a total of $10.50. The bookkeeper records that transaction as a $10.50 debit to cash, a $10.00 credit to sales, and a $0.50 credit to sales tax payable (a liability account). At the end of the quarter, the sales tax return is filled out, and a check is written out for the remittance amount. Then the bookkeeper records that transaction. Here, it would be a $0.50 debit to sales tax payable (as the liability has been satisfied) and a $0.50 credit to cash. (Need help with the accounting talk? See Chapter 18.)

Special Rules for When You Sell Your Shares

When the time comes for you to sell your shares of the corporation's stock, a number of tax issues will come into play. You may have sold stock before, the kind you've invested in and sold through your broker. That was simple. He sent you a form 1099-B at the end of the year, and you (or your accountant) plugged in some numbers on Schedule D of your Form 1040. This is a whole different ball game. Now you're not just selling off some shares from your portfolio, you're selling your business, and different tax rules may apply. As with all things that involve taxes and your corporation, talk with your accountant about what to expect and how to minimize any tax impact of the sale.

When you sell those shares, whether you're selling the entire company or selling your shares of the company to the remaining owners, one of two things can happen. You can make money on the deal, or lose money on the deal. The tax treatment is dependent on which way things go. When the deal goes south, and losses are sustained, Section 1244 tax treatment kicks in (the section number is just an IRS tax code reference).

With profitable circumstances, there are taxes to pay, and you (as a small-business owner) may benefit from special treatment under Section 1202.

Softening the Blow of Losses

Selling your shares for a loss (meaning less than you paid for them) is unpleasant. Section 1244 of the Internal Revenue Code softens that blow, at least a little bit, by granting you special tax breaks. The rule gets pretty technical, but the idea behind it is simple. You can treat up to $50,000 of the loss (or $100,000 for spouses filing a joint income tax return) as an ordinary loss rather than a capital loss.

When you sustain capital losses, as when regular investment securities get sold for less than you paid, you can apply up to $3,000 of those losses against regular (as opposed to capital gains) income in any one tax year. Here, the IRS is letting you offset $50,000 (or $100,000) of the capital loss you suffered from selling your business shares against the rest of your income, all at once.

As you might expect by now, you have to meet a list of IRS requirements to qualify for this amazing tax benefit:

1. You have to be the original owner of the shares in question.
2. You have to have paid for those shares with either money or property (but not corporate securities).
3. The corporation must have earned more than half of its revenues over the past five years from something other than passive investments.
4. The corporation cannot have received more than $1 million (in cash or property) in exchange for its shares.
5. When the loss occurs, you have to notify the IRS that you are electing to treat it as an ordinary loss per Section 1244.

Your accountant can help you determine whether or not you qualify for Section 1244 tax treatment. She can also help draft the statement for the IRS that notifies the agency of your intention to invoke Section 1244 (as there is no special form for this).

Keeping More of Your Gains

The tax code also helps you on the winning side of the field. When you sell the stock of a qualified small business, you get a break on the capital gains taxes due, thanks to Section 1202 of the Internal Revenue Code. Under this nifty provision, you may be able to exclude half of the gain on your stock sale, up to $10 million, from taxation. The price for this benefit isn't too steep, either. The taxable portion of your gain gets hit with the 28-percent capital gains tax rate, rather than the standard 15 percent, but you'll still come out ahead.

Once again, there are requirements to meet to qualify for this special tax treatment (though some exceptions and loopholes may apply—talk to your CPA):

1. You must have held the shares for at least five years.
2. The shares have to have been bought in exchange for money or property or received as part of employee compensation.
3. Back when the shares were issued to you, the corporation cannot have had more than $50 million of gross assets.
4. The business of the corporation can't be passive investment, professional services, or farming (or some other, much less common enterprises).

The sales transaction gets reported as part of your regular federal income tax return. Your tax advisor can help you fill out the forms properly to ensure you get this tax break.

 **TEST DRIVE**

Are you aware of all the tax filing requirements your corporation faces? No matter what kind of business you run or which form of corporation you have, there will be several taxes that come into play. Be aware of which apply to your corporation by considering these questions:

Sales tax: Does your corporation sell products to consumers? (Hint: customers who will resell the products don't count.)

Payroll taxes: Does your corporation have employees? (Hint: the answer to this one is always yes.)

Quarterly estimates: Must your corporation make quarterly estimated income tax payments? (Hint: this depends on which kind of corporation you have.)

PART **5**

Taxes, Taxes, Taxes

Why Set Up a Retirement Plan?

When it comes to building personal wealth, funneling money into a qualified retirement plan is one of the best things you can do. These plans allow you to sock away pre-tax cash, meaning you don't pay any income tax on the amount you contribute to your retirement plan at that time. On top of that, as your investment earns money, you get to skip the income tax payments on that as well, at least until you start taking the money out.

Pay a Professional Plan Administrator

Managing a retirement plan is hard; managing it properly, in accordance with myriad rules and restrictions, can make the most savvy entrepreneur bite his nails down to the quick. The downside of making a mistake here is huge. The plan loses its tax-advantaged status, and everyone—from the corporation to its employees—pays a price.

The tasks associated with perfect plan management are overwhelming. As plan manager, you must make sure all reports are filed accurately and on time, that you're making the best investment choices for all plan participants, and that you fully understand the intricacies of the plan. Unless this is your full-time job, it's virtually impossible to do. To keep the corporate retirement plan (and your retirement savings) intact, hire a pro.

So in one tidy package, you get to put away pre-tax income and defer the tax on those investment earnings—great benefits in and of themselves, but they do even more for you than is obvious at first glance. Because you don't have to deduct income taxes, your investment grows more quickly. For example, if you earn $100 and put that $100 into a retirement plan, you get to keep that whole $100. If your investment earns 5 percent in the first year, the entire $5 stays put. Then the next year's earnings are based on the full $105 investment. The same deal outside the shelter of a retirement plan starts with an immediate disadvantage. That $100 gets taxed at your current income tax rate, so you won't have a full $100 to invest. In turn, that reduces the earnings you'll receive, as 5 percent of less than $100 will never be as much as 5 percent of $100.

On top of the benefits you get from a retirement plan, providing one as a benefit may also help you attract better employees. In a very competitive hiring market, providing sought-after benefits (like retirement plans) can sway potential employees to accept your offer.

Choosing the Right Plan

Once you've decided to set up a retirement plan (and if you haven't decided that, re-read the previous section), the next step is choosing the type of plan that will be the most beneficial for your unique personal financial situation. Like business entities, you will not be locked into this choice forever, and you can make appropriate changes as your circumstances change. Here, you'll discover which factors are the most important when choosing your retirement plan now, as well as when it's time to consider transitioning to a different type of plan.

While there are several types of retirement plans to choose from, all fall under one of two large umbrellas: defined benefit or defined contribution. Defined benefit plans are much less common, as they are more difficult and expensive to administer; however, they do offer the biggest stash potential. Defined contribution plans are the norm for retirement plans. They're simple and cost-effective, but they come with lower maximum contribution caps.

Some of the most important factors you'll take into account when making this choice include the following:

- ➲ Your age
- ➲ How many employees you have
- ➲ Your existing retirement cash stash
- ➲ Your annual income

There are some other minor factors that may figure in, especially if you're struggling with two options. For example, administrative requirements and set-up fees vary greatly among the plan types. Also, some plans allow a great deal of contribution flexibility from year to year, while others simply do not. Finally, if it's down to the wire on being able to make any contribution at all for the current tax year, you may be limited in your choice for right now. In that case, you can set up whichever plan will let you put something away and switch to something more beneficial for the next year.

Meet ERISA

The ever-changing and always complex rules governing employee benefit plans fall under the federal Employment Retirement Income Security Act, commonly known as ERISA. This expansive act sets the guidelines for things like vesting rules, distributions, and reporting requirements. When a retirement plan falls under the ERISA umbrella, all employees must be allowed to participate, even if that wasn't what you wanted when the plan was initiated. For example, if your corporation implements a stock option plan for top employees, but the courts find that ERISA applies, your corporation could be forced to offer the stock option motivation plan to all employees.

Defined Contribution Plans

Defined contribution plans work by letting employees contribute specific amounts into a retirement fund, meaning you always know how much the current contribution will be. The big question mark surrounds how much cash there will be in the account when it's time to take money out (the benefits). The payouts are based partly on luck and can't be truly predicted ahead of time.

The factors that determine the eventual payout include the size of the contributions and when they start (both under your control) and the rate of return earned by the account (out of your control). The earlier you start, and the more you contribute, the better your chances of having a sizable nest egg at the end. There's no legal limit on how big that retirement account can grow, but there are limits on how much you can put into it in any given year.

Defined Benefit Plans

Defined benefit plans work in almost the exact opposite way of defined contribution plans. Here, the eventual payout is set in stone, and the contributions are adjusted constantly to hit that goal. As you might guess, this involves a lot of seriously complicated math and statistical analysis, which is why you need an actuary to come up with the annual contribution numbers. Some years, the contributions could be gigantic; other times may merit no current contribution at all.

How much you need to contribute in any given year depends on a bunch of factors, including these:

1. The current total account balance

2. How long you have left until retirement

3. How many years you'll spend in retirement (an actuarial statistic)

4. How much the account is expected to earn in the upcoming period, and

5. The target payouts themselves

Those factors come together to tell you the current desired account balance. When the actual balance is less, you have to deposit enough to bring it up to target; when it's more, you contribute nothing. That contribution question mark is the main reason most small companies stay away from defined benefit plans. Some years, the requirement can be so high as to be crippling, while other years, no contribution—and therefore no tax break—will be allowed.

Defining Your Goals

The first question to ask yourself when deciding which kind of retirement plan to choose is what you want to get out of it. Maybe you want to attract the very best employees to your brand-new corporation. Perhaps you want to take advantage of some very sweet tax breaks. Or maybe you just want an easy way to sock away a ton of cash for your retirement. Of course, it's possible (even likely) that all three of these goals apply, and it's your job to figure out which is the most important to you.

Some plans are easy to implement and maintain and inexpensive to set up; these plans are among the best choices when your primary aim is to make employees happy. Other plans let you put away lots of money now, with no taxes due now, to help you get a huge jump on your retirement nest egg. These plans serve the more personal goals, but can be more expensive and more complicated to create and administer. No one plan is perfect for all goals, and that's why clarifying your priorities is such an important part of this decision.

The Pension Benefit Guarantee Corporation

Only defined benefit plans are insured by the Pension Benefit Guarantee Corporation (PBGC), courtesy of the federal government. That's because employers offering this type of plan are legally obligated to ensure there's enough money inside the plan to pay out the guaranteed (that is, defined) benefits. However, in cases where the company doesn't meet that obligation, the PBGC steps in.

The purpose of the PBGC is to protect employees with a form of insurance. When your corporation's plan is covered, and the corporation goes belly up, the PBGC gets involved. They'll make benefit payments to employees to a pre-set maximum. Employees may not get their entire expected payments, but at least they get something.

When you want to put away the most money possible (for yourself), consider target benefit plans and profit-sharing plans. Should your primary goals be more along the lines of appealing to top-notch employees, look into one of the lower-cost alternatives, like a SEP, a 401(k), or a SIMPLE plan.

401(k) Plans

Companies with employees seem to offer 401(k) plans more than any other type of retirement plan. These retirement vehicles fall under the defined contribution umbrella, and employees are allowed to choose what portion of their paychecks to contribute to their 401(k) accounts. The most common version of the 401(k) is the thrift plan, where employees have a percentage of each paycheck withheld and put into a tax-advantaged investment account. The other, less common version is called a bonus plan. Here, employees may choose to have their year-end bonuses put into their 401(k) accounts rather than just getting the cash.

Whichever version of the 401(k) is used, both the employer and employees enjoy tax benefits. On the employee side (which includes you as an employee), all contributions are pre-tax, meaning they get deducted from your gross pay before income tax is assessed. Employer contributions aren't taxable to employees until they take the money out of the retirement plan. Plus, all of the earnings and growth experienced by the 401(k) account are tax-deferred. Again, there's no tax levied on any money while it remains in the account, only when it's removed. On the employer side, business tax deductions can be taken when the corporation contributes to the plan.

Speaking of contributions, there are legal maximums that control just how much anyone can put into his 401(k) account in a single year. For 2006, employees can put away up to $15,000; that includes you. Participants over age fifty are allowed to sock away an extra $5,000 (for 2006). Contribution limits are subject to change, and do so rather often.

Plan Requirements

As you consider setting up a 401(k) plan for your corporation's employees, consider the long list of rules you'll need to follow to hang on to the plan's tax advantages. It starts with some basic guidelines, like that the plan can only benefit employees or their beneficiaries, and that there has to be a written plan for employees to see.

Then the more detailed rules take shape, mainly to ensure that the plan is not discriminatory. All that really means is that it can't benefit highly compensated employees or owner-employees more than everybody else. Next, minimum vesting rules apply. Employees are considered fully vested when they own 100 percent of employer contributions made into their accounts. Here, employees must be fully vested after five years of employment. Also, employees must be allowed to participate by their first anniversary of working for the corporation.

Next come the reporting rules. Quite a bit of paperwork is involved with 401(k) plans. Reports must be filed periodically with different authorities, including the IRS, the Pension Benefit Guarantee Company (PBGC), and the

U.S. Department of Labor. Plus, to comply with ERISA, your corporation also has to provide periodic reports to plan participants and their beneficiaries.

Additional (and more complicated) rules may apply to your 401(k) plan, so have an experienced advisor help you with the set-up and maintenance. The corporation will pay a fee for this service, but that fee is money well spent, saving you a great deal of time and trouble to ensure the plan is run properly.

More Choices to Make

As you consider offering a 401(k) plan to your employees, you will have a few additional decisions to make regarding plan options. The first is whether or not the corporation will make matching contributions for participating employees. On the plus side, that matching benefits you as an employee. It also helps encourage other employees to join, and provides a deductible expense for the company. On the downside, it will put a big dent in your corporation's bottom line, as the match can get pretty expensive as more employees participate. It's not a controllable expense, either. Once you've decided on a matching percentage, you're stuck with it, regardless of how much or little employees contribute themselves. The more they put in, the more you'll have to match, though you are allowed to put a cap on the maximum match (like 5 percent of an employee's gross compensation).

Your second choice involves the investments. ▸▸ **All the funds in the 401(k) accounts have to be invested in something, even if it's just money market funds.** As the employer, you'll need to decide how much control the employees will have over their own accounts. You can give them a plan that allows a lot of investment options, but that can make the plan much more costly to administer. Narrowing down the options can save the corporation some money, but it narrows your investment options (as an employee) at the same time.

Third, you must decide whether or not employees will be able to borrow from their accounts. Allowing this option does encourage participation and allows you (as an employee) to borrow from your account as well. However, these loans are subject to very strict rules, including those regarding interest charged on the loan. Finally, letting employees borrow from their 401(k) accounts adds more administrative responsibilities to the plan administration, and that means higher costs for your corporation.

SIMPLE Plans

If your corporation has fewer than 100 employees, it's eligible for a SIMPLE (savings incentive match plan for employees) plan. While "simple" describes the administrative responsibilities, at least in comparison to other forms of retirement plans, it falls short as a modifier for the regulations surrounding the plan. Yes, this type of plan is cheaper and easier to deal with, but that big benefit comes at a big price: lower contribution caps than any other plan. Employees are limited to $10,000 contributions each year (as of 2006), though folks over age fifty can add $2,500 on to that.

In addition to the very low maximum contributions, employers don't have a lot of flexibility with these plans. When you offer a SIMPLE, it has to be the only plan offered. Employer matches are required, though you have some choice when it comes to how much you'll match. Plus, employees vest immediately, meaning once you make that contribution, the money is theirs for keeps.

The Basics

There are two ways in which your SIMPLE plan can be set up: with IRAs (individual retirement accounts) or 401(k) accounts. The differences between the two concern the required percentages of employer matches (as you'll see in the next section), how long employees have to wait to become eligible to participate, and which of the nondiscrimination rules your corporation may be exempt from.

With an IRA-based plan, the eligibility requirements are a little stiffer. Employees must have been paid at least $5,000 in each of the two preceding years and be reasonably expected to make that much (or more) again this year. Under the 401(k) plan option, employees can participate if they earned at least $5,000 last year and expect to earn at least that amount this year, also. The difference here allows your corporation to enforce stricter participation rules with the IRA form.

As for nondiscrimination rules, you get a better break with an IRA setup. Using a SIMPLE IRA plan allows your corporation to be exempt from all of the nondiscrimination and top-heavy (meaning in favor of the employees who earn the most) rules. With the 401(k) version of the plan, your corporation will only be exempt from special nondiscrimination rules and must comply with all the regular ones. This difference makes the IRA form easier to comply with and manage.

Both versions of the plan have the same reporting requirements, which are very simple. The only time an official report to the government is required is when the plan gets created. Employee reporting follows the same guidelines for other plans; the company has to keep them updated on account balances, investment performance, and the like.

Matching Contributions

Here's the big trade-off. In exchange for the simplicity of a SIMPLE plan, your corporation must make pre-set matching contributions. It doesn't matter if the company earned profits, nor does it matter if the company has cash. Employer contributions are required, period.

There is a little bit of flexibility in exactly how much the corporation contributes on behalf of each employee. Every year, the corporation either has to match the contribution of each participating employee, up to 3 percent of each employee's total gross annual income, or make a 2-percent-of-pay contribution for every eligible employee, even those who don't participate in the plan. Under the IRA version, the corporation gets an occasional, small break. In any two of five years, the corporation can choose to limit the across-the-board match to just 1 percent of each employee's total annual pay.

The SEP-IRA

SEP stands for "simplified employee pension," and retirement plans don't get much easier than this one. On top of its innate simplicity, SEPs are also extremely efficient (not terribly time-consuming for you) and relatively inexpensive to maintain. There are trade-offs, however. For example, these plans don't have nearly as much flexibility as other types when it comes to contributions, and that can spell trouble for struggling young companies.

Basically, a SEP-IRA is a collection of separate IRAs, just like the kind you can open for yourself. When the SEP is just for you, it gives you bigger benefits than a standard IRA without a lot of extra hassle. When you add employees into the mix, though, the simplicity dwindles a bit. The main reason for that is all eligible employees must participate; if even one doesn't, the plan may be dissolved.

When to Avoid a SEP

Though their low costs and light administrative burdens can make SEPs look extremely attractive to small-business owners, there are some cases in which they just don't make sense. First comes money. If your business earns a lot of profits, and you want to sock away the biggest pile possible, a SEP is not for you. This plan comes with a $44,000 absolute maximum limit, whereas some others will let you put away more toward your retirement nest egg.

Next up is employees. If you have seasonal or part-time employees, this is not the plan for you. You have to make contributions for every single eligible employee, even those who quit during the year, even if you don't know where they are. Plus, everyone has to participate or no one can.

Participation Rules

The guidelines for minimum eligibility requirements for a SEP are pretty generous—for the employees, that is. Everyone who meets these requirements is eligible:

- ➲ Twenty-one years of age (including those who reached this age during the year)
- ➲ Employees of your corporation during any three of the past five years
- ➲ Earning at least $450 this year (for 2006)

As long as an employee meets those requirements at any time during the year, he's an eligible employee for that year, and a contribution must be made on his behalf no matter what.

Consider this situation. John Flagmon has worked for you for three weeks every summer for the past two years. This year, he came back for one last three-week stint. By the end of that time, his total gross pay came to $600. In October, he turned twenty-one. Your corporation has to make a SEP contribution for John, along with everyone else who's eligible, no matter what comes next. If John moves to Europe, leaving no forwarding address, you still have to contribute. If, sadly, John dies, you still have to contribute.

The rules get even trickier. In order for the plan to qualify for its special tax treatment, every eligible employee has to participate—even if they don't want to. If an eligible employee doesn't set up an IRA, or closes his out, you have to establish one for him and notify him of that fact.

Vesting Rules

As soon as an employer contribution is made into an employee's SEP account, that cash is fully and immediately vested. That means it belongs to the employee, and you can't get it back. This rule is different than that of many other retirement plans, where employer contributions may vest according to a schedule. In those situations, when an employee leaves, the employer may be able to get some or all of those employer-made contributions back.

This is a bit of a drawback for a corporation with a lot of employee turnover. Since the participation rules weigh heavily in favor of the employees, without a big continuity requirement, your corporation could end up making irretrievable contributions for employees with no plans to stick around.

Profit-Sharing Plans

Profit-sharing plans can be a small employer's best friend. Their biggest advantage is the ability to not make contributions in a year when money is tight. Of course, that flexibility comes with a significant drawback. If your corporation skips making contributions in a lot of years, your account might come up short at retirement time.

Here's how profit-sharing plans work: each year, the corporation makes contributions based on a percentage of the profits earned. When there are no or little profits, the corporation can opt to make no contribution (or to make one anyway). So, each year, the contribution is defined— it's just that the definition for a particular year can be zero. When your corporation does start earning enviable profits, you can sock away up to 25 percent of compensation for every employee, not to exceed $44,000 for any one participant.

From the employee's perspective, these look very much like every other defined contribution retirement plan. That's especially true when the profit-sharing plan is set up like a 401(k) plan. In that form, employees make regular voluntary pre-tax contributions out of their salary, regardless of any employer match for the year.

Target Benefit Plans

A target benefit retirement plan combines the best features of a defined benefit plan with those of a defined contribution plan; that's why these are often called hybrid plans. These plans offer extra flexibility for business owners. You can structure this plan in a way that gives you better benefits than you could get with other plans.

Here's how they work. The employer (your corporation) sets a target benefit for employees. At the same time, each employee's pension is actually based on how much money is in his account. So the contribution follows the defined contribution pattern, and the target benefit is based on a formula, just like standard defined benefit plans. You can combine the mechanics of a target benefit plan with one of the different plan options, like profit sharing.

An Example with Numbers

The easiest way to get a good grasp on how target benefit plans can be better (especially for older business owners with younger employees) is to look at the numbers. In this example, George and Ringo each own 50 percent of Harrison-Starr Corp., and have for ten years. George (who's forty-eight) and Ringo (who's forty-seven) both take $50,000 a year in salary. They have two employees, John and Paul. John is twenty-seven years old, has been working for Harrison-Star Corp. for four years, and earns $30,000 a year. Paul is twenty-four, has been with the company for three years, and earns $25,000 per year. The corporation has a target benefit plan based on profit sharing.

If the corporation used a straight profit-sharing plan, each participant would get the same percentage of his salary, regardless of any other factors. With a profit-sharing rate of 10 percent, George and Ringo would each get $5,000; John would get $3,000; and Paul would get $2,500. That comes to a total of $15,500 paid out among all the employees, with George and John each getting about 32.3 percent of that pie.

Let's switch the view to add in the target benefit component. Now employee age and length of service play a part in the calculations; and that will put more of the pie on George's and John's plates. Based on actuarial computations, the new contributions fall out as follows: George gets $9,525, Ringo gets $9,475, John gets $1,180, and Paul gets $660. Now, both the overall contribution and George's and Ringo's relative shares are larger as well. Under this plan, the total pie is now $19,750; George's slice comes to 45.7 percent, and Ringo's to 45.5 percent.

A Definite Drawback

Though target benefit plans do offer some key advantages to the business owner, chiefly impressive flexibility, they do come with a distinct disadvantage: Benefits tend to get heavier as you go. Standard defined-benefit plans take expected salary increases into account as part of the mountain of numbers the actuaries work with, and that has the effect of spreading out those expected raises over the years, rather than in a big lump when they actually happen.

Under a target benefit plan, today's salary is the one the formulas taken into account, and that can lead to big contribution problems as you get older and make more money. Why does age matter? One of the key factors in calculating benefits and contributions is how long you have left until retirement. As you get closer to retirement age, you have less time left to fund your plan, and contributions tend to get bigger to catch you up. Combine that with a bigger salary on which benefits are based, and payments can get pretty steep toward the end.

Employee Stock Ownership Plans

Another great advantage to incorporating your business is the unique opportunity to offer a very special type of qualified retirement benefit plan, the ESOP (employee stock ownership plan). When you have employees and want to share ownership of the business with them (while you still retain control, of course), this is an excellent tax-advantaged way to do it.

▸▸ **An ESOP is pretty much like any other employee retirement plan, except that the biggest plan investment is in shares of your corporation.** With this plan, employees can buy shares through salary reductions or by paying cash for them. They get a piece of the pie, and your corporation gets more money. On top of that, the corporation can contribute to the ESOP by pouring cash or stock into the plan every year. Whatever the corporation contributes, it gets a tax deduction for that contribution, just as it would with any other retirement plan. But in effect—and here's the kicker—the corporation gets to keep the money, because the plan's major investment is in corporate shares.

With all of these advantages, though, come drawbacks. ESOPs are very complicated plans, and they absolutely require professional set-up and maintenance. Also, you've got to have employees to have an ESOP. When an employee leaves, he can opt to take his shares with him, rather than cashing out. That gives an ex-employee voting rights, which could cause trouble if the parting was not on good terms. In many cases, though, ESOPs foster employee loyalty and increase productivity; after all, now employees are working for themselves.

▸▸TEST DRIVE

If you're not sure which retirement plan best fits your situation, some basic criteria can help you make a decision. First, think hard about your primary purpose: getting a corporate tax break, saving for your own retirement, or attracting top-notch employees. Once you've prioritized your objectives, consider the relative ages of you and your employees, and how long their tenure is likely to be. Finally, be honest about how much your corporation can really afford, for both plan contributions and expenses. This combination of factors will help you narrow down the options and choose the best retirement plan for your business right now.

Appendixes

Appendix A
Glossary

Appendix B
State Business Development
Office Contact Information

accounting period

A defined block of time (such as a quarter or a year) for which financial statements are produced.

accrual basis accounting

A system of financial recordkeeping in which revenues are recorded as they are earned, and expenses are recorded as they are incurred, regardless of whether any money has actually changed hands.

alternative minimum tax (AMT)

A federal tax imposed on predetermined taxable income; tax preference items subject to inclusion in the income recalculation include accelerated depreciation and certain loss limitations, among other things.

angel investors

Business financiers who typically make relatively large investments in start-up companies while leaving managerial control in the hands of the business owners.

annual meeting of shareholders

A conference at which all (or effectively all) of the shareholders of a corporation debate and vote on corporate issues, including the election of members of the board of directors; most states require at least this annual meeting.

annual report

A document that furnishes state and federal governments with updated information about an existing corporation.

articles of incorporation

The formal documents that must be filed in the state where your corporation will be established, in accordance with the laws of that state.

asset

Anything of value owned by an individual or a business entity; assets may or may not take physical form. (See also intangible asset.)

assign

To give over a contractual right or obligation to another party. For example, if you sign a lease before your corporation is formed, you could later assign that lease over to the corporation.

at-risk rules

Special tax provisions that restrict the amount of tax-deductible loss for an S-corporation shareholder to the amount that he stands to personally lose. The amount considered at risk for a shareholder includes the combined value of cash and property contributed to the business plus any funds loaned to the corporation.

authorized shares

The total shares of stock that may be issued by a corporation, as determined by its founders and expressed explicitly in its articles of incorporation. For example, if a corporation authorizes 10,000 shares in its original formation papers, only 10,000 shares may be issued without a formal amendment to the articles of incorporation.

balance sheet

A financial statement which lays out the financial position of a company on a particular date. This report is broken into three distinct sections and includes the company's total assets, liabilities, and equity.

board of directors

The governing body of a corporation, as chosen by its shareholders. The board members (a.k.a. directors) each have a fiduciary responsibility to the corporation.

buy-sell provisions

Terms within a shareholders' agreement that dictate the allowable terms for the transfer of ownership interests in the corporation.

C corporation

A standard business corporation taxed under Subsection C of the Internal Revenue Code.

capital

Assets invested in a business in exchange for shares of ownership.

capital gain

The excess of the sales price of an income-producing asset over its current book value (a.k.a. adjusted basis).

capital structure

The makeup of a corporation's equity, comprised of various classes of stock, paid-in capital, and retained earnings.

cash basis accounting

A system of financial record keeping where transactions are recorded only when money changes hands, regardless of when the revenues were earned or expenses incurred.

cash flow

The movement of money into and out of a business.

certificate of authority

An official state document issued to a corporation not formed in that state (a foreign corporation) allowing it to transact business within that state.

charging order

A judgment by which an unpaid creditor is awarded the debtor's shares of a business.

close corporation

A special form of corporation, allowed by law in some states, that has the following attributes in exchange for relaxation of required corporate formalities: a small number of shareholders, active participation in the business by majority shareholders, and no public offering of the corporation's stock.

collateral

Assets pledged to lenders as a way to guarantee repayment of a loan should scheduled payments not be made.

common stock

The primary class of stock for every corporation, which gives shareholders the right to vote on corporate issues and receive a proportional share of dividends when they're declared.

corporate bylaws

A strictly internal document that contains the rules, regulations, and detailed operations of the corporation, generally including such items as rights and duties of both shareholders and board members. Bylaws are private documents, not subject to state filing.

corporate officers

A group of high-level employees, appointed by the board of directors, responsible for the day-to-day operations of the corporation. The four most common corporate officers are president, vice president, treasurer, and secretary. (In most states, one person can assume all officer roles.)

corporate record book

A binder or file that contains critical corporate documents, such as the articles of incorporation, the corporate bylaws, and all minutes of each meeting of the directors and of the shareholders.

corporate seal

A metal or rubber stamp of the corporate name and logo, used to authenticate corporate documents.

corporation

A distinct legal entity formed under state law; this entity can conduct business, enter into contracts, sue and be sued, and be held accountable under the law.

cost of sales

The total purchase price of inventory items that are resold to customers.

DBA

An acronym that stands for "doing business as," used when a corporation has both a legal name and a trade name (for example, Roger Princeton, Inc., DBA Princeton Art Supplies).

debt financing

Corporate funds obtained through borrowing (as with a bank loan) and which must be paid back, usually with interest.

depreciation

An accounting estimate of the natural decline in value of physical assets over time, measured for accounting or tax purposes.

dissolution

The official termination of the corporation's legal existence.

distributions

Transfers of cash and/or property from the corporation to a shareholder.

dividends

Distributions made to shareholders, on a per-share basis, out of the earnings of the corporation. These distributions can take the form of either cash or stock, and must be officially declared by the board before being distributed.

employee stock ownership plan (ESOP)

A mechanism by which employees receive shares of stock in the corporation they work for, giving them a vested interest in the success of the entity.

equity

The ownership interest in a business entity; contributed and earned capital, in the case of a corporation.

equity financing

Corporate funds raised by selling shares of stock (ownership) in the company.

estimated tax payments

Quarterly tax remittances made by taxpayers (including both C corporations and S-corporation shareholders) on any expected income not covered by withholding taxes.

expense

An expenditure made during the normal course of business, which usually serves as a deduction from income for tax purposes. Examples include salaries, telephone, and legal fees.

Federal employer identification number (EIN)

A federal tax registration number required of all corporations.

FICA

Social Security and Medicare taxes, a type of payroll tax.

fiduciary

An individual or entity entrusted with the assets of another party who has a legal duty to act in the best interests of that party.

financial statements

A set of accounting reports that details the financial position and results of operations for a business for a specific time period. The set typically includes a balance sheet, a statement of profit and loss, and a statement of cash flows.

fiscal year

Any twelve-month period designated by a business entity to be its annual accounting period.

foreign corporation

A corporation that conducts business in a state in which it was not originally formed; this requires filing for special corporate status in the not-home state.

Form 1120

The annual tax return that must be filed by C corporations for federal tax purposes.

Form 1120S

The annual informational tax return that must be filed by S corporations for federal tax purposes.

Form 1128

The federal form required when proposing a change in the corporation's tax year, called "Application to Adopt, Change, or Retain a Tax Year."

Form 8832

The IRS form on which a business entity can make a tax treatment election, such as a regular corporation applying for S-corporation status.

Form 940

The form on which federal unemployment tax obligations are reported by employers, usually filed annually.

Form 941

The form on which an employer reports federal income tax withholding, Social Security, and Medicare obligations, usually filed quarterly.

Form W-2

The form on which an employer reports annual wages and withholding taxes to each employee.

franchise tax

A state tax levied on corporations for the privilege of transacting business in that state. Different states charge the tax on different bases, but it is generally based on earnings, the value of outstanding stock, total assets, or total revenues.

fringe benefits

Non-cash compensation provided to owners and employees by the corporation in addition to regular salaries or other earned income; examples include health insurance and parking passes.

gross margin

A measure of profitability, calculated by deducting the cost of sales from total net sales.

incorporator

The person who prepares, files, and signs the articles of incorporation.

intangible asset

Property that has a monetary value but no physical form; examples include patents, copyrights, and trademarks.

inventory

The physical goods that a company holds for production (which could include raw materials and work in process) or for resale.

liability

Any legal obligation incurred by a business, usually involving a monetary debt. For accounting purposes, these debts are typically divided into long-term and short-term obligations.

limited liability

An advantage of corporations, by which personal losses are limited to investment in the business and personal assets are protected from claims by creditors of the corporation.

liquidating distribution

The assets given to a shareholder upon dissolution of a corporation.

LLC (limited liability company)

A business engaged in for profit by one or more individuals that provides limited liability protection for its owners (called members).

minutes

A written record of corporate events such as shareholder or directors meetings; these records are filed in the corporate records book.

net cash flow

The money remaining after all the cash disbursements for a defined time period are deducted from the cash receipts of the same period.

net profit

The excess of revenues over costs and expenses for a specified time period.

non-voting stock

Corporate shares that represent equity interests without the ability to affect changes in the corporation. These shares usually come with the right to receive dividends when declared.

no-par-value stock

Stock with no stated minimum value.

not-for-profit corporation

A special business form for entities that strive to use their earnings for charitable purposes.

operating expenses

Expenditures incurred as part of the normal course of business, unrelated to direct product costs. These expenditures may be categorized into general and administrative expenses and selling expenses.

paid-in capital

The excess over par value that is contributed to a corporation in exchange for shares.

par value

The stated minimum amount for which a share of stock may be issued and sold, as set forth in the articles of incorporation.

partnership

A business, legally owned by two or more individuals, that has not been incorporated or organized as an LLC.

passive-activity loss limitations

Rules under the IRC that disallow losses from passive activities to be offset against other types of income when determining tax liability.

passive owner

One who does not actively participate in the business of the S corporation

pass-through taxation

A situation in which an S corporation pays no taxes on its own income but instead passes all items of income, deduction, gain, loss, and credit directly through to its shareholders for reporting on their personal tax returns.

phantom income

A situation unique to pass-through tax entities that occurs when a shareholder has a tax liability for business income earned when he has not received any distributions of that income.

piercing the veil

A phenomenon that occurs when corporate shareholders are sued for corporate debts, and the courts find that the corporate entity is nonexistent for personal financial protection purposes.

preferred stock

A class of stock that generally grants its shareholders preferential payment of dividends but no voting rights; preferred stock must be authorized in the articles of incorporation.

private offering

A sale of corporate shares to individuals outside the circle of shareholder-employees, but limited to investors who either know corporate insiders or are considered sophisticated investors under securities law.

professional corporation

A business incorporated for the purpose of engaging in a licensed or learned profession, such as accounting or law; all shareholders must hold valid current licenses in that profession.

proxy

An authorization to vote on behalf of a shareholder.

quorum

The minimum number of individuals required to attend a meeting so that business may be conducted; may be measured as simple majorities or stated percentages.

registered agent

A person designated by a corporation to receive service of process and other official documents.

registered office

The business location, stated in the articles of incorporation, where the registered agent can be reached. This office need not be the principal place of business of the corporation.

resolution

A formal decision made for the corporation by either the shareholders or the board of directors; resolutions are filed in the corporate record book.

retained earnings

Profits that are kept inside the corporation to be used for future projects, rather than distributed as dividends to its shareholders.

S corporation

A corporation that elects special tax status under Subchapter S of the Internal Revenue Code. These entities pay no income tax on their earnings, instead passing those earnings through to their shareholders for inclusion on their personal tax returns.

SBA (Small Business Administration)

A federal agency that guarantees bank loans made to qualified small businesses.

Schedule E

The form on which a shareholder's portion of the ordinary income of the S corporation is reported for federal tax purposes; this schedule is included as part of the shareholder's annual individual tax return.

Schedule K-1

The form prepared by an S corporation for each shareholder to report that shareholder's proportional share of income, deductions, gains, losses, and credits; the S corporation also files a copy of this schedule with the IRS.

secured loans

Formal debt obligations obtained by pledging specifically named collateral, which may be seized or sold by the lender should the debtor fall behind in the repayment schedule.

Securities Exchange Commission

The federal agency charged with overseeing securities sales and publicly held corporations.

security

A financial instrument, such as a stock, bond, or mutual fund share.

share

A unit of ownership of a corporation.

shareholder

An individual or entity who owns shares of stock in a corporation.

shareholders' agreement

A written contract entered into by all shareholders of a corporation that will govern their conduct in relation to the corporation.

sole proprietorship

A business, owned by one person, that is not incorporated or organized as an LLC.

statement of cash flows

A financial report detailing the movement of cash into and out of a company for a specified period of time.

statement of profit and loss

A financial report that summarizes the results of operations of a business for a specified period of time.

stock

The capital of a corporation, measured in shares, with each share representing a unit of ownership of the company.

stock certificate

A formal printed document that represents ownership of shares of a corporation.

stock transfer book

A listing of all owners of shares of stock of a corporation.

title

A legal document representing ownership of a particular physical asset, such as a vehicle.

trademark

A distinctive symbol (words or pictures) used to identify a particular business and set it apart from others in the marketplace.

treasury stock

Shares of previously outstanding stock in a corporation that have been repurchased by that corporation.

unsecured loans

Debt obligations not guaranteed by any specific collateral.

voting rights

The decision-making powers granted to a corporate shareholder as set forth in the corporate by-laws or shareholders' agreement, typically based on the number of shares of stock he owns.

working capital

Funds available to cover the ongoing operating expenses of a company

Appendixes

This section lists the appropriate office for you to contact in order to receive information about the requirements to form your business entity. Many of the Web sites include fill-in forms for everything from articles of incorporation to applications for state sales tax ID numbers. All fees listed are for registration/incorporation of domestic for-profit organizations only. There may be additional fees for foreign corporations or other services or documents.

Alabama

Secretary of State
11 S. Union Street
State House, Room 207
Montgomery, AL 36103

Mailing address:
P.O. Box 5616
Montgomery, AL 36103-5616
Phone: 334-242-5324
Fax: 334-240-3138
www.sos.state.al.us
Filing Fee: $40

Alaska

Corporations Supervisor
333 W. Willoughby Avenue
9th Floor
Juneau, AK 99811

Mailing address:
P.O. Box 110808
Juneau, AK 99811-0808
Phone: 907-465-2530
Fax: 907-465-3257
E-mail: *corporations@commerce.state.ak.us*
www.dced.state.ak.us
Filing Fee: $250

Arizona

Secretary of State
Corporation Commission
1300 W. Washington
Phoenix, AZ 85007
or
400 W. Congress
Suite 221
Tucson, AZ 85701
Phone: 602-542-3135
Fax: 602-542-4990
www.cc.state.az.us
Filing Fee: $60

Arkansas

Corporation Commission
Suite 310
Building Services Building
501 Woodlane
Little Rock, AR 72201
or
State Capitol
Room 256
Little Rock, AR 72201
Phone: 501-682-3409
www.sosweb.state.ar.us
Filing Fee: $100

California

Secretary of State
1500 11th Street
Sacramento, CA 95814
Phone: 916-657-5448
www.ss.ca.gov
Filing Fee: $100
NOTE: Add your business type and
the word "unit" to reach the correct
office (for example, Corporate Unit).

Colorado

Secretary of State
1700 Broadway, Suite 200
Denver, CO 80209
Phone: 303-894-2200, press 2
Fax: 303-869-4864
www.sos.state.co.us
Filing Fee: $25 online, $125 if on paper

Connecticut

Secretary of State
30 Trinity Street
Hartford, CT 06106

Mailing address:
Secretary of State
Commercial Recordings Division
P.O. Box 150470
Hartford, CT 06115
Phone: 860-509-6002
Fax: 860-509-6069
E-mail: *crd@po.state.ct.us*
www.sots.ct.gov
Filing Fee: $200

Delaware

State of Delaware
Division of Corporations
401 Federal Street, Suite 4
Dover, DE 19901

Mailing address:
Division of Corporations
P.O. Box 898
Dover, DE 19903
Phone: 302-739-3073, press 2
Fax: 302-739-3812
E-mail: *DOSDOC_WEB@state.de.us*
www.state.de.us/sos/
Filing Fee: minimum $89

District of Columbia

Department of Consumer & Regulatory Affairs
941 N. Capitol Street, NE
Washington, D.C., 20002
Phone: 202-442-4432
E-mail: *dcra.concerns@dc.gov*
www.dcra.dc.gov
Filing Fee: minimum $185; exact fee var-
ies based on number of authorized shares

Florida

State Department
Division of Corporations
Corporate Filings
P.O. Box 6327
Tallahassee, FL 32314
Phone: 850-245-6052
E-mail: *corphelp@dos.state.fl.us*
www.dos.state.fl.us/doc
Filing Fee: $35

Georgia

Secretary of State
Corporations Division
315 West Tower
2 Martin Luther King Jr. Drive
Atlanta, GA 30334-1530
Phone: 404-656-2817
Fax: 404-657-2248
www.sos.state.ga.us
Filing Fee: $100

Hawaii

Department of Commerce
and Consumer Affairs
BREG Division
King Kalakaua Building
335 Merchant Street
Room 201
Honolulu, HI 96813

Mailing address:
P.O. Box 40
Honolulu, HI 96810
Phone: 808-586-2744
Fax: 808-586-2733
E-mail: *breg@dcca.hawaii.gov*
www.hawaii.gov/dcca/areas/breg
Filing Fee: $50

Idaho

Secretary of State
700 W. Jefferson Street
Boise, ID 83720
Phone: 208-334-2300
Fax: 208-334-2080
www.idsos.state.id.us
Filing Fee: $100 if typed, $120 if not typed

Illinois

Secretary of State
Suite 328
501 S. Second Street
Springfield, IL 62756
Phone: 217-782-6961
www.cyberdriveillinois.com
Filing Fee: $150

Chicago office:
69 W. Washington
Suite 1240
Chicago, IL 60602
Phone: 312-793-3380

Indiana

Secretary of State
Business Services Division
Room E-018
302 W. Washington Street
Indianapolis, IN 46204
Phone: 317-232-6576
E-mail: *links on Web site*
www.in.gov/sos/
Filing Fee: $90

Iowa

Secretary of State
Corporations Division
Lucas Building, 1st Floor
321 E 12th Street
Des Moines, IA 50319
Phone: 515-281-5204
Fax: 515-242-5953
E-mail: *sos@sos.state.ia.us*
www.sos.state.ia.us
Filing Fee: $50

Kansas

Secretary of State
Memorial Hall, 1st Floor
120 SW 10th Avenue
Topeka, KS 66612
Phone: 785-296-4564
E-mail: *corp@kssos.org*
www.kssos.org
Filing fee: $90

Kentucky

Secretary of State
700 Capitol Ave, Suite 152
Frankfort, KY 40601
Phone: 502-564-3490
E-mail form on Web site
www.kysos.com
Filing Fee: minimum $40; exact fee var-
ies based on number of authorized shares

Louisiana

Secretary of State
Corporations Section
P.O. Box 94125
Baton Rouge, LA 70804-9125
Phone: 225-925-4704
Fax: 225-925-4726
E-mail: *commercial@sos.louisiana.gov*
www.sec.state.la.us
Filing Fee: $85 (included $20 required
for reserving corporation name)
NOTE: The Louisiana Web site is a little
tough to navigate because of its design. To
avoid frustration, try calling the phone num-
ber listed before you brave the Web site.

Maine

State Department
Burton Cross Building
111 Sewall Street
4th Floor
Augusta, ME 04333
Mailing address:
101 State House Station
Augusta, ME 04333-0101
Phone: 207-624-7736
Fax: 207-287-5784
www.maine.gov
Filing Fee: $145

Maryland

Maryland Business Assistance Center.
Business & Economic Development
217 East Redwood Street
Baltimore, MD 21202
Phone: 1-888-CHOOSEMD or 410-767-6300
www.choosemaryland.org
Filing Fee: not listed

Massachusetts

Secretary of the Commonwealth
One Asburton Place, 17th Floor
Boston, MA 02108
Phone: 617-727-9640
Fax: 617-742-4538
E-mail: *corpinfo@sec.state.ma.us*
http://corp.sec.state.ma.us
Filing Fee: minimum $275; exact fee varies
depending on number of authorized shares

Michigan

Bureau of Commercial Services
2501 Woodlake Circle
Okemos, MI 48864

Mailing address:
P.O. Box 30054
Lansing, MI 48909
Phone: 517-241-6470
Fax: 517-241-0538
E-mail: *corpsmail@michigan.gov*
www.michigan.gov/cis
Filing Fee: minimum $60; exact fee var-
ies based on number of authorized shares

Minnesota

Secretary of State
60 Empire Drive
St. Paul, MN 55103
Phone: 651-296-2803 or 877-551-6767
Fax: 651-297-7067
www.sos.state.mn.us
Filing Fee: $135

Mississippi

Secretary of State
700 North Street
Jackson, MS 39202

Mailing address:
P.O. Box 136
Jackson, MS 39205-0136
Phone: 601-359-1350
Fax: 601-359-1499
www.sos.state.ms.us
Filing Fee: $50

Missouri

Secretary of State
Corporations Division
James Kirkpatrick State Info Center, Room 322
600 W. Main
Jefferson City, MO 65101-0778

Mailing address:
P.O. Box 778
Jefferson City, MO 65102
Phone: 573-751-4153
E-mail: *sosmain@sos.mo.gov*
www.sos.mo.gov
Filing Fee: minimum $58; exact fee varies
depending on number of authorized shares

Montana

Secretary of State
P.O. Box 202801
Helena, MT 59620-2801
Phone: 406-444-3665
Fax: 406-444-3976
E-mail: *sosbusiness@mt.gov*
www.sos.state.mt.us
Filing Fee: $70

Nebraska

Secretary of State
Room 1305
P.O. Box 94608
Lincoln, NE 68509-4608
Phone: 402-471-4079
Fax: 402-471-3666
E-mail: *Corporate_inquiries@sos.ne.gov*
www.sos.state.ne.us
Filing Fee: call or e-mail for fees

Nevada

Secretary of State
101 N. Carson Street
Carson City, NV 89701
Phone: 775-684-5708
Fax: 775-684-5725
E-mail: *sosmail@sos.nv.gov*
www.sos.state.nv.us/
Filing Fee: minimum $75

New Hampshire

Secretary of State
Corporation Division
107 N. Main Street
Concord, NH 03301
or
State House
Annex Room 341
25 Capitol Street
Concord, NH 03301
Phone: 603-271-3246
E-mail: *corporate@sos.state.nh.us*
www.state.nh.us
Filing Fee: $50

New Jersey

Commerce & Economic Growth Commission
State Capital Building
P.O. Box 820
Trenton, NJ 08625-0820
Phone: 609-777-0885
www.state.nj.us
Filing Fee: fees not listed on Web site
NOTE: New Jersey's Web site is difficult to navigate; the home page is very busy. You may be better off calling for information.

New Mexico

Public Regulation Commission
P.O. Box 1269
Santa Fe, NM 87504-1269
Phone: 505-827-4508 or 800-947-4722
Fax: 505-827-4387
www.nmprc.state.nm.us
Filing Fee: ranges from $100 to $1,000 based on number of authorized shares

New York

State Department
Division of Corporations
41 State Street
Albany, NY 12231-0001
Phone: 518-473-2492
Fax: 518-474-1418
E-mail: *corporations@dos.state.ny.us*
www.dos.state.ny.us
Filing Fee: $125

North Carolina

Corporations Division
2 South Salisbury Street
Raleigh, NC 27601-2903

Mailing address:
P.O. Box 29622
Raleigh, NC 27626-0622
Phone: 919-807-2225
Fax: 919-807-2039
E-mail: *corpinfo@sosnc.com*
www.secretary.state.nc.us/corporations
Filing Fee: $125

North Dakota

Secretary of State
Department 108
600 E. Boulevard Avenue
Bismarck, ND 58505-0500
Phone: 701-328-2900 or 800-352-0867
Fax: 701-328-2992
E-mail: *sos@nd.gov*
www.nd.gov/sos
Filing Fee: $30 plus capitalization fees

Ohio

Secretary of State
180 E. Broad Street, 16th Floor
Columbus, OH 43215

Mailing address:
P.O. Box 250
Columbus, OH 43216
Phone: 614-466-3910 or 877-SOS-FILE
www.serfrom.sos.state.oh.us
Filing Fee: $125

Oklahoma

Secretary of State
Room 101
2300 N. Lincoln Boulevard
Oklahoma City, OK 73105-4897
Phone: 405-521-3912
Fax: 405-521-3771
www.sos.state.ok.us/
Filing Fee: minimum is $50; total fee is $1
per $1,000 on total authorized capital

Oregon

Corporation Division
255 Capitol Street NE, Suite 151
Salem, OR 97310-1327
Phone: 503-986-2200
Fax: 503-378-4381
E-mail: *businessregistry.sos@state.or.us*
www.FilinginOregon.com
Filing Fee: $50

Pennsylvania

State Department
Commonwealth Avenue and North Street
206 North Office Building
Harrisburg, PA 17120

Mailing address:
P.O. Box 8722
Harrisburg, PA 17105-8722
Phone: 717-787-1057
Fax: 717-783-2244
www.dos.state.pa.us/corps/
Filing Fee: $125

Rhode Island

Corporations Division
148 W. River Street
Providence, RI 02903-1335
Phone: 401-222-3040
www.state.ri.us/
Filing Fee: $230 under 75 million shares

South Carolina

Secretary of State
Edgar Brown Building Capitol Complex
1205 Pendleton Street
Suite 525
Columbia, SC 29201

Mailing address:
P.O. Box 11350
Columbia, SC 29211
Phone: 803-734-2158
Fax: 803-734-1614
www.scsos.com
Filing Fee: $135

South Dakota

Secretary of State
500 E. Capital Avenue, Suite 204
Pierre, SD 57501-5070
Phone: 605-773-4845
Fax: 605-773-4550
E-mail: *corporations@state.sd.us*
www.state.sd.us/sos/
Filing Fee: $125

Tennessee

Division of Business Services
312 8th Avenue N
6th Floor, William Snodgrass Tower
Nashville, TN 37243
Phone: 615-741-2286
E-mail: *business.services@state.tn.us*
www.state.tn.us/sos
Filing Fee: $100

Texas

Secretary of State
Corporations Section
1019 Brazos
Austin, TX 78701

Mailing address:
P.O. Box 13697
Austin, TX 78711
Phone: 512-463-5583
Fax: 512-463-5709
E-mail: *corphelp@sos.state.tx.us*
www.sos.state.tx.us
Filing Fee: $300

Utah

Division of Corporation and Commercial Code
160 E. 300 S.
Salt Lake City, UT 84111
Phone: 801-530-4849
Live chat help available on Web site 24 hours
www.commerce.state.ut.us
Filing Fee: $22 to $52

Vermont

Secretary of State
Corporations Division
81 River Street, Drawer 09
Montpelier, VT 05609
Phone: 802-828-2386
Fax: 802-828-2853
www.sec.state.vt.us
Filing Fee: $75

Virginia

State Corporation Commission
Tyler Building
1300 E. Main Street
Richmond, VA 23219

Mailing address:
P.O. Box 1197
Richmond, VA 23218
Phone: 804-371-9967 or 800-552-7945
E-mail: *links on Web site*
www.state.va.us/scc/
Filing Fee: $50 to $2,500; exact fee varies based on number of authorized shares

Washington

Secretary of State
Dolliver Building
801 Capitol Way South
Olympia, WA

Mailing address:
P.O. Box 40234
Olympia, WA 98504-0234
Phone: 360-753-7115
E-mail: *corps@secstate.wa.gov*
www.secstate.wa.gov
Filing Fee: $175

West Virginia

Secretary of State
Corporations Division
Building 1, Suite 157-K
1900 Kanawha Boulevard E
Charleston, WV 25305-0770
Phone: 304-558-8000
Fax: 304-558-8381
E-mail: *links on Web site*
www.wvsos.com
Filing Fee: $50

Wisconsin

Corporations Section, Third Floor
P.O. Box 7846
Madison, WI 53707-7846
Phone: 608-261-7577
Fax: 608-267-6813
www.wdfi.org
Filing Fee: $100

Wyoming

Secretary of State
Corporations Division
State Capital, Room 110
200 W. 24th Street
Cheyenne, WY 82002-0020
Phone: 307-777-7311 / 7312
Fax: 307-777-5339
E-mail: *corporations@state.wy.us*
http://soswy.state.wy.us
Filing Fee: $100

Index

About the Author

Michele Cagan, C.P.A., focused much of her career on providing accounting, tax, and planning services to individuals and small business owners. She took that base of knowledge to a broader audience when she began writing articles for financial newsletters that detailed little-known investment strategies and opportunities.

Ms. Cagan is the author of *How to Legally Reduce Your Taxes Now* (a short booklet) and the books *A Beginner's Guide to Navigating Wall Street, An Insider's Guide to Surviving the Audit Process, Streetwise® Structuring Your Business, Streetwise® Business Plans with CD,* and *The Everything® Accounting Book*; she is also the coauthor of *The Everything® Investing Book, 2nd Edition*. In addition to her writing, Ms. Cagan has taught accounting and computer skills to community college students and private business owners since 1995.

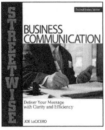

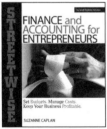
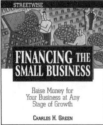

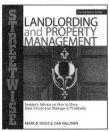

Streetwise® Landlording & Property Management
Weiss and Baldwin
$19.95; ISBN 10: 1-58062-766-8

Streetwise® Low-Cost Marketing
Mark Landsbaum
$19.95; ISBN 10: 1-58062-858-3

Streetwise® Low-Cost Web Site Promotion
Barry Feig
$19.95; ISBN 10: 1-58062-501-0

Streetwise® Managing a Nonprofit
John Riddle
$19.95; ISBN 10: 1-58062-698-X

Streetwise® Managing People
Bob Adams, et al.
$19.95; ISBN 10: 1-55850-726-4

Streetwise® Marketing Plan
Don Debelak
$19.95; ISBN 10: 1-58062-268-2

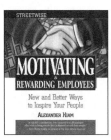

Streetwise® Motivating & Rewarding Employees
Alexander Hiam
$19.95; ISBN 10: 1-58062-130-9

Streetwise® Project Management
Michael Dobson
$19.95; ISBN 10: 1-58062-770-6

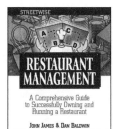

Streetwise® Restaurant Management
John James & Dan Baldwin
$19.95; ISBN 10: 1-58062-781-1

Streetwise® Sales Letters with CD
Reynard and Weiss
$29.95; ISBN 10: 1-58062-440-5

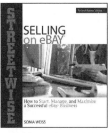

Streetwise® Selling on eBay®
Sonia Weiss
$19.95; ISBN 10: 1-59337-610-3

Streetwise® Small Business Book of Lists
Edited by Gene Marks
$19.95; ISBN 10: 1-59337-684-7

Streetwise® Small Business Start-Up
Bob Adams
$19.95; ISBN 10: 1-55850-581-4

Streetwise® Start Your Own Business Workbook
Gina Marie Mangiamele
$9.95; ISBN 10: 1-58062-506-1

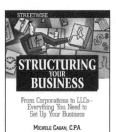

Streetwise® Structuring Your Business
Michele Cagan
$19.95; ISBN 10: 1-59337-177-2

Streetwise® Time Management
Marshall Cook
$19.95; ISBN 10: 1-58062-131-7